CANADIAN
CONSTITUTIONAL
CONVENTIONS

CANADIAN CONSTITUTIONAL CONVENTIONS

The Marriage of Law and Politics

ANDREW HEARD

Toronto
OXFORD UNIVERSITY PRESS
1991

Oxford University Press, 70 Wynford Drive, Don Mills, Ontario M3C 1J9

Toronto   Oxford   New York   Delhi   Bombay   Calcutta   Madras   Karachi
Petaling Jaya   Singapore   Hong Kong   Tokyo   Nairobi   Dar es Salaam
Cape Town   Melbourne   Auckland

and associated companies in
Berlin   Ibadan

CANADIAN CATALOGUING IN PUBLICATION DATA
Heard, Andrew David, 1957–
Canadian constitutional conventions
Includes bibliographical references and index.
ISBN 0–19–540719–9
1. Constitutional conventions – Canada
2. Canada – Constitutional law.   I. Title.
KE4199.h43 1991   342.71'0292   C91–093039–2
KF4482.A2H43 1991

Contents

Preface

The whole topic of constitutional conventions has been sadly overlooked in most discussions of the Canadian system of government. Political scientists, lawyers, and the public often ignore conventions, or dismiss them as merely the fleeting ethics of allegedly unethical politicians. But constitutional conventions, like politicians, have been greatly misunderstood. Canadian political actors have generally respected the most important of our conventions, and they have done so because conventions play a crucial role in shaping our political system. It is no great exaggeration to say that the Canadian system of government could not function if its most fundamental conventions were not faithfully observed.

This book offers a comprehensive look at the range of conventional rules that affect the constitution. The vast sweep of the constitution, ruled by conventions, is revealed in separate chapters on the powers of the governors and cabinet ministers, and on the legislatures, federalism, and the judiciary. These discussions are intended to convey the variety, complexity, and importance of our constitutional conventions. But I hope they will also show how conventions are founded on constitutional principles, not simply on the historical precedents of former times. Once-practised or newly suggested rules can be binding on contemporary politicians only if there is some generally supported principle to be respected.

The specific conventions I have selected for examination, and my discussions of the relationship between law and convention, are inevitably incomplete. But I did not set out to deal exhaustively with these subjects. Indeed, a truly thorough study of conventions would involve numbers of volumes without end. I have simply tried to give a brief but wide-ranging overview of some of the most important conventions in order to clarify and demonstrate the important role played in our system of government by this general class of constitutional rules. Once the variety and importance of conventions are brought into focus, the necessity of revising our views on the relationship between law and convention may become apparent.

As this book was completed, events relating to conventions continued to unfold. For example, we cannot know, at the end of 1990, how several court cases challenging the government's appointment of extra senators under section 26 of the Constitutional Act, 1867 will be decided. Actions are in progress where litigants are seeking to establish that the previous lack of use of this provision has led to its obsolescence. Whether or not a convention has arisen to block the appointment of extra senators offers a challenge to Canadian courts to confront the very nature of conventions. Since section 26 had never been used before to appoint extra senators, one hopes that the courts do not confuse the absence of precedents (where legal provisions have not been resorted to because of a lack of suitable opportunities) with negative precedents (arising when legal powers are deliberately not used because a convention supports a constitutional principle that goes against the legal rule). In any event, these cases will underline how important it is for the courts to have a full understanding of conventions and their relationship to law.

I am indebted to many people who have helped me over the years towards writing this book. I am grateful to Murray Beck, Professor Emeritus, Dalhousie University, whose lectures not only awoke my interest in constitutional issues but also saved me from pursuing a degree in biochemistry. I am especially thankful for the kind guidance of Professors Peter Russell and Stefan Dupré of the University of Toronto, and Peter Hogg of Osgoode Hall, who supervised my doctoral dissertation, which forms the basis of several chapters of this book. Many of my ideas have been refined through long chats with Geoffrey Marshall of Oxford University, who may not have realized he made any dent on me. I also wish to acknowledge many illuminating conversations with David Conklin Jr., and the congenial company of other neighbours and colleagues at Trinity College, University of Toronto, where much of this book was written. On a more practical note, I am grateful to the Social Sciences and Humanities Research Council of Canada for financing my research. Once the bulk of the writing was completed I was greatly helped by my editor, William Toye, and his desire for clarity.

My deepest gratitude I owe to my parents, whose long careers as educators have set high examples for me and whose support has meant so much.

1

The Role and Nature
of Conventions

The Canadian political system is shaped by a wide variety of constitutional rules that go well beyond the provisions of our formal Constitution. While section 52 of the 1982 Constitution Act declares that some two dozen British and Canadian statutes and orders-in-council comprise our Constitution, and are the 'supreme law of Canada', Canadian constitutional law also includes many other legal rules found in statutes, orders-in-council, and judicial decisions relating to the executive, the judiciary, and the legislature. But even when they are added to the Constitution, we have only an incomplete and distorted view of our political system. The whole *constitution* is actually composed of three elements: the formal *Constitution*; the legal rules relating to the three branches of government; and, in addition, vitally important informal rules, called conventions, that have arisen through political practice.* As many areas of the constitution are structured by archaic or incomplete laws, the political arena has given birth to binding conventions and customary usages that not only direct political actors in these matters, but ultimately determine the full substance and character of the Canadian constitution. Even the 'supreme law' of the Constitution is often remoulded by the force of conventions, which both complete the constitution and allow it to evolve with changes in prevailing values.

Every major aspect of the constitution depends on conventions. The sweeping legal powers of the Governor General are transferred by con-

---

*In the discussions that follow I shall maintain this distinction between the whole *constitution*, and the subset of rules found in the entrenched documents of the *Constitution* that are described in s. 52 and in the Schedule of the Constitution Act, 1982.

vention to the Cabinet. The very basis of responsible government—with the requirements that both individual ministers and the Cabinet collectively must account to the legislature for the activities of the executive branch of government—is a vital matter that has been entirely left out of the formal Constitution. Both the operation of disciplined parties, which give the basic character to our legislatures, and the relationship between the House of Commons and the Senate, are similarly determined by convention. Many of the rules giving effect to the federal principle have arisen from political practice rather than from the formal division of powers, found in the original Constitution Act of 1867 and in subsequent judicial pronouncements. The basic independence of the judiciary has grown to a large extent out of informal rules as well as legal guarantees.

With the role conventions play in transforming the formal Constitution, it is crucial to have a full appreciation of the manner in which the legal and conventional rules of the constitution interact. Perhaps the greatest weakness of traditional examinations of the Canadian constitution is the oversimplification of both the character of constitutional conventions and their relationship with the positive laws of the constitution.

Two distinct and somewhat contradictory trends relating to constitutional conventions appear to be at play in Canada. One tendency is to draw a clear boundary between law and convention. In its opinions on the 1981 reference questions about the amendment of the Constitution, the Supreme Court of Canada drew a sharp distinction between conventions, as political rules, and the legal rules enforced by the courts. The majority summarized their views with the formula: 'Constitutional conventions plus constitutional law equal the total [c]onstitution of the country.'[1] Although this statement illustrates the importance of conventions, it drastically oversimplifies the variety of rules that make up the constitution, as well as how they interrelate.

The second major trend lies in an increasing propensity to seek the legal regulation or judicial resolution of issues normally governed by convention. The justiciability of conventions may become an increasingly important issue in Canadian constitutional theory. Peter Russell has noted that Canadian political culture has become more litigious in recent decades, with legal solutions sought for political disputes.[2] In recent years a number of cases explicitly involving constitutional conventions have come before Canadian courts for judicial determination.[3] The inclination to seek a legal resolution of matters involving conventions was further exemplified after the 1985 general election in Ontario. When the Liberals and the New Democratic Party announced they had reached an agreement ensuring that the NDP would support a Liberal government for two years, Premier Frank Miller immediately sought legal advice about whether this agreement could be challenged in the courts—even though it clearly related only to matters governed by convention. For his part, Lieutenant

Governor John B. Aird consulted with a noted constitutional lawyer, J.J. Robinette, about the avenues of action open to him. Thus a trend seems to be developing where legal solutions are sought for problems involving conventions.

The outcome of these two trends should be of great interest to students of the Canadian constitution. If conventional rules come to inhabit some legal dimension, there may be significant consequences for the constitutional process. Any increased propensity to seek judicial remedies for matters involving conventions could further enhance the power of the judiciary to regulate the activities of elected officials. Some concern might be expressed at this prospect, since conventions have always represented a valued method by which a constitution may evolve informally through the actions of politicians who both respond and are accountable to the electorate. If conventions become increasingly justiciable, there is some danger that the democratic quality of constitutional evolution might be eroded. On the other hand, too clear a boundary between court-enforceable constitutional laws and conventional rules might see the courts enforcing outdated rules that not only lack any political legitimacy but may also be destructive.

THE NATURE OF CONVENTIONS

In the interests of clarity, a working definition of conventions is needed before proceeding further. What exactly is meant by a constitutional convention may be most easily explained by citing the formulation of Geoffrey Marshall and Graeme Moodie:

> By conventions of the constitution, we mean binding rules of constitutional behaviour which are considered to be binding by and upon those who operate the Constitution, but which are not enforced by the law courts (although the courts may recognise their existence), nor by the presiding officers in the Houses of Parliament.[4]

Curiously few Canadian writers have ventured their own definitions of conventions. Eugene Forsey calls them 'the acknowledged, binding, extra-legal customs, usages, practices and understandings by which our system of government operates.'[5] Peter Hogg refers to conventions as 'rules of the [c]onstitution that are not enforced by the law courts.'[6] Both of these definitions, however, fail to distinguish conventions from the 'laws and customs of Parliament', a distinction insisted upon by most British authors.

Despite the importance of conventions to the Canadian constitution, surprisingly little has been written on the subject by Canadian scholars. Canadian constitutional lawyers seldom seem to give much attention to the topic, perhaps heeding A.V. Dicey's injunction of over a century ago that the subject of conventions 'is not one of law but of politics, and need trouble no lawyer or the class of any professor of law.'[7] A few constitutional lawyers have included interesting, if brief, discussions in their texts; Hogg[8] is perhaps the best example among anglophone law teachers, while Henri Brun and Guy Tremblay provide the superior coverage found in the French-Canadian literature.[9] Apart from these general discussions, particular constitutional conventions have occasionally been examined in greater detail: Paul Gérin-Lajoie's work on constitutional amendment,[10] Frank Mackinnon's on the monarchy,[11] John T. Saywell's book on Lieutenant Governors,[12] and Forsey's series of papers[13] on different aspects of parliamentary government are among the better-known examples. The Supreme Court's handling of the Patriation case prompted a reawakening of academic interest in conventions.[14] The Quebec Veto case (1982) also prompted some speculation on the nature of conventions in an article by Marc Gold.[15] In general, however, much of the discussion in the Canadian literature has focused over the years on the terms of particular conventions. Very little attention has been paid by Canadian scholars to the nature of conventions and how they may relate to other constitutional rules.

The most rigorous discussions of constitutional theory and the nature of conventions may be found in a number of works by British scholars. Dicey[16] and Sir Ivor Jennings[17] remain the most prominent earlier authors, but quite a few British scholars have recently undertaken wide-ranging examinations of conventions.[18] Geoffrey Marshall has given conventions the most comprehensive treatment to date.[19] The only other full-length book to examine constitutional conventions was published in 1979 in Australia by L.J.M. Cooray.[20]

The distinction between law and convention is often implicitly treated by constitutional writers as dating from A.V. Dicey's *An Introduction to the Law of the Constitution*, first published in 1885. Certainly Dicey's examination of conventional rules was more thorough than any previous work and has come to be one of the leading texts in British constitutional theory. However, scholarly attention to the difference between the legal rules and the political practices and principles of the constitution predates Dicey's work considerably. Hood Phillips has detailed the evolution of British constitutional theory and the growing distinction made between law and political practice.[21] The existence of these two types of rules was noted by Edmund Burke in the eighteenth century and was progressively expanded upon by later authors. But Dicey laid much of the foundation of modern constitutional theory when he drew a fundamental distinction between

'the law of the constitution', which, consisting (as it does) of rules enforced or recognised by the courts, makes up a body of 'law' in the proper sense of that term, and the 'conventions of the constitution', which, consisting (as they do) of customs, practices, maxims, or precepts which are not enforced or recognised by the courts, make up a body not of laws, but of constitutional or political ethics . . .[22]

Dicey's clear separation of law and convention, on the grounds of court-enforceability, has been a pervasive element in theories of constitutional law ever since.

There is a clear consensus among scholars since Dicey's time about the general purposes that conventions serve. Their main function is to allow the exercise of legal powers in some manner other than that prescribed by the letter of the law. As Jennings put it, ' . . . they provide the flesh which clothes the dry bones of the law.'[23] Some conventions stipulate that the powers of a certain office be exercised only in certain circumstances; for example, the Governor General's power of dissolution is limited to a few situations. Other conventions ensure that one actor's legal power is effectively exercised in practice by someone else; thus much of the prerogative power of the Crown is determined exclusively by Cabinet rather than by the monarch. Finally, a few conventions negate some existing legal power or duty; for instance, a convention now releases the Governor General from the duty imposed in s.56 of the 1867 Constitution Act to send copies to the Queen of all federal legislation enacted into law. The primary benefit of these functions of conventions is that they permit the adaptation of constitutional rules to changes in the general political principles and values of the day, without the need for formal amendment of existing positive law.

There is, however, some uncertainty over how conventions come to be established and how they may be identified. Moreover, there is a fundamental division of opinion concerning the legal character of conventions. The neat dichotomy that Dicey drew is both hotly defended and criticized.

LAW AND CONVENTION

Dicey set the battle-lines for a continuing debate on the nature of conventions in 1885, when he declared that conventions 'are not in reality laws at all since they are not enforced by the Courts.'[24] A good number of modern-day authorities continue to stress that a distinction between legal rules and conventions based on court enforceability should be maintained, especially because conventions primarily inhabit the political dimension.[25] As Forsey put it: 'First and foremost, they are political: political in their birth, political in their growth and decay, and political in their applications and sanctions.'[26] Laws are enforced in the courts, while conventions are said to be enforced in the political arena alone; this is the essence of the distinction made between law and convention.

Some authors, however, have taken issue with the neatness of this dividing line. Jennings has been the most influential constitutional theorist to argue that conventions are not so easily separated from legal rules as the judicial-enforcement test implies. He has claimed that, in their substance, laws and conventions are often inextricably interrelated;[27] for example, laws that refer to the prime minister or the government presuppose the conventions that create those offices.[28] As a consequence, the courts have had to resort to conventions for guidance and interpretation in a number of cases involving constitutional issues. E.C.S. Wade has also echoed these points in his assertion that a distinction based on judicial enforceability cannot consistently serve one in discussing the nature and functions of both law and convention.[29] Although both authors willingly point out certain differences between law and convention, neither would accept Dicey's assertion that these rules are 'of a totally different character'.

The main bone of contention between these two schools of thought is the role conventions may play in judicial proceedings. The debate focuses not only on the more empirical question of how judges have treated conventions, but also on the normative issue of how the courts should treat them. The issues involved relate to whether some legal character has been attributed to conventions through the use made of them by the courts, as well as to whether one can say that conventions have been 'enforced' in some manner in these cases.

J.R. Mallory has argued that conventions have occasionally been absorbed into law by the courts, despite their usual reticence to deal with them:

> Generally speaking the courts do not concern themselves with conventions of the constitution but only with matters of strict law. However, it is possible for a court to assimilate a constitutional convention into the law of the constitution if the rule appears to be clear and certain.[30]

In his reference to 'clear and certain' conventional rules, Mallory appears to distinguish between the courts' treatment of ambiguous or controversial conventions and of those that are generally accepted and easily formulated. Unfortunately Mallory gives no specific examples of where conventions have actually been assimilated into the law; indeed, this assertion is left without further support in his discussion.

Colin Munro, on the other hand, has written a forceful defence of Dicey's separation of law from convention. Drawing principally from two decisions of the Judicial Committee of the Privy Council,[31] Munro pronounced flatly that conventions have not been, nor can be, enforced in the courts as legal rules:

The validity of conventions cannot be the subject of proceedings in a court of law. Reparation for breaches of such rules will not be effected by any legal sanction. There are no cases which contradict these propositions.[32]

A number of authors have argued that not only have conventions not been enforced in the courts but neither should they be. For example, Rodney Brazier and St J. Robilliard object to the notion that conventions should be treated as legal rules because of the informal origins of constitutional conventions:

> To say that a convention can become a rule of law would be to challenge the proposition that Parliament makes laws which are recognised as such by virtue of the act of law-making, whereas conventions, on the other hand, evolve in a manner which is not necessarily appreciated by those participating in their development and which in any case has not been perceived by them as law-making.[33]

Eugene Forsey has also taken great exception to the possibility that courts could declare what the terms of a conventions are:

> The courts have not, nor should they have, the right to decide what the conventions of the Constitution are. If they attempt to do so, the decision has no force at all, legal or other. It is not desirable or even safe, to have the courts making such decisions. On the contrary, it is most dangerous. Acceptance of the Supreme Court's decisions on conventions would mean a Quiet Revolution in our system of government. It would blur the distinction between convention and law. It could lead to the supersession of the law set out in the Constitution by judicially determined 'convention'. It could provide a means of circumventing the explicit provision for constitutional amendment set out in the Constitution Act, 1982. It could subvert parliamentary government.[34]

All arguments that have been rallied against the justiciability of constitutional conventions, however, can be seriously challenged. Munro is mistaken in his assertion that the validity of conventions has not been dealt with in the courts; forthcoming chapters will demonstrate the manner in which conventions have been treated in a variety of relevant cases around the Commonwealth. The legislative formalism inherent in Brazier's and Robilliard's normative argument against justiciable conventions is curious, given the law-making role of the courts in refining both statutory and common law. Forsey's impassioned attack seems to bolt the proverbial door too late. Conventions have been discussed and defined in a number of cases over the years without the ensuing demise of parliamentary government. Forsey appears to ignore the judicial interpretation of our formal Constitution that has effected substantial constitutional change since very soon after Confederation, thereby side-stepping the previous amending procedures; indeed, judicial interpretation is a fundamental avenue of constitutional evolution. Furthermore, one must point out in just as strong terms that the development of constitutional conventions, regardless of their treatment in the courts, has also brought fundamental alterations to the constitution without recourse to the formal amending procedures. The very basis of parliamentary government Forsey wishes to uphold is founded on conventional rules that arose outside the existing formal amending procedures.

No author has seriously contended that a formal legal remedy, such as a prerogative writ, will be granted by the courts purely on the grounds that a convention has been broken. There is no evidence that in judicial proceedings conventions have been treated in exactly the same way as statute or common law.[35] Nevertheless Jennings,[36] Russell,[37] Allan,[38] and Marshall[39] have clearly shown that various Commonwealth courts have on occasion referred to conventions for guidance and defined their terms in the course of interpreting statutes and extending particular common-law principles.

The Supreme Court of Canada's handling of the reference questions on the amendment of the Constitution illustrates both aspects of the treatment of conventions given by the judiciary: the Court was prepared to discuss in detail the conventions, but not to consider them as court-enforceable rules. On the one hand the majority said:

> The conventional rules of the Constitution present one striking peculiarity. In contradistinction to the laws of the Constitution, they are not enforced by the courts. . . . [T]he legal system from which they are distinct does not contemplate formal sanctions for their breach.[40]

On the other hand they also argued that they would be following judicial practice in discussing the existence and content of a convention:

> We are asked to recognize if it exists. Courts have done this very thing many times in England and the Commonwealth to provide aid for and background to constitutional statutory construction. . . . In so recognizing conventional rules, the Courts have described them, sometimes commented upon them and given them such precision as is derived from the written form of judgment.[41]

The explicit discussion of particular conventional rules in both the Patriation and Quebec Veto reference cases appears to have settled the issue in Canada about the justiciability of constitutional conventions in Canada. In these two cases the Supreme Court was asked to decide whether a convention existed and, if so, what its terms were. Marshall, however, denies that the Court's answering of these reference questions implied that conventions were dealt with as legal rules, claiming that it dealt with them as questions of fact rather than of law:

> The Canadian courts only felt able to declare the existence of the convention because under widely drawn provincial and federal statutes providing for the furnishing of advisory opinions, they were specifically authorized to give such opinions on questions either of law or of fact. The power to recognize the conventions derived therefore from statute. Where such statutes exist the law will treat the existence of a convention simply as a question of fact—though not a simple question of fact . . .[42]

There is legislation to permit reference questions in all federal and provincial jurisdictions in Canada. Although there are slight variations in the phrasing of the various acts, they essentially provide that the governor-in-council may refer *any* matter to the appeal court of that jurisdiction for an opinion. The Supreme Court of Canada intimated that the courts could place their own restrictions on what matters they would hear: 'The scope of the authority in each case is wide enough to saddle the respective Courts with the determination of questions which may not be justiciable and there is no doubt that those Courts, and this Court on appeal, have a discretion to refuse to answer such questions.'[43] However, the Supreme Court also held that the questions relating to constitutional conventions in the Patriation case should be answered. The majority did not reach this position because they would be answering questions of fact, as Marshall suggested. Rather the majority opinion stated that the question about the existence and terms of the convention dealing with amendments to the constitution

> . . . is not confined to an issue of pure legality but it has to do with a fundamental issue of constitutionality and legitimacy. Given the broad statutory basis upon which the Governments of Manitoba, Newfoundland and Quebec are empowered to put questions to their respective courts of Appeal, they are in our view entitled to an answer to a question of this type.[44]

Thus Canadian courts have been enjoined to answer reference questions raising matters of 'constitutionality and legitimacy'.

The justiciability of conventions should not be denigrated simply because they can be most clearly litigated in reference questions. As Gerald Rubin concluded after a review of the treatment of reference cases in subsequent litigation: 'Theoretically in law, reference opinions are "advisory only"—no doubt about that. But in practice they are treated with the respect due to judgements.'[45] In some ways the status of reference opinions is moving towards that of the 'opinions' of the Judicial Committee of the Privy Council, which are now conventionally taken to be legal decisions of a court of law.[46]

Furthermore, the judicial consideration of conventions is not restricted to reference questions. In two cases decided before the Patriation reference, the Supreme Court relied heavily on the conventional relationship between a legislature and its government: in *Arseneau v. The Queen*[47] this relationship was relied upon to allow prosecution, under a charge of bribing a member of the legislature, of a person who had corruptly paid money to a minister; in *Blaikie* (No. 2, 1981),[48] it was used to explain an earlier decision to extend the bilingualism required under s. 133 of the 1867 Constitution Act to cover regulations enacted by the government of Quebec. Constitutional conventions are clearly rules with which Canadian constitutional lawyers must become more familiar.

The dichotomy between law and convention may not be as distinct as many constitutional theorists would have us believe. The later chapters of this book dealing with the operation of particular conventions will include discussions of the use made of conventions in a number of court decisions that involve a good deal of litigation outside the context of reference legislation.

THE GENESIS OF CONVENTIONAL RULES

There is general agreement that conventions may arise in at least two ways: through some practice acquiring a strong obligatory character over time, or through the explicit agreement of the relevant actors. When conventions arise from practice, however, it is often difficult to ascertain when or if a usage has become sufficiently accepted as binding that it constitutes a convention. Some writers have downplayed the importance of distinguishing between obligatory conventions and non-binding usages. As Peter Hogg has written:

> The distinction between convention and usage, although insisted upon by some constitutional lawyers, is not ordinarily useful, because conventions are as unenforceable as usages. The most that can be said is that there is a stronger moral obligation to follow a convention than a usage, and that departure from convention may be criticized more severely than departure from usage.[49]

In one of the most recent treatments of conventions, Colin Munro has argued that usages and conventions belong to the same continuum.[50] Nevertheless political actors and observers must concern themselves with the distinction between them, however ambiguous it may be, precisely because greater moral obligation occurs in convention than usage. When constitutional dilemmas emerge, it is the degree of obligation to follow, or abstain from, one course of action rather than another that ought to guide politicians in their actions; when rules conflict, one needs to be able to discern which rule should be observed. It is crucial that distinctions be drawn between rules of different orders of obligation. Thus the pertinent criticism of the convention/usage dichotomy is that the distinction needs to be made clearer.

What is evidently important to the establishment of a convention is the level of agreement involved. Conventions may be created or altered by the express agreement of the main political actors; thus the Imperial Conferences in the inter-war period laid the foundation of the conventional rules that gave Canada and the other Dominions their political independence from the British Empire. However, most conventions arise, as Marshall puts it, 'from a series of precedents that are agreed to have given rise to a binding rule of behaviour.'[51] The essential place of this agreement is stressed by Brun and Tremblay in their discussion of conventions. They assert that an 'entente' among several political actors forms the basis of any conventional rule; in short, they characterize a convention as a type of contract:

> La convention constitutionnelle s'élabore sous la forme d'une entente. Un usage, une practique ou une façon de faire y fait l'objet d'un accord. La convention est nécessairement bilatérale ou multilatérale; elle implique plusieurs parties. Elle est une sorte de contrat. Une façon de faire se trouve consacrée par entente plutôt que par le temps qu'il a en droit coutumier; l'élément déterminant de la convention est l'entente en vertu de laquelle les gouvernants se considèrent liés.[52]

At the heart of Brun's and Tremblay's view of conventions is a sort of contractual agreement among the relevant actors. While this notion is readily applicable to those conventions that arise from explicit accords, such as many Commonwealth rules, it is more difficult to apply to conventions that emerge from past practice, as more and more actors come to feel bound by a particular pattern of behaviour. In being established by the growth of a consensus, however, such conventions are difficult to view in the contractual terms expressed by Brun and Tremblay, who may have anticipated this criticism when they went on to say: 'Cette entente . . . peut être écrite, orale ou tacite.'[53] Unfortunately the assertion of this tacit entente poses many problems, not the least of which is trying to establish its existence. The conventional rules that are generally accepted in principle are those the relevant actors have clearly agreed exist. Perhaps tacit agreement, or understanding, may be the necessary element a practice acquires while it is gaining credence as an obligatory rule; once explicit acceptance is expressed, there can be little doubt that the convention is firmly established.

The conclusion about the role and importance of agreement among the actors, however, is complicated when one tries to apply it to a number of particular conventions about which few if any statements by the main actors are to be found. The absence of any explicit agreement by the prime office-holders is especially problematic in those conventions relating to the personal powers of the Queen and her governors. One of the rules among this group of conventions is that these office-holders normally shall not speak publicly about their prerogative powers. Consequently there is virtually no record of explicit recognition by them of the terms of the specific conventions that limit the exercise of their legal powers; in examining these conventions one cannot rely on any express agreement by past monarchs or their governors. Marc Gold raised this dilemma in his criticism of the Supreme Court of Canada's emphasis in the Quebec Veto case on statements by political actors concerning a conventional rule's existence.[54]

Perhaps the difficulties posed by relying on an entente among the principal actors are only properly resolved when one escapes the notion that conventions are primarily a matter of the internal morality of political actors. That view is exemplified in Hood Phillips' definition of conventions as the 'rules of political practice which are regarded as binding by those to whom they apply. . . .';[55] in short, the terms of conventions are what the actors believe them to be. But a fallacious conclusion is reached when they are viewed solely in this light: if conventions are only what the actors feel bound by, or state they are bound by, they are not truly bound, since any contrary statement or belief on their part would negate their obligation to the so-called rule. Marshall takes a more sensible approach in arguing that conventions must be rules of critical morality, rules that the political actors *ought* to feel bound by.[56] This approach is reflected when he says: 'It would seem better to define conventions as the rules of behaviour that ought to be regarded as binding by those concerned in working the constitution when they have correctly interpreted the precedents and the relevant constitutional principles.'[57] Implicit in this view is the notion that there is a standard of behaviour that in some sense may be independent from the actual beliefs of the political actors in a given situation. But the recognition of conventions as rules of critical morality should not imply that they are some sort of natural law of the constitution. Instead, the force of conventions as critical morality derives from the support of the general political community.

THE WEAKNESS OF VIEWING CONVENTIONS AS ESTABLISHED RULES

When constitutional writers focus on the *establishment* of conventions through practice or explicit agreement, they create a particular notion of conventions. For instance, when conventions are seen to originate through usage, the temptation then is to think of a convention chiefly as a behaviour pattern, rather than as a political principle that has become obligatory. This perspective is reflected in a passage by Hogg: 'If a practice is invariably followed over a long period of time, it may become regarded as obligatory and thus cease to be merely a usage.'[58] Traditional views of conventions emphasize the *established* rules that are either time-honoured or created by express agreement; they do not easily accommodate the way vague principles, such as constitutionalism, may be occasionally invoked as binding rules of behaviour. Furthermore, the traditional views of conventions fail to provide a way to distinguish among even established conventions. Some method to draw broad distinctions is essential if one is to try to resolve the conflicts between several rules that might arise in some unprecedented constitutional crisis.

The emphasis on the established nature of conventions is clearly reflected in the test that has been widely accepted for identifying conventional rules. Sir Ivor Jennings set three questions to be posed when seeking to establish a convention's existence: 'first, what are the precedents; secondly, did the actors in the precedents believe they were bound by a rule; thirdly, is there a reason for the rule?'[59] In Jennings' view, precedent appears essential to the establishment of a convention; two parts of his test concern historical precedents. Furthermore, although he asserts that long historical practice is not always necessary, at least one precedent appears essential: 'A single precedent with a good reason may be enough to establish the rule.'[60] The notion that the rule did not exist before the precedent is implicit but clear in this statement. This requirement of a precedent has been strongly underlined by Forsey: 'A constitutional convention without a single precedent to support it is a house without any foundation . . . [I]ndisputably, at least one precedent is essential. If there is no precedent, there is no convention.'[61]

THE PROBLEMS OF PRECEDENT

The greatest weakness of traditional views of conventions lies in this emphasis on rules' becoming established only after a precedent occurs. Most clearly, this view fails to allow for conventions that are altered or created *de novo* by the express agreement of the prime political actors. For instance, no one doubted after the 1930 Imperial Conference that British ministers could no longer advise the monarch on the appointment of governors to the Dominions. Very little time transpired between the meeting, which agreed that these appointments would be made on the advice of Dominion ministers, and the first use of this new power in Australia and Ireland; but in the interim it was quite evident that powers of British ministers in the area were extinct and that new powers for Dominion ministers existed.

Furthermore, this emphasis placed on precedent not only tightens the reins of history on constitutional development but also introduces the ambiguity and contradiction inherent in precedent. If one searches for a rule among historical events, a number of dilemmas arise from conflicting precedents. Does the contradictory evidence demonstrate that no binding rule exists? Is there a rule, but is one or more of the actors mistaken in assessing its terms? Did one rule give way to another higher rule? Finally, did the actors knowingly breach the rule, but publicly deny its existence, as an act of political self-interest? Furthermore, in weighing the statements of various office-holders concerning particular rules, one must also be able to account for an institutional bias; for instance, one would expect some difference of opinion between provincial premiers and the prime minister on the rules governing federal-provincial relations, and between Opposition and Government politicians on ministerial responsibility. Unfortunately no clear method for resolving these problems of interpretation has been presented by those who stress the importance of precedent in the creation of a convention. These ambiguities will remain in any approach to constitutional disputes that relies on precedent.

The traditional approach fails to provide for the operation of binding rules or principles prior to, or during, the first precedents that establish the convention. Where constitutional theory concentrates on established rules, one can find little or no guidance for hard cases that lack any historical parallels and are not covered by established conventions.

THE TASK AHEAD

A significant challenge lies in tackling the problems posed by the traditional emphasis on historical precedent both to the practical resolution of hard cases and to general theories concerning the nature of constitutional conventions. One potential answer lies in the role that constitutional principles may play in generating obligations political actors must respect. While some authors mention that conventional rules arise from either precedent or special agreement, Marshall has posed a third avenue. He notes that convention 'may be formulated on the basis of some acknowledged principle of government which provides a reason or justification for it' and explains this idea with an example:

> Though it is rarely formulated as a conventional rule the most obvious and undisputed convention of the British constitutional system is that Parliament does not use its unlimited sovereign power of legislation in an oppressive or tyrannical way. That is a vague but clearly accepted conventional rule resting on the principle of constitutionalism and the rule of law.[62]

Marshall's brief reference to a third source of conventions provides a starting-point for examining the ways in which broad constitutional principles at some times only underlie conventions but at others operate as binding rules in the absence of more specific, established conventions.

These broad, fundamental principles may hold the key to understanding the nature, role, operation, and content of the informal rules that have arisen to adapt the positive law of the Constitution. Under closer examination, the traditional distinctions between usage, binding convention, and positive law may seem over-simplified and inadequate to describe the many informal rules that give substance to constitutional structures and processes.

The main task of this book, then, is to provide an insight into the nature of the conventional rules at work in the Canadian constitution: what are they? how do they arise? how are they enforced? Also, it is important to know what the terms of the conventions of the Canadian constitution actually are. To these ends chapters will be devoted to a review of the principal conventions governing each of the major areas of the Canadian constitution: the prerogative powers of the Governor General and Lieutenant Governors; the operation of responsible cabinet government; the workings of the legislatures; federalism; and judicial independence. In the examinations of these conventions, just how completely the legal provisions of the Constitution are transformed by convention will be underlined, and reference will be made to the court cases dealing with these conventions. The book concludes with the proposal of a hierarchical series of classifications for informal constitutional rules, which, it is hoped, may help provide both a clearer understanding of the variety of constitutional conventions and a firmer basis from which to begin to analyse the relationship between law and convention. This scheme may help to explain how the informal rules of the constitution range from non-binding traditions or usages through to the fundamental conventions that determine the basic character of the Canadian constitution and that must always be obeyed.

2

Conventions of the Governors' Powers

Constitutional conventions have forged fundamental changes in the powers of the Queen and her representatives in Canada. Although the Queen remains Canada's legal head of state, the only area in which she plays any ongoing role lies in the appointment of the Governor General. Apart from that act, the monarch has only a symbolic role in the political and constitutional affairs of Canada. The functions of the head of state are performed instead by the Governor General and Lieutenant Governors. But even though the Canadian governors have a host of legal powers, some of the most important conventions of the Canadian constitution ensure that these powers are exercised in practice by the Prime Minister and Cabinet.

Although the Governor General is mentioned frequently in the original Constitution Act of 1867, there is no provision there for his or her appointment; indeed, the Act assumes the pre-existence of a Governor General. In fact the office of Governor General is constituted by royal Letters Patent, most recently issued in 1947 by King George VI.[1] This document declares that the Governor may 'exercise all powers and authorities lawfully belonging to Us in respect of Canada'.[2] As the appointment of a Governor General is made through a commission granted under the Great Seal of Canada, it must involve the federal Cabinet. A firmly established convention dictates that the initiative for selecting a new Governor General lies with the Canadian Prime Minister personally.[3] The traditional period of tenure for Governors General is now generally limited to five years, although they serve 'at pleasure'.

Since the appointment in 1952 of Vincent Massey as Governor General, a Canadian has always been chosen for the position. Massey's appointment climaxed a developing Canadianization of the office, which had begun with the agreement at the 1930 Imperial Conference that Dominion ministers, rather than British, would henceforth advise the monarch on the appointment of Governors General; until 1952, however, the Canadian Prime Minister had chosen from a list of British candidates. Despite the possibility raised by some Canadians in recent years that one of the Queen's sons might be appointed, this idea has generally been considered inappropriate. The appointment of any non-Canadian would likely be opposed because of the resulting diminution of visible Canadian independence from Britain, and also because it would exacerbate the division between anglophones and francophones in Canada.[4] Thus the practice of appointing only Canadians has probably become obligatory, although there have been few, if any, firm public statements made on the issue by leading federal politicians.[5] These past thirty years have also seen the unvarying alternation between anglophone and francophone appointees. It would seem that this tradition will also be faithfully observed in the future because of the symbolic importance of representing the two main cultures of Canada in the office.[6]

The 1867 Constitution Act did provide for the appointment of the Lieutenant Governors by the Governor General in Council; but in practice the choice of the appointee is made by the Prime Minister.[7] In the early years after Confederation there was some conflict over the constitutional status of the Lieutenant Governors; a reading of several provisions of the 1867 Act can give the impression that Lieutenant Governors are actually the representatives of the national government in the provinces. However, the Judicial Committee of the Privy Council ruled in 1892 that a Lieutenant Governor is 'as much a representative of Her Majesty for all purposes of provincial government as the Governor General is for all purposes of Dominion government'.[8] Thus the Lieutenant Governor is vested with the prerogatives of the Crown for all aspects relevant to the governing of the province.[9]

THE CONTRAST BETWEEN LEGAL AND CONVENTIONAL POWERS

The legal status of the Governor General conveys the impression of an office of considerable power. Either through orders-in-council or proclamations under the Great Seal of Canada, the Governor General may summon and dissolve Parliament, as well as appoint and remove Lieutenant Governors, Senators, the Speaker of the Senate, and the judges for the Superior, District, and County Courts in each province. The necessity for acting in tandem with the Privy Council might appear to be a matter of only slight inconvenience, since the Constitution Act of 1867 provides that the Governor General may summon and remove persons to and from the Council at his unfettered pleasure. In addition, the Letters Patent of 1947 'require and command' all ministers 'to be obedient, aiding, and assisting unto Our Governor General'. The position of the Governor General is further strengthened by the power expressly granted in the 1867 Act to refuse royal assent to any bill passed by Parliament, or to reserve a bill for the Queen's pleasure. Finally, any measure to raise or spend public money must be recommended to the House of Commons by the Governor General. Thus the positive law of the Constitution provides a Governor General with a great range of potential powers. Many of these legal powers are also extended to the Lieutenant Governors for purposes of provincial government.

In reality, however, the Governor General is prevented from exercising the bulk of these powers on his or her own initiative by some of the most firmly established conventions. Indeed, it is only because of these conventional restraints that the broad legal powers of this monarchical office are tolerated within Canada's democratic constitution: first, the Governor General appoints to the Privy Council as Prime Minister the leader of the party (or parties) that can command a majority in the House of Commons; second, the Governor General appoints as ministers only those chosen by the Prime Minister; third, only the current members of the Privy Council who hold ministerial positions can partake in the decision-making process; fourth, the Governor General is bound to act on the 'advice' of the Cabinet in virtually all circumstances. Furthermore, governors should not involve themselves in any political debate about potentially controversial or partisan policy issues. Either the Prime Minister personally, or the Cabinet collectively, makes the decisions relevant to the exercise of almost of the governors' legal powers.

Within the constraints of these rules, Governors General might retain some small measure of personal influence through the rights formulated by Walter Bagehot: 'the right to be consulted, the right to encourage, the right to warn'.[10] The Governor General is able to exercise these rights through regular meetings with the Prime Minister. Just how much influence Governors General enjoy through these meetings will depend entirely on their own political experience, authority, and particularly on their personal relations with the Prime Minister. Although this is a generally valued convention that allows for the governor to give impartial advice to the government and remain informed of the affairs of state in case of a constitutional crisis, there is little that could be done if a Prime Minister refused to meet regularly or to talk about any substantial matters during whatever meetings were held. These conventional rights, however, seem to be more honoured in the breach at the provincial level. For instance, René Lévesque chose to all but ignore his Lieutenant Governors during his term of office as Premier of Quebec and there was nothing they could do about it; the delicate position of monarchical offices in Quebec precluded any public protests by the officeholders.[11] Thus this constitutional right of consultation is one that appears to lack any practicable sanction, beyond the mild opprobrium that may or may not be generated by public knowledge of the situation; as the Quebec example illustrates, however, not even that small measure of leverage may be available to a governor.

Perhaps the clearest way to convey an impression of the position of the governors is to state that broad conventions normally operate to remove any element of personal discretion from a governor's exercise of his or her powers. Thus the main constitutional conventions either delegate the expansive legal powers of the governor to the first minister and cabinet, or determine that the powers may be exercised only in such a way that the governor has no freedom to select among alternative courses of action. In the normal course of events the governor acts strictly in accordance with the 'advice' tendered by the Cabinet and merely provides the legal sanction for its decisions. The only duty always performed without formal advice is the appointment of the first minister, but the outcome of an election usually becomes clear in a short enough time that the governor has no option but to appoint the leader of the winning party.

THE GOVERNORS' PERSONAL POWERS

Nevertheless, exceptions to these broad conventions also exist that permit the very rare exercise of personal discretion by a governor in order to defend the basic operation of the political process, or the existence of some fundamental principle of the constitution. As Chief Justice Sir William Ritchie said in *R. v. McLoed* (1883) with respect to the royal prerogatives in general:

> These prerogatives of the Crown must not be treated as personal to the sovereign; they are great constitutional rights, conferred on the sovereign, upon principle of public policy, for the benefit of the people, and not, as it is said, 'for the gratification of the sovereign'—they form part of and are generally speaking 'as ancient as the law itself'.[12]

The personal prerogative powers of the monarch may be divided between those that are absolutely essential to the basic functioning of any political system based on the Westminster model of parliamentary government, and those that may be desirable as part of a larger system of checks and balances that protect other aspects of the constitution. The greatest level of agreement exists with respect to the first group of powers. Only a few would deny the necessity of having *someone* within the political structure who might help to sort out the appointment of a prime minister when the results of an election are not clear, or remove a Prime Minister who might obstinately hang onto power when clearly defeated in the House or, more especially, in a general election.[13] As a majority of the Supreme Court of Canada said in the Patriation Reference:

> [I]f after a general election where the Opposition obtained the majority at the polls the Government refused to resign and clung to office, it would thereby commit a fundamental breach of conventions, one so serious that it could be regarded as tantamount to a coup d'état. The remedy in this case lies with the Governor General or the Lieutenant Governor as the case may be who would be justified in dismissing the Ministry and calling on the Opposition to form the Government.[14]

Unfortunately the specific circumstances in which a governor may exercise these emergency powers remain controversial. A basic division may be made between those, on the one hand, who feel that a certain narrowly defined range of circumstances can be described in which the exercise of certain prerogative powers is justified, and those on the other who argue that the precise nature of future constitutional crises cannot be foretold and, accordingly, believe that no attempt should be made to dismiss absolutely some prerogative power. Another reason why the prerogative powers remain controversial is that some underlying principles and facts of life about parliamentary democracy are still either misunderstood or are inherently open to various interpretations.

THE POWER OF APPOINTMENT

Although the appointment of a first minister is the most important duty of a Governor General or Lieutenant Governor, it involves the one act of a governor that is never done on formal advice.[15] All other Cabinet appointments are performed on the first minister's advice. The governor seldom has any practical discretion in the matter, even though he or she has complete legal freedom in appointments. The governor is bound by convention to appoint as first minister a person who is likely to command a majority in the legislature. This convention exists to ensure that the basic principles of responsible government are respected. Usually the results of a general election are sufficiently clear that the governor has no doubt who that individual is. When a party has won a majority of seats, its leader is appointed to head the ministry. Even when an election gives no one party a clear majority, a bargain is usually struck between two parties to command a combined majority in a short enough time that the person the governor must appoint is quite evident. Thus in most instances a governor does not have long to wait before the political arena has placed a single candidate in the spotlight, ready for appointment.

It appears, however, that with parliamentary government some measure of discretion *must* be left to the functional head of state in choosing whom to appoint as the head of government. In Commonwealth constitutions based on the Westminster model, some discretion has been left to the Governor General or President.[16] (Indeed, much discretion is left to the head of state in non-Commonwealth countries with parliamentary forms of government. Valentine Herman and Françoise Mendel point out that in such countries as Belgium, Israel, Italy, and the Netherlands, 'where there is usually no political party with a majority in the House, the Head of State plays a major role in the appointment of the Government.'[17]) There are two general scenarios in which a governor may be faced with real difficulties in appointing someone to be first minister. A situation might arise when a Governor General has to replace a Prime Minister who resigns either immediately following an election defeat or following a defeat in the legislature soon after an election. The governor can face serious difficulties if all parties are in a minority position and cannot subsequently agree among themselves on the composition of a new government. The second scenario arises when a Governor General must replace a Prime Minister who dies suddenly or resigns from office. A few writers have argued that even in these problematic situations, a governor should not exercise any personal discretion.[18] But most have recognized that personal discretion may have to be exercised in very rare cases, even though the range of that discretion should be minimized as much as possible. Forsey expressed the sentiments of many when he said:

> Sometimes the Crown has to exercise a discretion, even at the risk of being accused of bias. But it seems clearly desirable to reduce the risk as much as possible. It is hardly necessary to add that this applies with even more force to a Governor General or Lieutenant Governor than to the King or Queen, because the representatives of the sovereign ... are more likely to be accused of bias.[19]

Charges of bias have sometimes arisen in Canada because of suspicions that partisan loyalties remained from the active political backgrounds of those appointed to the vice-regal posts at both levels of government.[20]

In order to limit the influence of monarchical offices in the democratic process, several authors have proposed rules-of-thumb that would reduce, if not eliminate, the element of discretion that might be exercised in the first scenario mentioned above. For instance, Jennings has proposed, in the British political context, that the Leader of the Opposition must be sent for after a government resigns; but this solution was offered in the era of legislatures dominated by only two parties.[21] Forsey adapted Jennings' principle to a multi-party House when he suggested that the rule might rather be that the leader of the largest party should be given the chance to form a government.[22] Geoffrey Marshall, however, challenges this by pointing out that it might be clear that a third party leader would have a better chance to manage a minority or coalition government than the leader of a larger party.[23] Nevertheless, Forsey emphasizes that his suggestion has the desirable effect of reducing the risk that a governor will be charged with favouring one party over another:

> If the leader of the largest party has had a chance to form a government, and has either declined or failed, he and his supporters can have no possible grounds for complaint. But if the Crown sends for anyone else first, there is always the possibility that the largest party will allege bias.[24]

It is interesting to note that in all these discussions reference is made uniquely to the appointment of party *leaders* following an election. Canadian and British practice appears to preclude the appointment of someone other than a party leader as first minister, which sometimes happens in European countries.

Some discretion may have to be exercised after an election where the parties have roughly equal numbers. It is not immediately clear whether governors should restrict their actions to asking a particular party leader to try to form a government, and then step aside while the politicians thrash it out, or whether the governor should attempt mediation among various party leaders (in the manner pursued by the Italian President) before choosing the new Prime Minister.[25] While J.R. Mallory mentions vaguely that in some circumstances the governor 'enjoys a real freedom of choice', he fails to give any illustration of what he meant.[26] But Frank MacKinnon limits the personal intervention of a governor to 'encouraging and helping others to do the picking themselves'; he does not feel that governors have any right to do the actual selection.[27] Unfortunately it is not evident what a governor might do in order to 'encourage and help'. Perhaps he or she might hold private talks with party leaders, in order to encourage them to overcome their differences, before inviting one of them to try to form a government. Like MacKinnon, Brun and Tremblay also suggest that some minimal personal intervention may be undertaken by a governor, but not to the extent of making the decision personally: 'Son intervention ne pourrait aller au-delà de ce qui est nécessaire pour permettre le bon fonctionnement des institutions desquelles découle ce choix.'[28]

Those who argue in favour of restricting as much as possible the degree to which the vice-regal office-holder can intervene in the democratic process would likely agree that the proper course of action for the governor is to invite the leader of the largest opposition party to try to form a government, and then retire to the sidelines, allowing the party leaders to sort out the problem for themselves. Should the first leader fail, another might be enjoined to try, especially if there are enough small parties represented in the legislature to permit a variety of combinations that could form a majority. However, should all leaders fail to reach an agreement, a new election would have to be held. Sometimes an election produces legislatures that simply cannot function, and fresh elections are an absolute necessity.[29] Indeed, new elections were held in Prince Edward Island in 1859, and in Newfoundland in 1909, before the Assemblies formally met, because no Speaker could be elected—a fundamental sign that no government could possibly win the support of a majority.

All the authors reviewed have based their views on the number of seats held by parties after an election. No one suggested that a governor should pay attention to the share of votes received by parties in the election, even though it is quite possible that one party may win more seats but with fewer votes than another party.[30] The disparity between seats and votes could lead to some difficulties for a governor. For instance, after the 1975 Ontario elections the Conservatives remained in power, but only with the support of the New Democratic Party. Had the Conservatives viewed the election results as a moral defeat and resigned, the Lieutenant Governor might have faced a conundrum in deciding whom to ask to form the new government. The difficulty lay in the fact that the NDP had won more seats than the Liberals, 38 to 36, although their share of the vote (28.9%) was much lower than that of the Liberals (34.3%). Since the NDP was the largest opposition party, it would appear to have had the first chance to form a government; but such adherence to parliamentary form might well be viewed as an injustice to the Liberals, who had won more votes.

The appointment of a new government becomes relevant, however, only when the incumbent government has resigned. All constitutional authorities are agreed that a government has the right to remain in office to meet the legislature when an election results in no majority position for any party. This right exists because parliamentary government involves, both in theory and in practice, the determination of a government's composition by the legislature, and not directly by the electorate. As Hugh Clokie has written: 'The House of Commons may be regarded as the Canadian "electoral college", but an electoral college which does not disband after performing its function . . . '[31] Sometimes the results of an election make it clear what party will receive the support of a majority in the legislature before it has met, but this is not evident until the legislature has convened. When the results are not clear in advance, the existing government has a right to continue in office until the legislature has had an opportunity to meet.

There was much confusion after the 1985 Ontario elections deprived any party of a majority. The Conservative party decided, as was its right, to remain in office and meet the legislature. However, Premier Frank Miller appeared not to understand the conventions governing the appointment of new ministries after elections, because he believed he had a right to another election if he was defeated by the legislature when it met. Just before the legislature was to meet, the NDP made a formal agreement with the Liberals that would see them combine to defeat the government on the Speech from the Throne and then support a Liberal government. When this was announced, Miller still declared that it was a 'reasonable conclusion' that he would ask for a dissolution when defeated.[32] This was plainly nonsense, because his defeat would mean only that the legislature was pronouncing its verdict on who should govern after the election. The Lieutenant Governor had no choice but to appoint the Liberals to power. In a parliamentary system the legislature determines the final outcome of an election because the government must have the support of a majority there. Michael Atkinson was quite mistaken in his general assertion that, 'Whatever responsible government might have meant in pre-Confederation Canada, it does not mean, in the 1980s, that the House of Commons can choose the government.'[33] The confusion following the 1985 Ontario election demonstrates just how important it is to realize that the legislature ultimately decides who shall govern.

In the end it appears that a governor may have little, if any, personal discretion to exercise in the appointment of a first minister after an election. It is clear that in a minority situation the governor takes no formal action until the government has resigned. Virtually all observers agree that once the resignation is accepted, the governor is initially bound to invite another party leader to try to form a government according to a predetermined order arising from the number and size of the parties. It seems generally assumed that in a multiparty legislature the leader of the largest opposition party is automatically asked first. If the first opposition leader fails to receive sufficient commitment from other parties to form a government, another opposition leader might be asked whether he or she would try. In practice it is highly unlikely that the governor has any discretion beyond asking a particular party leader to try to form a government. There is a clear consensus that governors should minimize their intervention in the political process as much as possible. Furthermore, it seems that this discretion involves not so much a consideration of who should be asked to try to form a government, as this seems to be a matter of following the order of declining party size, but rather whether there is any likelihood of *any* government's being formed; if there is not, then an election is necessary.

In order to remain abreast of the political climate a governor has a right to consult, or receive unsolicited opinions from, the various party leaders. In the uncertain circumstances after both the 1985 Ontario election and the 1971 Newfoundland election the Lieutenant Governors received information from the opposition party leaders outlining their views of the situation; indeed, Ontario NDP leader Bob Rae even visited Lieutenant Governor Aird in order to inform him of the party's disposition to support the Liberals.

The other general scenario, in which the governor might have some problem in finding a candidate to appoint a first minister, would arise when a prime minister dies or resigns suddenly, leaving a governing party or coalition divided over a successor. In this situation there appears to be some willingness among political observers to concede the possibility for a personal choice to be made by the governor. For instance Peter Hogg, Richard Van Loon and Michael Whittington, and MacGregor Dawson all allow that the sudden death or resignation of a prime minister may be the one circumstance that necessitates a discretionary choice to be made by the governor.[34]

The past few decades, however, have seen a narrowing of the discretion afforded a governor in making such an appointment. The most recent discussions of this issue remain divided in their opinions of the range of discretion still left to a governor in appointing a new prime minister who can command a majority in the legislature. On the one hand, Forsey and Mackinnon both maintain that a governor may have to make a personal choice based on wide-ranging discussions with senior members of the governing party.[35] Forsey makes this argument on the basis that the only formal machinery existing in Canadian political parties for the election of a new party leader depends on the lengthy convention process. On the other hand, Hogg has strongly suggested that a governor no longer possesses any real personal discretion beyond the appointing of an interim prime minister, because the governing party would insist on making its own choice of leader:

> The utmost initiative which I can conceive of the Governor General exercising would be the appointment of a caretaker Prime Minister for the period when the party is making its choice; but even in this circumstance it is likely that the party, perhaps by vote of its parliamentary caucus, would also wish to designate the caretaker, and, in the absence of some gross impropriety in the mode of selection, a Governor General would be obliged to defer to the party's wish.[36]

In the context of a developing limitation on the governor's personal freedom in appointing a prime minister, it is likely that Hogg's view is prevalent among contemporary political observers in Canada. Thus, the only discretion that a governor might properly exercise today is in the appointment of an interim prime minister, and even then it would have to be in circumstances where the party could not reach a decision after a prime minister had died or resigned suddenly. There does not appear to be any agreement on guiding rules that might direct a governor in this choice. Both Hogg and Mallory dismiss the idea that the Deputy Prime Minister, if one exists, should be considered the automatic choice.[37] The increasing importance of the Deputy Prime Minister during the 1980s, however, may come in the future to direct a governor's first choice to this person.

One consideration that might limit a Governor General's discretion is the common view that it is no longer acceptable for a prime minister to be a member of the Upper House.[38] This restriction has arisen because of the principle that the government must be responsible to the elected chamber; the first minister, it is felt, should be in the Commons to be personally answerable for the government's conduct. However, there seems little harm in appointing a Senator who clearly intends to seek a seat in the Commons at the earliest opportunity. Indeed, if John Turner can be appointed Prime Minister while not holding a parliamentary seat, it appears excessive to insist that a prime minister could not sit for a short period in the Upper House.

It is perhaps worth noting the degree of flexibility that a governor has in order to deal with an extreme emergency, because he or she has broad legal powers limited only by convention. The crucial roles played by the Governors General in Grenada and Fiji following the coups in those countries underline the importance of some broad power's being retained in the event of a fundamental civil crisis. Should a provincial or federal government be plunged into upheaval by an act of war or terrorism, or by a catastrophic accident, the governors do have the legal power to appoint immediately new ministers to take charge of the situation. For instance, if a bomb were to explode inside a legislature and kill or incapacitate most of the members, the governor would be freed of the constraints that remove his or her discretion, because conventional rules presuppose the existence of a functioning legislature. An emergency interim government could be appointed to take charge of affairs until an election is held and a new government constituted. In appointing this interim government, it would appear that the governor would have to exercise almost total personal judgement in summoning a ministry. In the absence of a legislature for a government to be responsible to, the conventions that uphold responsible government would become temporarily meaningless.

THE POWER OF DISMISSAL

Just as governors have total legal freedom in appointing a government, they also have complete freedom in law to dismiss it. This legal power of dismissal, however, is also severely limited by conventional rules. In the normal course of events, a change of government is brought about not by dismissal, but when a prime minister in effect offers formal advice by submitting the government's resignation. Individual ministers may also resign during the life of a government, but their dismissal is carried out only on the advice of the prime minister. The power of dismissal left to a governor by convention is uniquely that of dismissing the prime minister and thus the government as a whole. Mackenzie King's rather forced resignation came in 1926, but Canada has witnessed five outright dismiss-

als of provincial governments by Lieutenant Governors since Confederation, with the latest true dismissal occurring in British Columbia in 1903.
(Other examples of dismissal can be found in the more recent political
history of other Commonwealth countries.[39]) However, as Saywell has
written about the dismissals in the Canadian provinces, 'to say that the
Lieutenant Governors succeeded [in their dismissals] is not to say that
they were right, that they were justified in using their undoubted powers
as they did.'[40]

Virtually all constitutional authorities appear to allow that a governor
may dismiss a government with propriety either if an opposition party has
won a majority in an election and the existing government refuses to
resign, or if a government has been defeated on a clear vote of confidence
and neither calls an election nor resigns. The power to dismiss a government in these circumstances is absolutely essential to the functioning of
responsible government. It does not seem to have been utilized, however,
since the Lieutenant Governor of British Columbia dismissed the government in 1897 after an election had reduced the government benches to the
same number as the Opposition.[41] Nevertheless, no one has suggested
that this power has died through disuse, as is often argued to have happened to the power to refuse assent to legislation in Britain. Perhaps the
reason that it still survives is that there is no other effective means in the
constitution at present to remove a government wrongly clinging to
power.[42]

Controversy surrounds the suggestion of several scholars that the governor may also dismiss a government for some other gross constitutional
improprieties, be they breaches of convention or of positive law. Opinion
on this issue is divided according to conflicting constitutional principles.

On the one hand, there are those who adamantly insist that the governor should refrain from dismissing a government for any other reason
than that it clearly can no longer command a majority in the legislature, in
which case the intrusion of a governor into the democratic process is
justified only in order to defend the most essential principle of responsible
government. Edward McWhinney has attacked the notion that the prerogative powers should protect against abuses of other constitutional conventions; rather, he claims that the best sanctions 'are the self-restraint of
legislative majorities and the corrective of public opinion as expressed
through the ballot.'[43] Peter Hogg has argued that a governor should not
remove a government for illegal activities, because 'questions of illegality
are properly justiciable and remediable in the courts.'[44] Furthermore,
Hogg echoes a position first drawn by H.V. Evatt[45] when he asserts that a
governor 'has neither the competence nor the authority to assume to
adjudicate a question of law and to provide a remedy for a finding of
illegality.'[46]

On the other hand there are those who firmly believe that the Queen and her representatives can and should act in some way as a 'guardian of the constitution'. Dawson has argued that a governor should intervene to remove a criminally corrupt regime from office. 'If, for example, a prime minister were shown beyond any reasonable doubt to have accepted a bribe and he then refused to resign or advise that Parliament be immediately summoned to deal with the matter, the governor would have an undoubted right to dismiss him from office.'[47] In this instance, however, the governor would not redress the breach of law—prosecution in the courts would still be pursued—but would defend the principle that the Cabinet must act with basic honesty, integrity, and respect for the rule of law. Marshall has asserted that a government might be removed from office for illegal administrative activities or ones that breached convention, but adds an important qualification: 'It would be necessary for the breach to be a profound one for which no other remedy could be found, either political or legal.'[48] Thus he views the power of dismissal to be one of absolute last resort, when the courts are powerless to provide a remedy.

But recourse to the courts can prove completely ineffective in some cases, despite the variety of remedies that may be available. The slow pace of the judicial process may render a remedy moot, or the government may corruptly try to suppress prosecution or to ensure a decision in favour of the government. Especially where the unconstitutional activity of a government involves a gross violation of judicial independence or the rule of law, the governor might provide the only effective check upon a government. Sometimes, as well, a ministry may not be legally liable for corruption and illegalities they knowingly turned a blind eye to. Ministers may also behave in a technically legal, yet immoral and dishonest, manner. The basic limitation of judicial remedies is that they redress only a specific breach of law, and do not deal with the political consequences of illegal activities.

There have been two instances in Canadian political history where a government has been dismissed for scandalous behaviour. In 1891 the Mercier government in Quebec was cajoled by the Lieutenant Governor into agreeing to a Royal Commission to probe widely believed allegations of corruption. This Commission revealed the difficulty of relying on court sanctions to discipline a corrupt government. It concluded that fraudulent payments had been made by the government to its supporters with the knowledge, but not the direct action, of the cabinet; thus criminal charges against the ministers were unsuitable. Nevertheless, the Lieutenant Governor dismissed Mercier. The other case occurred in 1903 when the Lieutenant Governor of British Columbia dismissed the government after a scandal involving corrupt relations between two ministers and railway interests. It should be noted that in both instances the Lieutenant Governors dismissed the governments only after some committee or commission had investigated and established the fact of corrupt activities. In another incident in 1915, the Lieutenant Governor of Manitoba threatened the Premier, Sir Rodmond Roblin, with dismissal if he did not agree to set up a Royal Commission to investigate allegations of corruption in the government. The Commission was agreed to, and such misdeeds were eventually uncovered that Roblin resigned.[49]

Few modern writers discuss the propriety of a governor's dismissing a government on account of some scandal. In 1977, however, André Bernard reviewed the first two cases cited above, and concluded that it was doubtful whether a governor could still act to remedy a government scandal by dismissing it.[50] If the right to dismiss a corrupt government does exist, it would appear that a governor could consider removing a government only when it was found to have committed gross acts of corruption and could continue in office with the support of the legislature only through party discipline.

Thus there is still much controversy surrounding a governor's ability to act as a guardian of the constitution by dismissing a government for some scandalous, illegal, or unconstitutional action other than clinging to office after a clear defeat in the legislature or at the polls. This power is far from generally accepted because many people believe that the principles of democratic government demand that the intrusion of the appointed official who acts as governor should be as limited as possible. The only dismissal that would be widely accepted, it appears, is the removal of a defeated government that tried to remain in office.

One aspect of the power of dismissal is unanimously accepted: a governor may dismiss a government, for whatever reason, only if the likelihood of forming some alternative government is apparent. In what can best be described as an outrageous abuse of the power of dismissal, the Lieutenant Governor of British Columbia dismissed a government in 1900 after it was defeated on a motion of confidence, only to replace it with an administration that had a single member in the legislature![51] In a lesson that should warn any other deluded governor, the Lieutenant Governor himself was dismissed by the federal government, through the Governor General, after the new provincial government had been defeated at the election that followed relatively soon after its appointment.

A governor's right to dismiss a government is sometimes exercised in a curious, indirect manner. Rather than remove outright a government from office, a governor can induce a change in government by refusing its advice on some important matter, such as advising that an election should be held. It was for this reason that Mackenzie King resigned in 1926 when Lord Byng, the Governor General, refused his advice to dissolve parliament. It is often suggested that the proper course for prime ministers who find their advice refused by the governor is to offer their resignation. This is rather anachronistic in a modern parliamentary system where a government is said to be responsible to the elected legislature. However, it is the principle that a government must also retain the confidence of the sovereign (hence, the governor) that permits, in a strict sense, any dismissal of a government.[52] A prime minister is sometimes thought to have some choice to stay on in office 'to force the issue' after advice is refused, although it is assumed that the preponderance of obligation lies on the side of resigning. The obligation to resign appears to be nullified in circumstances where the principle that a prime minister must retain the governor's confidence comes in conflict with a far more important principle: that the governor must act on any constitutionally correct advice given by a prime minister who has the confidence of the legislature. Therefore the justification for staying in office in such a situation is likely to turn on whether a prime minister has a right to have the particular advice in question acted upon by the governor.

The power of dismissal is sometimes mooted as a means to carry out the Crown's prerogative power to insist on an election. The Australian constitutional crisis of 1975 provides a rich example to illustrate the controversies involved when a governor takes it upon himself to dismiss the government because he felt an election was necessary.[53] The difficulties arose when the Opposition-controlled elected Senate refused to pass supply in protest against a complicated financial scandal the government had embroiled itself in. After a while the government started to run out of money and considered a scheme by which funds could be raised on the commercial market to keep the wheels of government in motion. The government under Gough Whitlam was in firm control of the House of Representatives and felt that the Upper House had no conventional right to exercise its legal power to block supply. The Opposition, led by Malcolm Fraser, was equally adamant that the Senate had both the legal power and the conventional right to block supply on a crucial issue such as the one at hand. The Governor General, Sir John Kerr, held discussions with both the Prime Minister and the Leader of the Opposition, looking for a resolution to the impasse. Whitlam argued that the blockage of supply by the Senate was unconstitutional, and he felt that supply would not run out before he could force the bill through by weakening the resolve of enough individual senators and by having an extraordinary election for half the Senate. Fraser, on the other hand, informed the Governor General that the Senate would remain firm.

Kerr brought an end to the immediate problem by dismissing Whitlam and installing Fraser in his place. He did this on the grounds that Whitlam was being refused supply and could not guarantee that it would be granted in time; Kerr believed that the government had thus lost the confidence of parliament and that a fresh election of both Houses was needed, which Whitlam had refused to advise. Kerr gained a promise from Fraser that supply would immediately be granted by the Senate and an election advised if he were appointed Prime Minister; this, in fact, is what transpired. Although Kerr resolved the problems of the moment and was in some indirect sense vindicated by Whitlam's crushing defeat in the election, this particular exercise of the power of dismissal sparked a raging controversy.[54]

The actions by several of the principal actors in the incident illustrate the damage that can be done when positive law is allowed to prevail over the conventions that have arisen to produce the contemporary functioning constitution. Fraser was at fault for sparking the crisis by using the legal power of the Senate to block supply, despite a long-respected principle that the Upper House should never refuse supply. Also, the Governor General asked for a constitutional opinion from the Chief Justice of the High Court, Sir Garfield Barwick, who wrote back: 'The Senate has the constitutional power to refuse to pass a money bill; it has the power to refuse supply to the Government of the day.'[55] However, in this instance Barwick was using 'constitutional power' synonymously with the *legal* provisions of the formal Constitution. In formulating his course of action, Kerr relied explicitly on the legality of the Senate's actions, as well as on the broad legal power he possessed to dismiss a ministry. As he explained at the time: 'The Constitution must prevail over any convention because in determining the question how far the conventions of responsible government have been grafted on to the federal compact, the Constitution itself must in the end control the situation.'[56] In addition, Kerr seemed to rely on a populist notion that the electorate should be allowed to pronounce their judgement on a serious constitutional confrontation. In his own defence Whitlam argued strenuously that the convention that the government is responsible only to the Lower House should prevail over the arguments based on the legal powers of the Senate and the Governor General, and that a government that is supported by the Lower House should be given every opportunity to resolve the confrontation. The academic analyses of this crisis appear to favour overwhelmingly the constitutional position taken by Whitlam, and to condemn Kerr for an ill-considered intrusion into the democratic processes.[57]

THE POWER TO SUMMON AND DISSOLVE THE LEGISLATURE

It is a firm convention in Canada that the Prime Minister normally decides when to recall the legislature or to dissolve it in order to hold an election. But the Australian constitutional crisis of 1975 raises the important question of whether a governor has a right to demand that an election be held. If such a right exists, it would only work through the reversal of the normal flow of advice from the Prime Minister to the Governor General. Although both the Constitution Act, 1867, and the Letters Patent of 1947 expressly mention the Governor General's power of dissolution, these legal provisions have been superseded by the specific details of the Elections Act. In strict law, the dissolution of the legislature now requires the concurrence of both the first minister and the governor in the issuance of the writ of election; indeed, the federal writ states that the call is to be made 'by and with the advice of our prime minister'.[58] Thus if a governor were to demand an election, the Prime Minister's agreement would be essential. The questions are: does a governor have the right to demand that the Prime Minister agree? and, if the Prime Minster does not agree, can the governor dismiss the government and appoint one that will advise an election? If this right does exist, it has been hardly exercised at all. Apparently there has been only one instance in Canadian history of a forced dissolution, which occurred in New Brunswick in 1856.[59]

Modern constitutional opinion takes rather a dim view of a prerogative right to dissolve the legislature. Forsey is quite emphatic that a governor should not possess such a right: 'To concede him the power to dissolve of his own motion would be to put responsible government at his mercy.'[60] Although Jennings has mused, 'There is something to be said for a power to dismiss an unconstitutional Ministry or to dissolve a corrupt Parliament . . .', he went on to conclude that 'while the Queen's personal prerogative is maintained in theory, it can hardly be exercised in practice.'[61] He believed that the Queen should not dissolve Parliament just because it was passing legislation opposed by a majority of the populace:

> Every government takes decisions which would not be approved of by the electorate. It is neither practicable nor desirable that an election should be held whenever it is suspected that a particular decision is not approved. The electorate is asked to approve not a particular decision but a course of policy.[62]

One might add that in the present era of multiparty political systems, it is rare for any government to be elected with a majority of votes, let alone maintain majority support for most of its policies.

However, there may be occasions when a government is proposing quite radical and lasting alterations to the fundamental fabric of the political system, or to society, that were not approved of in an election. It has been suggested by some writers that in such a situation the governor might have a right to insist that the matter be put to the electorate.[63]

This whole problem was raised briefly in 1982 when the then Governor General, Edward Schreyer, revealed publicly that he might have considered forcing an election over the Patriation issue. In an interview with Canadian Press, Schreyer speculated that a situation could have developed that would have justified his intervention. If the federal-provincial conference held after the Supreme Court's ruling had not resulted in any agreement, and Prime Minister Trudeau had continued to press for unilateral amendment while 'there was an absolute absence of willingness to discuss anything any further, the only way out ... would have been to cause an election to be held and the Canadian people asked to decide.'[64]

In this case the Governor General would have intervened to protect the federal principles of the Canadian Constitution from unilateral amendment by the federal government. The Supreme Court had quite clearly ruled that unilateral patriation would violate a fundamental convention requiring substantial provincial agreement to changes that affect provincial jurisdiction. With this statement the Court offered the only judicial remedy available for a breach of convention alone. If negotiations had broken down and the government had continued in its course, it appears that the only practical check in its way would have been the Governor General. If he had insisted on an election, the Governor General would have called on the electorate to act as the guardian of the rights of provinces to agree to any amendment that would substantially alter their jurisdiction.

Reaction to Schreyer's speculation was quite mixed. Forsey felt that Schreyer was wrong to contemplate forcing an election; he also complained that a Governor General should never talk about such matters until he has been out of office for many years. Gil Rémillard and Gerald Beaudouin were also both skeptical that a governor could properly exercise his legal powers in the manner suggested by Schreyer. Mallory, on the other hand, supported Schreyer by saying that a Governor General has the right to dismiss a prime minister who is 'behaving totally unreasonably or going against the constitution ... He would have been a brave man but he would have been within his rights as Governor General.'[65]

Thus the forcing of an election by a governor would certainly be one of the more controversial exercises of reserve power because there appears to be little consensus about its propriety. If this extreme action were ever seriously contemplated by a governor, the resulting controversy might be lessened sufficiently to allow a governor to survive its exercise only if the matter to be put to the electorate involved a deep and permanent disruption of the constitution (such as secession), and on which the government had not allowed the electorate to voice its opinion. Indeed, it would have to involve something that the majority of the public were plainly outraged over.

In Canada, however, the history of constitutional development does not give much support to the notion that the people must give a mandate for deep constitutional change. The initial Confederation agreement that created Canada was never put to the electorate, nor even formally approved of by all of the provincial legislatures.[66] Even the recent constitutional package that finally provided for an amending formula and the Charter of Rights was not put before the electorate in any jurisdiction. Two notable exceptions to this trend are the 1980 Quebec referendum on sovereignty association and the 1988 federal election, which was forced by the

Senate over the Free Trade Agreement. But the democratic principle that the electorate should be consulted on any fundamental and lasting constitutional change holds sufficient appeal that some constitutional observers will continue to argue that a governor might insist on an election in certain rare situations.

A far less controversial right of a governor involves the summoning of the legislature. As with the dissolution of the legislature, the writs calling Canadian legislators to assemble require the agreement of both the governor and the first minister. There is an evident consensus that a governor may at times insist that the legislature be called together, and the Prime Minister is obliged to comply. When an election has deprived a government of its obvious support and the government appears to be trying to avoid meeting its fate in the legislature, a governor may insist that the legislature be summoned within some reasonable time in order that the support for the present or a new government be made clear.[67] Eugene Forsey and Graham Eglington have also argued that a governor should insist on the recall of the legislature in order that supply be passed, rather than allowing the government to rely for any extended period on financial warrants.[68] However, there has been little support among other observers for action on financial warrants.

THE REFUSAL OF ADVICE

In strict legal terms there is no obligation that the governors accept any advice given to them by their first ministers, cabinets, or even the legislatures.[69] This broad power to veto the policies of the elected decision-makers, however, has been greatly restricted by convention. The development of modern responsible government has given rise to an essential rule binding the governors to abide by all advice that is constitutionally correct, regardless of their personal view of the wisdom or merits of the advice. Indeed, most observers would also add that governors should give their assent even to advice that is unconstitutional, provided there is some effective remedy for the consequences of that advice. However, there are still some instances where a governor may properly refuse unconstitutional advice—separate categories that are best examined individually in order to determine when, or if, a governor may stand firm and refuse to endorse some advice: the refusal of a prime minster's recommendation to call an election, the refusal of royal assent to legislation, and the rejection of a cabinet recommendation to endorse some administrative measure.

In *The Royal Power of Dissolution of Parliament in the British Commonwealth* (1943) Eugene Forsey wrote the authoritative text on the prerogative to refuse dissolution, which has been accepted by many scholars as firmly demonstrating the rectitude of this power.[70] He reveals that there have been 51 refusals in Imperial and Commonwealth history, from the advent of responsible government until 1939. A general rule prohibits the granting of elections to a government within a relatively short, but undetermined, length of time after it had already been granted an election. This rule appears to apply specially when the legislature has not had a chance to meet, or if the government is defeated immediately after the legislature first meets. The one allowable exception is where a legislature cannot plainly function, or even elect a speaker. Forsey proposed that a second dissolution should be refused to a government, 'unless (a) no alternative government was possible, or (b) some great new issue of public policy had arisen, or (c) there had been a major change in the political situation, or (d) the Opposition has explicitly invited or agreed to a dissolution.'[71] The basic formulation of these points has been echoed by several writers dealing with this issue.[72] The justification for allowing a governor to refuse to grant a dissolution is usually that it is necessary to prevent a 'diet of dissolutions', as well as to act as a brake upon a prime minister's power. As Ronald Cheffins and Ronald Tucker have argued:

> In view of the tremendous power possessed by the Prime Minister in the Canadian Constitutional system, surely we should attempt to retain some element of countervailing power to protect us from an excessively ruthless and ambitious Prime Minister, or one who seeks an endless number of dissolutions, in order to achieve his political ends.[73]

Nevertheless, the Crown's right to refuse dissolution has also been denied by some political actors and observers. The unfortunate King-Byng affair of 1926 sparked a flurry of articles that condemned the exercise of such a power as an arbitrary intrusion of monarchical power into the democratic process.[74] There have also been other more recent writers who have doubted or protested the existence of this reserve power.[75] It would appear, however, that the denial of *any* power to refuse a dissolution with propriety is a minority position among constitutional observers today.

Whether or not a governor may refuse royal assent to a bill duly passed by the legislature is a particularly contentious question. This power is most adamantly denied by British writers, or those who rely on British precedent, because no British monarch has refused to give royal assent to legislation since 1707. Even by 1867, Bagehot was able to claim that 'the Queen has no such veto. She must sign her own death-warrant if the two Houses unanimously send it up to her.'[76] The inability to refuse assent has been cited by many British constitutional writers ever since.[77]

The colonial experience in Canada, however, has meant that in this regard Canadian political culture has drawn on a completely different range of practice than has British politics. Colonial governors played an active part in the legislative process, readily vetoing or referring back to

London any legislation that ran counter to British Imperial policy or legislation. Thus Lieutenant Governors felt little compunction about refusing assent to provincial legislation, especially during the first half-century after Confederation.

Legislation may fail to gain assent after passage in the legislature in a variety of ways. Saywell has counted 28 bills that have been refused assent outright, although most of these occasions have been with either the advice or the acquiescence of Cabinet.[78] In addition, British Columbia possesses a curious provision in its Constitution Act that permits the Lieutenant Governor to refer bills back to the legislature for reconsideration with his or her own proposed amendments; by 1944, 88 bills had failed initially to gain assent in this manner.[79] Finally, Canadian governors at both levels of government, in order to express their personal displeasure with legislation, have relied on their legal power to reserve a bill for the approval of a higher authority—the Governor General or the Queen. The Governor General's legal power to reserve bills on his or her own initiative for the monarch's pleasure, however, has been negated by convention since an Imperial Conference in 1887 agreed that the practice should be ended.[80] A total of 22 reservations of Dominion bills had occurred by the time the last was reserved in 1886, with 7 bills failing to gain royal assent in the end.[81] Of the 70 provincial bills reserved, only 14 were eventually assented to by the Governor General. Saywell says that 12 of these instances of reservation of provincial legislation were motivated primarily by the Lieutenant Governor's disapproval of the bills.[82] Thus a total of 186 provincial and 22 federal bills initially failed to gain assent after being passed by the legislature because the governors had vetoed or reserved them, or sent them back to their legislatures; 99 of these bills never finally received royal assent. However, in recent decades the practice of refusing assent or reserving a bill has become almost unheard of. The last veto came in 1945, while there has only been one instance of reservation in the last half-century—in 1961.

It has become quite unconstitutional for a Lieutenant Governor to avoid granting assent by reserving legislation on his or her own discretion. The reservation of three bills in 1937 by the Lieutenant Governor of Alberta caused such surprise that a reference question was put to the Supreme Court of Canada concerning the continued existence of the power of reservation; unsurprisingly, the Court ruled that the power still remained fully extant—in law.[83] Nevertheless, opinion continued to develop against the exercise of that power; at the 1950 Constitutional Conference five provincial premiers stated publicly that they favoured the abolition of the power of reservation. By the time the Lieutenant Governor of Saskatchewan reserved a bill concerning mineral rights in 1961 there was widespread outrage, and the bill was immediately assented to by the Governor General on Prime Minister Diefenbaker's advice.[84]

In a governor's outright refusal to assent to legislation, a distinction should be made between a refusal of assent made on the advice of the Cabinet and a refusal based on the governor's personal discretion. Governors simply cannot refuse assent to a bill on their own initiative, but there a few circumstances where a governor can properly refuse assent on the advice of the Cabinet.

Some refusals may be advised by Cabinet because a bill contains some fatal technical flaw that was realized only after the bill had passed third reading. An example of a technical flaw is found in a criminal-code amendment bill passed in 1968-9, in which a section provided that an individual had a right to independent testing of a breathalyzer sample; however, it was not practically possible to save a breath sample for such testing. This particular flaw was overcome by the novel procedure of not proclaiming the particular section into force, but it illustrates a type of difficulty that might arise.[85]

A government might also advise that royal assent be refused or reserved for a measure that had been passed by the House despite the government's attempts to defeat the bill. This situation was repeated on many occasions in the late nineteenth century when party discipline was still undeveloped. In modern times it might occur when a minority government sees a bill amended by the combined forces of the Opposition. If a governor were advised to refuse assent to a bill passed or amended by the Opposition, he or she would have to choose between the duty to follow the Cabinet's advice and the equally important duty of respecting the will of the legislature; in essence the choice would have to be made between the principle that upholds Cabinet government, and that which requires the legislature's final control over the Cabinet. But a Cabinet ought not to advise a normative refusal of assent in the first place.

A few constitutional observers still reckon that some crisis might arise in the future that could possibly justify the veto of legislation by a governor on his or her own initiative. Although they do not completely rule out the refusal of assent in order to prevent as serious a move as to abolish the Opposition, such an event has been termed 'extremely unlikely' by Cheffins and Tucker.[86] Marshall concedes that the power to refuse assent in Britain may well be dead, but suggests that some major development in the future might require the monarch to block legislation when no judicial remedy would be available. Rather than dismiss a government that tried to pass an Abolition of General Elections Act, Marshall viewed the refusal of assent as 'the more immediate and less radical remedy'.[87]

The consensus, however, clearly seems to support a conventional rule that would nullify a governor's legal power to refuse assent on his or her own initiative; this rule protects the supremacy that must be granted the legislature in a parliamentary system of government. A number of Canadian scholars and politicians state starkly that assent can never be withheld. For instance, Van Loon and Whittington have argued that the Governor General could never refuse assent; to do so, they say, the Governor General 'would be violating a fundamental norm of our system of government, by claiming to represent the public interest better than the public's elected representatives.'[88] Furthermore, the entrenchment of a Charter of Rights in Canada has greatly bolstered the role of the courts in protecting many of the most basic political rights. In the Patriation reference a majority of the Supreme court said that by convention neither the Queen nor her representatives can 'of their own motion refuse assent to any such bill on any ground. . . .'[89] If assent were ever to be refused, it might possibly be done with any hope of correctness only if the legislation were to eradicate the very foundations of parliamentary democracy that the convention exists to protect.

It is clear that no matter how deeply it would contravene constitutional convention for the governors to refuse assent on their own initiative, no court would hold that the Bill that had been refused assent should nevertheless be considered to be valid law. Indeed, the Supreme Court of Prince Edward Island ruled in 1949 that not only did the Lieutenant Governor have the legal power to refuse assent to a Bill in 1945, but that his successor could not subsequently grant assent to that Bill unless the legislature formally presented it to him again.[90]

The third general area of advice involves all the other matters not relating to dissolution or legislation on which a governor may be advised by the first minister or Cabinet. Once again, the general rule is that the governor must agree to any constitutional measure. However, there are strong indications that some unconstitutional advice may be refused by the governor, if such advice is either illegal or conventionally improper for the Prime Minister or Cabinet to give. For instance, it is often suggested that a defeated government may tender only a limited range of advice before it leaves office.[91]

Several instances can be found in Canadian political history to illustrate the refusal of advice in this third area. In 1896 the Governor General rejected the advice of the Prime Minister to make appointments to the Senate and to several judicial posts on the grounds that the government had just been defeated in a general election; MacKinnon, Hogg, and Mallory have all supported this refusal as a protection of the rights of the incoming government.[92] A number of provincial precedents can also be found for refusing to make appointments recommended by a defeated government. In both 1878 and 1882, appointments were refused by the Lieutenant Governor of Nova Scotia, as they were in Quebec in 1897 and in New Brunswick in 1908.[93] In these cases the governments had lost the right to have their advice acted on because they clearly would not possess the confidence of the new legislature when it met. The Lieutenant Governor of PEI in 1924 refused his premier's advice to dismiss one of the cabinet ministers because he discovered that the minute of censure the premier claimed had been approved by cabinet was in fact quite bogus and that the rest of the cabinet supported the minister.[94] One cannot imagine why such plainly dishonest advice should be agreed to by a governor.

The legal right to refuse advice was reinforced in 1986 when the Nova Scotia Supreme Court ruled that the Lieutenant Governor *could* have refused the advice of his Attorney General concerning the Lieutenant Governor's warrants for the criminally insane. Indeed, Mr Justice Doane Hallett appeared to urge the Lieutenant Governor to make a personal decision in such matters, rather than rely on the Attorney General's advice:

> The Lieutenant Governor is entitled to, but does not have to, follow the Attorney General's recommendation just as the Lieutenant Governor does not have to follow the recommendation of the Review Board appointed under Section 547 of the *Criminal Code*. Parliament . . . has imposed on the Lieutenant Governor the duty of making the decision respecting an insane person's custody and rehabilitation; the Lieutenant Governor is the decision maker, not the Attorney General. The Lieutenant Governor is not a figure-head with respect to matters which he is obliged to deal with under this Section of the *Criminal Code*.[95]

Hallett also implicitly recognized an existing convention when he added: 'The Attorney General has the right to make recommendations to the Lieutenant Governor . . .', even though the relevant passages of the Criminal Code make no mention at all of the Attorney General.[96]

One positive incentive to refuse certain illegal advice is the bare protection for personal liability a Canadian governor enjoys, even for acts undertaken in an official capacity. As T. Franck has pointed out, a governor is not immune from 'civil or criminal suit for official acts done in contravention or excess of his authority or function.'[97] A court may well find that a governor's official approval of an illegal act is not part of his or her required duties. In order to make such an assessment the court would probably have to make full use of the conventions relating to the duties of a governor. One possible scenario in which this could arise is in the case of the appointment of someone to a public office whom the governor knew had bribed the prime minister to nominate him; in that situation the governor could be a party to the criminal offence of selling or purchasing public offices. Another example might arise if a person sought damages for being unjustly held under a lieutenant governor's warrant. This lack of complete immunity stems from the common-law position that colonial governors were not *in loco regis* and thus could not claim the protection of the rule that 'the Queen can do no wrong'. In 1916 the Judicial Committee of the Privy Council stated *in obiter* that because of several limitations found in the 1867 Constitution Act, the Governor General is not 'a viceroy in the full sense'.[98] Since the granting of the new Letters Patent in 1947, however, a good case could be made that the Governor General is now truly a viceroy and might claim the monarch's personal immunity from suit. But a similar claim could not be made for the Lieutenant Governors.

THE REMOVAL OF A GOVERNOR

This discussion of the reserve powers has focused up to now on the role the governors play in protecting the constitution from breakdowns in the political process and from abuses of power by the elected politicians. With such a broad range of legal power at a governor's disposal, one might wonder how the constitution can be protected from abuses of power by a Governor General or Lieutenant Governor. The ultimate sanction against an abuse of power by a governor is plainly that of dismissal. In such a matter the Canadian political system is in a more fortunate position than the British, which can only resort to a forced abdication or the abolition of the monarchy; either measure would prove far more traumatic to the nation than would the removal of a Canadian governor, who holds office for only a limited period in any case.

There is some confusion about who exactly has the right to advise the removal of a governor. Although both Governors General and Lieutenant Governors are appointed on the recommendation of the Prime Minister, it is not clear if the Prime Minister alone can advise that a governor be dismissed. In the two instances where Lieutenant Governors have been removed, the advice came from the Cabinet. In the first case the Governor General, Lord Lorne, even insisted that the Cabinet be unanimous in its recommendation, although such an insistence seems improper.[99] Thus it appears that the removal of a Lieutenant Governor requires the advice of not just the Prime Minister but of the Cabinet as well. In the two instances where the monarch has removed Commonwealth governors, however, the advice came from the Prime Minister alone; and in the speculation surrounding Whitlam's supposed consideration of advising the Queen to dismiss Kerr, it was assumed that he could do so alone. It is an open question whether the Commonwealth or Canadian provincial precedents would apply in removing our Governor General. Commonwealth precedents suggest that the advice of only the Prime Minister was sufficient, but Canadian precedents involved the whole Cabinet. Forsey and Eglington presume that the Commonwealth precedents have established a rule granting a Canadian prime minister the right to give such advice, although they did not consider the provincial cases.[100] However, prudence would seem to favour the Canadian precedents, which add a desirable impediment to the Prime Minister's power by requiring the whole Cabinet's approval; it is by no means clear that a prime minister could count on the support of other Cabinet ministers in such a drastic move as the removal of a governor.

It seems quite certain that a governor may be easily removed from office if he or she insists on continuing despite suffering from some obvious mental or physical incapacity. In such a case the Governor General would revoke the commission of a Lieutenant Governor on the advice of the federal Cabinet, but the Queen would remove the Governor General. In the case of an incapacitated Lieutenant Governor the federal government would likely await a petition from the provincial government. One difference between the dismissal of a Governor General and of a Lieutenant Governor lies in s.59 of the 1867 Constitution Act, which provides that a Lieutenant Governor 'shall not be removable within five years from his appointment, except for cause assigned, which shall be communicated to him in writing . . . and shall be communicated by message to the Senate and to the House of Commons. . . .' In contrast, the Governor General holds office entirely at pleasure and no cause need be formally given if a new person is appointed to succeed an incumbent at any time.

Unfortunately the justification and procedures necessary to remove a governor for incompetence or gross excess of power are far less certain. The only action needed at the federal level is for the Queen to be advised that the Governor General's commission should be revoked, because this position is held 'at pleasure'. The problem, however, is whether the Queen ought to refuse a request for the removal of a Governor General in some circumstances.

Former Governor General Roland Michener told a Senate committee in 1978 that he had always believed that the Queen would, and should, agree in the end to a prime minister's request to remove a Governor General in the event of a confrontation:

> If a conflict developed between the two, it would be a simple matter for the Prime Minister to recommend the appointment of another person as Governor General and solve his problem that way. The Governor General has no right to object, and the Queen has no right to refuse to make the appointment, so that would oust him, even if it were the first year of his term. The only restraint on that kind of thing is that prime ministers . . . would not dare lay hands on the Governor General if it were something on which they did not have public support.[101]

There is substantial evidence to suggest that the monarch would in the end agree to any request to remove a Governor General. When the Imperial Conference of 1930 established that the appointment of a Governor General would be made only on the recommendation of the advice of Dominion ministers, King George V is reported to have realized that each newly elected government might expect to appoint a new Governor General.[102] In 1932, A.B. Keith concluded: 'In the case of removal from office it seems clear that, under the existing arrangements, the Governor General can be deprived of office on the recommendation of the Executive Council, and that the Crown could not resist such a recommendation.'[103] Indeed, later that same year the Prime Minister of the Irish Free State advised the King to remove the Governor General—advice that was duly followed. Marshall reviewed this incident and concluded 'that there was no choice but to comply.' He then added: 'But on that occasion no significant constitutional disagreement between Ministers and the Governor General was in issue.'[104] It appears, however, that Marshall is mistaken in that qualification. Although there was no immediate division between the Governor General and the ministry, the advice to remove him was clearly given in anticipation of such a problem. The de Valera government intended to pass a bill removing the Oath to the Crown from the Constitution, and it was widely assumed at the time that the current Governor General would refuse assent on the grounds that such a measure was blatantly *ultra vires*.[105] There is another, more modern example where the monarch has removed a Commonwealth governor. In 1962 the Queen dismissed the Governor of the Western Region of Nigeria, the Oni of Ife, during a tempestuous period in the political life of that province. Earlier that year, the Oni had removed the regional prime minister, Akintola, after a majority of the legislative assembly had signed a petition demanding his dismissal. The Nigerian federal government subsequently intervened and appointed an Administrator to take the place of the new Prime Minister appointed by the Oni. This Administrator subsequently empowered Akintola to handle the affairs of government. One of Akintola's immediate acts was to advise the dismissal of the Oni of Ife who had dismissed him; the Queen promptly complied.[106] Thus there are two precedents of a monarch's removing a governor on the advice of the first minister, during or in anticipation of a showdown between the two officials.

There is also very recent evidence to suggest that the Queen personally believes that the overriding principle guiding her actions is that ministerial advice *must* in the end be acted upon. During the summer of 1986 much speculation arose over a split between the Queen and Prime Minister Margaret Thatcher concerning the damage the British government was causing to Commonwealth unity by resisting any sanctions against South Africa. This episode revealed something of the Queen's view of how she should treat advice from her ministers. As the Queen's private secretary, Sir William Heseltine, wrote to the London *Sunday Times*:

> 1. The sovereign has the right—indeed a duty—to counsel, encourage and warn her Government. She is thus entitled to express her opinions on Government policy and to express them to her chief minister.

2. Whatever personal opinions the sovereign may hold or may have expressed to her Government, she is bound to accept and act on the advice of her ministers ...

After 34 years of unvarying adherence to these principles, it is preposterous to suggest that Her Majesty might suddenly depart from them. No sensible person would give a moment's credence to such a proposition.[107]

Even if Sir William's letter indicates that the Queen believes she would have no choice but to grant a dismissal when so advised, her views do not exclusively determine the content of a conventional rule guiding her behaviour. The nature of conventions as rules of critical morality implies that she can be mistaken in her belief. Indeed, there are strong arguments to be made against such an automatic grant of dismissal.[108] Franck is explicit in his condemnation of this notion:

If the *de facto* head of state is to exercise his functions properly, he must not be dependent for his tenure solely upon the pleasure of his ministers. A fixed term of office ought to be written into the British North America Act, with the provision for removal or recall only upon a joint address of both houses being submitted to the Queen.[109]

When the federal government proposed legislative changes in 1978 that would have made the Governor General dismissable on the advice of the federal Cabinet, the provincial premiers met and issued a communiqué endorsed by all ten:

Provinces agree that the system of democratic parliamentary government requires an ultimate authority to ensure its responsible nature and to safeguard against abuses of power. That ultimate power must not be an instrument of the federal Cabinet. The Premiers, therefore, oppose constitutional changes that substitute for the Queen as ultimate authority, a Governor General whose appointment and dismissal would be solely at the pleasure of the federal Cabinet.[110]

Indeed, the notion that a prime minister can be automatically granted the removal of a governor virtually negates the reserve powers of the Governor General. Governors General would be all but powerless if they could be removed any time they resisted the Prime Minister's will; and it is clear that there is a firm consensus that the Crown has a duty to refuse unconstitutional advice in certain circumstances.

While the Queen is bound to grant a dismissal when properly advised, there may be another related rule: that a government ought never to advise a governor's dismissal except when the public clearly supports its contention that the constitution would be flagrantly violated by his or her continuance in office. The Queen might be justified in refusing advice to remove a Governor General if the dismissal were an attempt to overturn a decision taken with all constitutional propriety by the governor, such as refusing a dissolution. Nevertheless one could strongly argue that the Prime Minister should be judged by the electorate by means of a lost election if it does not approve of his or her decision to remove a Governor General. Some writers have pointed out that even a modest delay by the Queen, while considering the Prime Minister's advice to appoint a new Governor General, would open the possibility of the Governor General's dismissing the Prime Minister in the meantime.[111] However, when the Queen was advised in 1974 by the Prime Minister of Grenada to replace the Governor, she did not do so immediately; the Governor instead resigned of her own accord the following day.[112]

What is abundantly clear from this discussion is that the Queen's reaction to a request for dismissal is subject to several guiding, if conflicting, principles. Even in the absence of definitive rules, there are clear obligations that the Queen would have to balance, involving the duties to follow ministerial advice and to protect the constitution from abuses of power by an irresponsible Cabinet. The broad principles of the constitution impose obligations on the Queen, despite the lack of established conventions in this area, and greatly limit the choice of action she can consider.

The dismissal of a Lieutenant Governor presents an added dimension, in that it is carried out by another level of government: a provincial government that wished to remove its governor would have to appeal to the federal cabinet. Thus a body of elected ministers would decide the fate of the provincial government's petition. Two Lieutenant Governors have been removed from office, in Quebec in 1879 and in British Columbia in 1900.[113] The main reason in both cases was that each had dismissed a government on his own initiative only to have his new appointees repudiated at an ensuing election; this was taken as evidence that the governor had wrongly meddled and had acted against the interests of the people. Although the dismissal of T.R. McInnes in British Columbia raised few problems because he had removed two governments from office during his tenure and finally installed a government with only one member from the existing legislature, the Quebec case was far more partisan and raised the issue of the extent to which the federal government could interfere in provincial affairs.

THE FORMAL AMENDMENT OF GOVERNORS' POWERS

The importance of the conventions regulating the prerogative powers is underlined by the problems raised by the Constitution Act, 1982, in the amendment of the legal framework of these powers. According to s.41(a), 'the office of the Queen, the Governor General, and the Lieutenant Governor of a province' can be amended only by the unanimous consent of all eleven federal and provincial legislatures. Cheffins and Johnson have warned of some far-reaching consequences of this entrenchment:

At first glance this does not seem to be particularly significant in terms of the scope of the provision. However, after reflecting upon the decision in the case of *Re the Initiative and Referendum Act*,[114] one realizes that the phrase 'office' involves more than the dealings with the office holder, encompassing also the powers relating to the office. That decision held that any change in these powers involved an amendment to the office. . . . Taken to its logical conclusion, this result means that any change in the powers of the Crown and its representatives requires the unanimous agreement of the legislatures of the eleven governments. . . . In fact the legal powers of the Crown are so intrinsically interwoven with the system of cabinet government and thus any attempt to change cabinet government would invariably change the legal powers of the office of governor general or the lieutenant governor of a province, the authors contend that by virtue of section 41(a) this means that the cabinet system of government has become entrenched.[115]

It is debatable, however, whether the effect of s.41(a) is so extensive. Certainly the provisions relating to the Queen and governors contained in the Constitution Act, 1867 are covered by the unanimity rule; but provincial governments have never been able to amend those provisions relating to their Lieutenant Governors. Thus what innovation has been brought about by the new Constitution Act affects only the federal level of government. It is not clear, either, that the federal parliament possessed any great competence to amend the provisions of the Constitution Act, 1867 relating to the Queen and the Governor General. Even though the Constitution Act (No.2), 1949, gave the national parliament some express authority to amend the 'Constitution of Canada', the Supreme Court of Canada unanimously held that the power afforded by the 1949 Act 'relates to the constitution of the federal government in matters of interest only to that government.'[116] This might appear to have put many of the sections dealing with the Governor General out of reach of the national parliament, since those sections also serve as the direct or indirect models for the powers of provincial Lieutenant Governors; some of the other provisions, such as the vesting of the executive power in the Queen, would also be protected because they are of concern to the whole country, rather than just the 'juristic federal unit' referred to by the Court. However, the federal parliament has passed some legislation relating to the monarchy without causing any controversy: for example, the Succession to the Throne Act in 1937, which gave legal effect in Canada to the abdication, and the Royal Styles and Titles Act in 1952.

Peter Russell has also cast doubt on the sweeping inclusion of 'cabinet government' by Cheffins and Johnson into the protection of unanimous amendment.[117] Some of the most fundamental aspects of Cabinet government are not directly related to the legal powers of the Crown; for example, neither the party discipline that permits Cabinet government, nor the individual and collective responsibilities of Cabinet ministers to the legislature, directly affects the legal powers of the Crown.

The conventions adapting the legal basis of the powers of the Queen and governors are by no means 'frozen' as a result of s.41(a). Conventions have always adapted legal provisions—be they entrenched, statutory, or common law—in a continuous and evolving fashion. So long as the powers of the monarchic offices continue to be defined by convention, they can evolve and adapt to changing political values without resort to the formal amending procedure. However, if a government wished to effect some change by legislation, it could now do so only by the unanimous consent of the eleven legislatures. Many conventions relating to the prerogative powers of the Crown are protected from legislative intrusion by s.41(a), but these conventions have not lost any of their adaptive nature because of this section.

CONCLUSIONS

Conventions play an absolutely crucial role in regulating the practical use of the governors' enormous legal powers. The positive law of the Canadian Constitution provides the governors with the legal right to appoint and dismiss their ministers at will, to reject any advice of the Cabinet, and to refuse assent to the bills passed by the legislature. But parliamentary democracy is assured in the Canadian constitution by the transfer through conventional rules of virtually all these powers to ministers who are responsible to the legislature. The only vestiges of effective power that a governor has left to exercise, according to his or her own discretion, are those that are essential to the fundamental functioning and protection of the constitution.

The adaptation by convention of the constitution's legal framework has allowed an evolution without the need to resort to formal amendment. Just as the prevailing constitutional principles have varied in relative importance in Canadian political culture, so have the informal rules concerning the exercise of the governors' prerogative powers evolved. The disappearance of the colonial character from the office of the Governor General of Canada is perhaps the most pronounced example of this trend. The appointment of Canadians to this position, on the recommendation of Canadian ministers, developed as the principle of Canada's independence from Britain gained precedence in the constitution. Similarly, the governors' powers of reservation and refusal of assent have been nullified by convention as the principle of democratic responsibility crystallized.

Although a vast number of the conventions regulating this area of the constitution are unanimously agreed upon, much controversy remains over the range of prerogative powers that may be properly exercised by the governors during some constitutional difficulty. The controversies arise in part because constitutional observers cannot agree on the nature of the crises that might develop at some time in the future. A number of authors rule out the practical possibility of situations that would justify the exercise of some power, such as the refusal of royal assent. Similarly they would also restrict in advance the exercise of certain powers to particular situations; thus, the right to dismiss a government is allowed by some only when a government has either lost an election and will not resign, or has lost the confidence of the legislature and will neither resign nor advise an election. However, many writers cannot bring themselves to exclude categorically the possibility of these powers' being exercised, because they allow that some undefinable crisis might possibly arise in the future to justify their use; for this group the legal powers of the governors exist as an insurance against the unforeseeable.

Much deeper division of opinion is created by a lack of consensus on the principles that should guide the exercise of the prerogative powers and the relative weight to be afforded these principles. On the one hand, there is substantial support for the notion that the governors should intrude into the democratic process only to the minimum extent absolutely required for the basic functioning of parliamentary government. In this view a governor's intervention is justified only in order to ensure that a government exists that is responsible to the legislature. This principle is coupled with one other: the necessity to follow the advice of a government enjoying the support of the legislature. In this view, the range of powers that may be exercised according to the governor's discretion is therefore very restricted. On the other hand, many scholars would argue strongly that a governor also has a right and duty to protect other important principles of the constitution, especially in situations where the reserve power of the Crown provides the only effective defence for those principles; thus federalism, the rule of law, and the independence of the judiciary, as well as the non-corruption of governments and legislatures, are among the matters that a governor might possibly defend.

The greatest acceptance of an exercise of personal prerogative power will occur only at times when the basic functioning of parliamentary government is at stake. When a hard case emerges, the best course of action should be deduced from an examination of what measure is necessary for the proper operation of parliamentary government. Great controversy would likely arise if a governor were to exercise personal powers to defend other principles of the constitution.

Regardless of the disputes that the rare exercise of some prerogative power might engender, the normal course of government transpires in Canada without the slightest problems rising out of the vast legal powers of the governors. The conventions that transfer the usual control of these legal powers to the government of the day are firmly established and universally accepted. Without them the legal framework of the Constitution would have to be fundamentally altered.

3

Cabinet, Ministers, and the Civil Service

The conventions relating to the Cabinet are crucial to the Canadian constitution, since the Cabinet is barely known in positive law. No constitutional document or statute creates the Cabinet, determines who should sit in it, or details its powers; no law describes the relationship between the Cabinet and the legislature. Indeed, the whole enterprise of Cabinet government is left almost untouched by the positive law of the constitution. The principles of individual and collective ministerial responsibility take form mostly in the informal rules that have arisen to modify the positive legal framework of the constitution. The importance of these rules of responsible government cannot be overstated; without them the nature of our system of government would be fundamentally transformed.

CABINET FORMATION

Although the federal Cabinet has no specific genesis in law, it is a committee of the Privy Council that was created by s.11 of the Constitution Act, 1867, in order to 'aid and advise in the Government of Canada'. Before a minister is sworn in, he or she is made a member of the Privy Council, and usually remains a member for life. In addition to present and former cabinet ministers, the Privy Council also contains a number of honorary appointees, such as provincial premiers, Opposition-party leaders, members of the Security and Intelligence Review Committee, elder statesmen, senior judges, and some members of the royal family. It is a firm convention that only those members of the Privy Council who hold ministerial positions, be they with or without portfolio, may participate in the committee known universally, but colloquially, as the Cabinet.

Just whom the governor may appoint to ministerial positions is also firmly determined by convention. As we noted in the previous chapter, the governor must first appoint a prime minister who can command a majority in the legislature. The prime minister then advises the governor whom to appoint to which ministerial positions; at the federal level these nominations have been made since 1953 in the form of a letter called an Instrument of Advice.[1] It is a longstanding principle that a government exists only so long as there is a prime minister, because the prime minister is the only person who can offer advice to the governor.[2] If a prime minister suddenly dies, a Cabinet no longer exists—even though the other ministers remain in their individual offices. Particular ministerial positions all have some statutory basis in Canada.

The prime minister's choice of ministers is determined not only by intraparty and electoral considerations of good political choices, but also by conventional rules. At both the provincial and national levels, anyone appointed to the cabinet must either be a member of the legislature or seek a seat within a reasonably short period. It is not uncommon to see members appointed initially from outside the legislature. Between 1867 and 1984, 76 people were brought into the federal Cabinet who did not belong to either House.[3] And in 1985 Quebec Premier Pierre-Marc Johnson appointed four people to his cabinet who did not hold seats in the National Assembly. The requirement that ministers should become members of the legislature results directly from one of the most basic principles of our constitution, that the government should be responsible to the electorate through the legislature. The operation of this rule as a convention in Canada contrasts with the situation in Australia, where s.64 of the Commonwealth of Australia Constitution Act provides that 'no minister shall hold office for a longer period than three months unless he is or becomes a senator or a member of the House of Representatives.' New Zealand used to have a far more stringent stipulation in the Civil List Act, which required that anyone appointed as a Minister of the Crown or as a member of the Executive Council must be a member of the House of Representatives at the time of appointment. This provision was loosened in the 1986 Constitution Act by allowing candidates defeated in the previous general election to be appointed as ministers, provided they win a by-election within 40 days.

Since the first cabinet was formed after Confederation in 1867, it has been a firm principle that the federal Cabinet should be filled on a representational basis. Perhaps the most fundamental rule in this regard is that every province, if possible, should have at least one representative in the Cabinet; however, PEI has often been an exception and gone without a minister.[4] Another representational consideration that a prime minister must take into account when forming the Cabinet is the number of francophone ministers.[5] There have always been a considerable number of francophone members of the Cabinet; for instance, between 1867 and 1965, 28 per cent of all Cabinet positions were held by francophones, which is close to the francophone portion of the population.[6] While religious representation used to be a consideration, modern prime ministers are no longer obliged to balance Catholics and Protestants.[7]

Another major constraint faced in the composition of the federal Cabinet is an apparent obligation to include as few senators as possible. Since the turn of the century there have never been more than three senators in the Cabinet—usually only one. During almost five years of Diefenbaker's term as Prime Minister, there was no senator in the Cabinet. The general practice in this century has been to restrict senatorial ministers to positions without portfolio; usually the sole representative in the Cabinet from the Senate only functions formally as the Leader of the Government in the Senate. The move to bar senators from holding portfolios is of long duration, with the Liberals missing by one vote the passage of a bill in 1871 that would have legally established such a rule. It may not be clear if this practice can be viewed as an established convention today. Dawson does refer to it as a rule that 'has suffered some major infractions',[8] but these infractions have amounted to 12 instances since 1925—six since 1979. Incidents that go contrary to a rule, however, may signify that other more important rules have taken precedence, rather than that the rule does not exist at all. For example, the five senators holding portfolios in the Clark and Trudeau governments between 1979 and 1984 did so only in the context of insufficient elected MPs from important regions of the country. The earlier instances mostly involved temporary or short-lived situations while newly appointed ministers waited for a by-election to run in. A general rule against senators' holding portfolios might have to give way in particular circumstances to the requisites of linguistic or provincial representation, or to the requirement that a minister must hold a seat in either House of parliament. Its breach would not bring with it very serious consequences, since questions could still be addressed to the Prime Minister, an acting minister, or another minister in the Commons who has charge of duties in the same policy area as the senator.

RESPONSIBLE GOVERNMENT

The principle of responsible government figures prominently in the rules relating to the formation and operation of the Cabinet, since the government must be held continually accountable to the elected representatives in the legislature. This principle involves two general aspects: the responsibility of individual ministers for their departments and their own personal activities, and the collective responsibility of the Cabinet as a whole. Both individual ministers and the government collectively must answer to the legislature for their actions and resign if the legislature loses confidence in their performance.

Although responsible government has taken shape through conventions, the courts have several times relied on their combined effect in settling points of law. Two cases from the Supreme Court of Canada illustrate the use the judiciary can make of conventions. The Supreme Court did not actually mention conventions in either case, yet their use is evident. In the 1979 *Arseneau* decision, the Court allowed a prosecution against someone who had paid monies to a minister, under a charge of corruptly paying a member of a legislature. The reasons that Mr Justice Ritchie gave in his unanimous opinion are worth quoting at length:

> In the absence of evidence to the contrary, I am prepared to proceed on the basis that it was as a member of the Legislature that Van Horne was appointed to be Minister of Tourism. This would be in accord with the generally accepted practice in this country whereby ministers are accountable to the elected representatives of the people in Parliament or the Legislature as the case may be, and it is in his capacity as a member of the Legislature that a Cabinet Minister participates in the process of securing legislative authority for the implementation of the policies which he proposed. In the final analysis, it is as a member and not as a minister that he approves the expenditures which he may have recommended as a minister. In view of the above, I am unable to accept that Van Horne's capacity as a member of the Legislature can be so severed from the functions he performs as a Minister of Tourism as to make it an offence under s.108 to corruptly pay money to him as a member of the Legislature and no offence to corruptly pay money to the same man in his capacity as minister.[9]

Thus the Court used the conventional relationship between the Cabinet and the legislature to extend the circumstances in which a criminal charge could be laid.

In *Blaikie* (No.2),[10] the Court relied on the relationship between the Quebec legislature and the provincial executive council (the cabinet) to extend s.133 of the 1867 Constitution Act to executive regulations. In reaching this conclusion, the Court mentioned that the Lieutenant Governor would appoint to the Executive Council only persons who, 'according to constitutional principles of a customary nature referred to in the preamble of the B.N.A. act as well as in some statutory provisions . . ., must be or become members of the Legislature and are expected, individually and collectively, to enjoy the confidence of the elected branch.' Thus:

> The Government of the province is not a body of the Legislature's own creation. It has a constitutional status and is not subordinate to the Legislature in the same sense as other provincial agencies established by the Legislature. Indeed, it is the Government which, through its majority, does in

practice control the operations of the elected branch of the Legislature on a day to day basis, allocates time, gives priority to its own measures, and in most cases decides whether or not the legislative power is to be delegated and, if so, whether it is to hold it itself or to have it entrusted to some other body. Legislative powers so delegated by the Legislature to a constitutional body which is part of itself must be viewed as an extension of the legislative power of the Legislature and the enactments of the Government under such delegation must clearly be considered as the enactments of the Legislature for the purposes of s.133 of the B.N.A. Act.[11]

In this case, as in *Arseneau*, the conventions were used as an interpretative means to extend a rule of positive law.

INDIVIDUAL RESPONSIBILITY

Two particular meanings are generally attributed to the responsibility of individual ministers: first, questions concerning a department may be directed in the legislature to the minister; second, the minister carries a culpability for wrongful actions and will have to correct the wrong and/or, depending on the circumstances, suffer the penalty of loss of office. In what might be called the classic theory, ministers were responsible in both these senses for the activities of their officials as well as for their own actions. As Herbert Morrison once told the British House of Commons, a minister 'is responsible for every stamp stuck on an envelope'.[12] However, post-war political practice has seen great changes in the rules of individual responsibility, and the classic view no longer holds.

Informational Answerability

The most widely accepted aspect of ministerial responsibility is the doctrine that members of the legislature may direct questions to ministers concerning their administrative responsibilities. Indeed, this is one of the characteristic features of the Westminster model of parliamentary government adopted by Canada.

The practical operation of ministerial answerability, in this informational sense, illustrates the interaction between the conventions of the constitution and the 'laws and customs' of parliament enforced by the presiding officers in the legislature. The Standing Orders of the Canadian House of Commons provide the formal framework within which ministerial answerability may occur in the national legislature. An Oral Question Period is provided for, during which time members of the House may pose questions of any minister present without giving notice of the issue to be raised. In addition, provision is made for written questions to be submitted to ministers on matters that require some research; answers to these questions are usually merely inserted into *Hansard* without an oral response.

However, there is a contradiction involved in the relationship between the convention of answerability and the parliamentary rules that allow its practical operation, because the Speaker also enforces traditional rules that can work to negate the accountability of a minister. As Speaker James Jerome once declared, 'there is no obligation upon any minister to answer any question.'[13] This contradictory rule is most authoritatively stated in *Beauchesne's Rules and Forms of the House of Commons of Canada*, which Speakers use as a guide for their decisions in procedural rulings:

> A Minister may decline to answer a question without stating the reason for refusing, and insistence on an answer is out of order, with no debate being allowed. A refusal to answer cannot be raised as a question of privilege, nor is it regular to comment upon such a refusal. A member may put a question but has no right to insist upon an answer.[14]

And as Jerome pointed out, '. . . in the final analysis, the Chair cannot compel an answer—it is public opinion which compels an answer.'[15] But the usual provision of some response by a minister, even if the content of the answer is often unsatisfactory to the Opposition, is evidence of a general obligation that ministers feel to reply to questions in the legislature.

The answerability of ministers may also be diluted by restrictions regulating the content of questions that may be properly put to a minister.[16] For example, several decisions by Speaker Jerome in the 1970s extended an existing rule that former ministers could not be questioned in the House, and limited questions to the portfolio currently held by a minister.[17] The issue arose when Opposition members tried to question several Liberal ministers about their knowledge of wrongdoings that had occurred when they had held previous portfolios. The Speaker's rulings severely hampered the Opposition's efforts to determine the role played by past Solicitors General in a series of RCMP wrongdoings in the early and mid-1970s.[18]

Another restriction on the answerability of ministers arises because questions in the House must relate solely to the official duties of a minister. A prohibition has been consistently placed by Speakers against putting a question to a minister about responsibilities that might arise because of his or her informal role in representing a province or group in Cabinet.[19] As *Beauchesne* states: 'A question cannot be asked of a minister in another capacity, such as being responsible for a province, or part of a province, or as spokesman for a racial or religious group.'[20] Thus some important aspects of a minister's actual work may escape questioning in the legislature.

Culpability

The other major aspect of individual ministerial responsibility involves the political culpability and legal liability of ministers for actions undertaken within their departmental areas. Ministers are legally liable for the actions of most of their officials by virtue of the statutes that create their departments. T.M. Denton points out that for these legal purposes, 'The minister, like a company, is a legal fiction.'[21] In 1988 the Minister of Employment and Immigration and the Secretary of State for External Affairs were jointly found guilty of contempt of court because they were said to be vicariously responsible for the failure of their officials to produce some documents demanded by the federal Court.[22] Ministers have also been held liable to laws that bind 'officials' of a department.[23] However, the doctrine of individual responsibility also means that ministers may be held politically culpable for their own actions and those of their officials.

The past thirty years have seen a marshalling of academic opinion against the notion that ministers are responsible in the politically culpable sense for everything that transpires within their departments. This shift in opinion was generated by the realization that actual practice ran counter to this supposed rule. The size and complexity of operations in a modern government department preclude a minister's knowing all that his or her officials do. S.E. Finer launched the assault on the classic theory of individual responsibility with an article published in 1956, dealing with the application of the theory to British politics, and concluded that there was in fact no rule of individual ministerial responsibility that compelled a minister to resign because of the actions of his or her officials.[24] Finer's conclusions have since been expressly embraced by British scholars who have dealt with the subject.[25]

However, some British writers argue that a minister still bears some culpable responsibility for a subordinate. Philip Norton has argued that a distinction must be made between bureaucratic acts that a minister could reasonably have known about, and illegal or incompetent acts carried out by junior personnel that the minister would not have normally known about. He then asserted: 'In the former case, the minister would be expected to resign. In the latter case, the minister would probably be expected to answer questions in the House, explain what happened, and announce the taking of corrective actions.'[26] Marshall and Moodie also argue that ministers may bear responsibility for the actions of their officials, but only when the matter may be 'construed as a *personal* fault' of the minister.[27] In both these views, however, the minister is not being held culpable so much for the particular actions of an official as for his or her own personal failings in directing the department.

Opinion in Canada closely mirrors the British views of individual responsibility. There is a clear consensus that ministers are no longer held culpably responsible for all the actions of their subordinates. Indeed, T.M. Denton claims that he has not found a single instance in Canadian politics where a minister has been forced to resign because of some malfeasance by departmental officials.[28] Kenneth Kernaghan has concluded that the culpable aspect of ministerial responsibility has been almost lost in modern political experience: 'In practice, ministers do not resign to atone for either serious mismanagement by their officials or personal administrative mistakes.'[29]

It is sometimes argued that certain instances of ministerial resignation demonstrate that ministers are still under an obligation to resign if a major scandal or administrative problem develops as a result of some action or inaction on their own part. For instance, Lord Carrington's resignation as British Foreign Secretary at the start of the Falklands war is described by Marshall as a 'clear precedent for the existence of a rule requiring a Minister who is personally culpable for misjudgment or negligence to offer his resignation.'[30] Two resignations from the Mulroney cabinet might also serve as precedents for such a rule. When it was revealed that Robert Coates had spent some time in a German bar talking to a stripper, he resigned in 1985 after Opposition cries that no Minister of Defence should place himself in a situation where national security could be compromised. John Fraser, Minister of Fisheries and Oceans, resigned later that same year after he overruled one of his departmental inspectors and allowed the sale of tainted tuna. However, a closer examination of these events may dilute their suitability as precedents for the rule. First of all, Lord Carrington's resignation was accepted only after Margaret Thatcher had tried several times to dissuade him from resigning.[31] Secondly, there was little public outcry for Coates's resignation, and he claimed he resigned only in order to pursue a civil suit against the newspaper that first published the story.[32] In the third case, Fraser was finally forced to resign only when his version of the handling of the problem directly conflicted with that given by the Prime Minister's Office. Each of these examples of ministerial resignation appears in the end to support Finer's contention that the resignation of a minister depends on the 'fortuitous conjuncture' of three factors: his or her own resolve, the Prime Minister's judgement of where political advantage lies, and the feelings of the governing party's caucus.[33]

The vast majority of ministerial resignations in Canada have transpired because the minister has been caught in some morally or legally compromising position, rather than as the result of some administrative misjudgement involving ministerial responsibilities. Kenneth Kernaghan argues that this culpability may survive as a dimension of individual ministerial responsibility because 'a number of recent cases in Canada show that a minister will almost invariably resign if personal misconduct in the form of unethical, immoral or illegal activities is revealed.'[34] Resignations are demanded, and secured, in instances of personal wrongdoing because they demonstrate the basic unfitness of an individual to be entrusted with the management of the affairs of state. For example, Trudeau secured the resignation of Solicitor General Francis Fox in 1978 when it was confirmed that Fox had forged a signature on a hospital admittance form in order to procure an abortion for his married lover.

Perhaps the most fertile ground for culpable resignations in contemporary Canadian politics arises from conflict-of-interest activities, especially where a minister may have financially profited from government business.[35] Prime Minister Mulroney initially resisted Opposition pressure in 1986 to remove Sinclair Stevens, Minister of Regional Industrial Expansion, but Stevens resigned from Cabinet and Mulroney finally gave in to intense public pressure and set up an inquiry; since then he has been quick to accept or demand the resignations of two other ministers, André Bissonette and Roch LaSalle. There have also been a number of resignations at the provincial level in recent years as a result of conflict-of-interest allegations. Ontario Premier David Peterson let two of his ministers go in 1986, while an inquiry was held; the Manitoba Minister of Energy and Mines, Wilson Parasiuk, resigned while a judicial inquiry examined allegations against him—of which he was found innocent; British Columbia Minister of Lands and Forests, Jack Kempf, resigned and eventually left his party after it was revealed that much of his travel allowance was unaccounted for; the B.C. Minister of Health, Stephen Rogers, quit the cabinet in 1986 after being charged with failing to reveal all his investments; yet another B.C. Cabinet minister, Clifford Michael, resigned in November 1987 over conflict-of-interest allegations; also, Billy Joe MacLean was forced to resign in 1985 after being charged with defrauding the Nova Scotia government while Minister of Culture. The doctrine of individual responsibility clearly still has force in applying to a minister's personal wrongdoings, and often entails resignations when an alleged conflict of interest and personal enrichment are plainly apparent.

Ministerial resignations may involve the concurrent and independent operation of both internal and critical rules of morality. For instance, John P. Mackintosh points out that 'a minister may, like a private individual, feel responsible if he could by greater wisdom or exertion have prevented some unfortunate occurrence'; the minister may feel 'the point of honour or of punctilio that after all, this had happened in his department and therefore some degree of moral culpability should be accepted, even if not deserved.'[36] Thus ministers may be compelled, as Lord Carrington apparently was, by their own personal ethical code to do the 'proper thing' and resign, rather than feeling that they are under an obligation imposed by the demands and expectations of others that they resign. Another example of a point of personal punctiliousness is found in the resignation of Darcy McKeough in 1972 as the Treasurer of Ontario. A real-estate company in which Mckeough had an indirect financial interest had received the approval for a development permit from one of his subordinates, but it soon became clear that McKeough had had no personal involvement in the matter. Nevertheless he resigned within a few days of the story's coming to light and made the following statement: 'It is my conclusion that doubts have been raised and that these doubts may continue to be raised as long as I remain in this Ministry and Cabinet . . . I cannot tolerate these doubts knowing in my own mind that I do not deserve them.'[37] Where such a resignation occurs for reasons of personal morality, the incident is difficult to apply as a precedent for some rule of critical morality that obliges all ministers to resign in similar circumstances.

One particular view of individual ministerial responsibility occasionally surfaces in the form of an argument that the Finance Minister faces a special obligation with respect to the secrecy of the budget. If a significant leak of an item occurs before the budget has been presented, there will be loud cries that the Finance Minister must resign. Supporters of this view rely on one incident in British politics dating from 1947, when Hugh Dalton resigned after a delay in the presentation of the budget allowed a newspaper to publish details of it before the budget speech was given. In this case the minister had given the details to a reporter on his way into the House.

However, the reaction to a series of budget leaks during the 1980s in Canada has illustrated that the consensus of opinion here does not favour such a broad application of culpability. Marc Lalonde inadvertently allowed a television reporter to film a page of his 1983 budget during a general photo opportunity a few days before the budget was due to be delivered; when this was discovered, he raised the one leaked figure by $200 million when he actually presented the budget to the House, but he did not resign. Ontario Treasurer Frank Miller did not resign later that same year when budget material was discovered in the garbage of the company printing the budget for the government. A news report of some of the details of the 1986 Nova Scotia budget did not result in Finance Minister John G. Kerr's resignation. The announcement by a newspaper of a plan to encourage employee stock purchases three days before the 1986 Ontario budget was made known was lightly dismissed by Treasurer Robert Nixon. The Quebec Minister of Finance, Gérard Lévesque, faced no calls for his resignation outside of the National Assembly when the major details of his 1987 budget were leaked a week before it was due to be presented; although Lévesque immediately offered his resignation to the Premier, it was refused. In that instance the government called on the Speaker to recall the Assembly and presented the budget only hours after the leak had been broadcast by a television station. And in 1989, Michael Wilson did not resign after the main points of his budget had been leaked by Doug Small on Global Television.

The public reaction to the 1989 incident gives a clear indication of the consensus of opinion on this particular application of ministerial responsibility. Newspaper editorials and columnists argued strongly that Wilson should not resign.[38] The same position was taken by a number of political analysts, such as John Holtby,[39] Paul Fox, and Ron Blair.[40] Political scientists Reg Whitaker and Kenneth Kernaghan appeared to be in the minority in claiming that the rules of ministerial responsibility required Wilson to resign.[41] The key element in all the arguments made against Wilson's resignation was that he could not be held culpably responsible for the actions of the large number of people involved in the preparation of the budget and in producing its documents. It seems safe to conclude that the Minister of Finance's responsibility for the budget does not differ from any other aspect of individual ministerial responsibility: culpability enters the picture only when the minister has made a personal error.

Some of the ambiguities involved in individual responsibility arise because many political actors and observers have misperceived the operation of the basic principles involved. Constitutional principles may be affected by the interplay of other factors, and operate in practice in an unfamiliar guise. The principle that ministers bear a culpable responsibility for their actions may well continue to exist, but not in the form expected. The combination of party discipline and collective responsibility has effectively transformed the way in which the principle of ministerial responsibility operates in practice by transferring the effective power of enforcement from the legislature to the Prime Minister. The difficulty in placing this sanction with the Prime Minister is that the rule operates as a question of the Prime Minister's internal morality as much as a rule of critical morality. The Prime Minister, however, can ultimately be held responsible to the legislature for his or her handling of ministerial malfeasance.

The operation of individual ministerial responsibility may be further obscured because the Prime Minister might not dismiss a minister at the time of some major mistake, but might later demote or remove him or her during a general Cabinet shuffle involving several ministers. In 1987 Michel Côté was quietly moved from the Department of Regional Industrial Expansion to Supply and Services after it had been discovered that his department had overspent its budget by $80 million. In this fashion the action taken against an individual minister, although actually prompted by a particular misdeed or continuing incompetence, will be presented to the public as part of a managerial re-ordering of Cabinet personnel rather than as punishment for some wrongdoing on the minister's part. Nevertheless the Prime Minister may privately make it clear to the minister that such an administrative shuffle out of the Cabinet or demotion to a less-important position was indeed a punishment.

There is little doubt that the culpable dimension of ministerial responsibility is assumed to exist among most parliamentarians. As Geoffrey Marshall has mentioned in the British context, this aspect of individual responsibility is 'a convention whose existence is certainly not doubted in the House.'[42] The difficulty in formulating precisely when a Prime Minister should ask for a minister's resignation does not in itself prove that there is no longer any principle at play in our constitution requiring a minister either to resign or be dismissed for personal wrongdoing or gross mismanagement. Popular expectations, as well as the behaviour and language of politicians, are clearly modelled on the existence of such an obligation. The shift in the focus of sanctions from the legislature to the Prime Minister has not destroyed the basic principle that ministers are finally accountable to the legislature for their proper conduct as ministers—even though the principle may not be as rigorously enforced as many would like.

POLITICAL NEUTRALITY AND ANONYMITY OF CIVIL SERVANTS

The notion of an apolitical or non-partisan civil service has been an important foundation of modern responsible government.[43] The traditional doctrine of individual ministerial responsibility holds that a government department is accountable to the legislature only through its minister. This has traditionally resulted in the anonymity of civil servants in parliamentary discussions. One reason for this principle is to allow civil servants to have the freedom to offer advice to the minister without fear of public recrimination. Perhaps a more important reason for the anonymity of public servants is that it ensures the political neutrality of the permanent bureaucracy, which is a prime characteristic of the Westminster model of parliamentary government. Both these aspects of individual responsibility, however, have come under some pressure in recent decades.

In 1986 the Supreme Court of Canada upheld the dismissal of a federal official who had publicly campaigned against several government policies, although not in the context of an election. Chief Justice Brian Dickson clearly laid out the necessity of a politically neutral bureaucracy in his decision:

> As a general rule, federal public servants should be loyal to their employer, the Government of Canada. The loyalty is owed to the Government of Canada, and not to the political party in power at any one time. A public servant need not vote for the governing party. Nor need he or she publicly espouse its policies. And indeed, in some circumstances a public servant may actively and publicly express opposition to the policies of the government. This would be appropriate if, for example, the government were engaged in illegal acts, or if its policies jeopardized the life, health or safety of a public servant or others, or if the public servant's criticism had no impact on his or her ability to perform effectively the duties of a public servant or on the public perception of that ability. But having stated these qualifications

(and there may be others), it is my view that a public servant must not engage, as the appellant did in the present case, in sustained and highly visible attacks on major government policies ...

As the adjudicator pointed out, there is a powerful reason for this general requirement of loyalty, namely, the public interest in both the actual, and apparent, impartiality of the public servant.[44]

In a later case, also decided without recourse to the Charter of Rights, the Supreme Court upheld Ontario's legislative restrictions on partisan political activities of its civil servants. In so doing the majority decision explicitly referred to the importance of the principle of a politically neutral bureaucracy.[45]

However, the general legislative prohibitions against political activities have also been held to contradict the Charter of Rights in two separate court actions. The Nova Scotia government chose to bring forward new legislation after the Trial Division of the provincial Supreme Court ruled the existing legislative provisions invalid.[46] The federal Court of Appeal also struck down the federal ban against a civil servant's engaging in any kind of work for, or against, any political party. In this case the federal government argued that the convention gave rise to a right, under s.26 of the Charter, to be served by a politically neutral bureaucracy. Although the Court accepted this claim, it did not allow this right to prevail over the civil servants' right of association enumerated in s.2(d); the Court struck down the application of the provisions, except with respect to the most senior civil servants.[47] In both decisions the courts explicitly recognized the value of the constitutional convention of political neutrality, which the pieces of legislation were meant to protect, but held that the statutory measures were too broad to be justified.

Parliamentary practice has begun to demonstrate that it is no longer desirable or feasible to adhere to the notion that civil servants should remain anonymous and accountable solely through their ministers. As a result of the sheer complexity of departmental operations, deputy ministers and other senior officials have become regular witnesses before parliamentary committees to answer questions relating to the administration and to technical implementation of the duties assigned to their departments. Yet such appearances only occur with the approval of the minister.[48]

There has been some movement towards making a distinction between the political responsibility of ministers for the general policies of a department and the administrative responsibility of deputy ministers for the management and operation of the department's resources.[49] A federal Royal Commission, headed by Allen Lambert, proposed in its final report of 1979 that deputy ministers be given formal authority for the administration of their departments and that they should be held accountable to the Public Accounts Committee.[50] Although these proposals largely went unheeded in Ottawa, the Ontario legislature's Public Accounts Committee has since adopted several of the Lambert Commission's suggestions.[51]

It is still quite rare in Canada for ministers to name the official who is responsible for some mistake in their departments. A couple of instances have occurred, however, that have eroded the anonymity of civil servants. In 1972 Jean Chrétien referred to a report prepared by a named official in his department as a 'shabby piece of work' with 'stupid' conclusions.[52]

In 1978 Minister of Supply and Services Jean-Pierre Goyer created a stir when he castigated one of his officials by name in the House, announced the man's dismissal, and then repeated the remarks to the press outside the chamber.[53] He declared that he had not been properly informed by the deputy head of the project, Lawrence Stopforth, of financial negotiations with Lockheed about a possible long-range patrol aircraft, and as a result had given inaccurate information to the House. Stopforth sued Goyer for the remarks made outside the House and was initially awarded $10,000 in damages for being libelled. In order to dismiss one of the arguments made by the defence, the trial judge relied on the convention that civil servants must remain anonymous. It was argued that the minister could claim a 'partial privilege' because there was a duty to inform the public; however, Mr Justice Lieff pointed out that the obligation that existed appeared to require the minister to protect the official's anonymity.[54] Thus this case provides an example of the use to which constitutional conventions may be put in a judicial decision, with the convention being used to consider whether a common-law defence applied. However, Goyer later won the case when it went to the Ontario Court of Appeal. Mr Justice Arthur Jessup dismissed the trial judge's rationale and concluded that the constitutional convention relied on by the trial judge could not 'be permitted the effect of either enlarging or abridging the law of defamation.'[55]

Kenneth Kernaghan has concluded that these episodes have somewhat eroded the principle of anonymity: 'Although the instances in which ministers have publicly criticized their officials are exceptional, it is clear that officials cannot invariably rely on their minister to protect their anonymity.'[56] It is one thing, however, to observe that civil servants 'cannot invariably rely' on anonymity, and quite another to conclude that ministers are not obliged to refrain from naming the officials directly at fault.

One wrinkle in the relationship between ministers and their officials emerged briefly in the last Trudeau government. It involved the resignation or reassignment of deputy ministers following some grave administrative or policy problem in their departments: the deputy minister of finance, Ian Stewart, was removed from his position in 1982, some months after a disastrous budget; and the deputy minister of national revenue, Bruce MacDonald, was transferred to a position in the Privy Council Office in 1984 after severe political problems arose for the government over the use of performance quotas in the department.[57] Nevertheless, when administrative misdeeds are discussed, the prevalent parliamentary practice clearly seems to respect the anonymity of the officials working under their ministers. It is remarkable how few incidents to the contrary can be found, considering the temptations ministers must feel at times to pass the blame along to some subordinate.

COLLECTIVE RESPONSIBILITY

The collective responsibility of the Cabinet as a whole provides some of the basic characteristics of our system of government, where a body of ministers directs the affairs of state with a single public voice and retains office only so long as a majority of the elected representatives of the public have confidence in their abilities. There are three different dimensions to collective responsibility: the Cabinet is responsible to the monarch, to itself, and to the elected chamber of the legislature. The responsibility of the Cabinet to the monarch is often overlooked in discussions of responsible government, because it is 'true only in law'.[58] Ministers are legally servants of the Crown, appointed to direct the executive powers and departments of the Crown, and hold office at the governor's pleasure. But the governor's removal of a minister must be the consequence of the minister's having lost the confidence of the Prime Minister or of a government's losing the confidence of the legislature or electorate.

Cabinet Solidarity

Cabinet ministers have a responsibility to each other that takes two forms: they must maintain a public posture of unanimity in support of the policies decided upon by the Cabinet, and they must respect the confidentiality of the materials reviewed and of discussions held in reaching those decisions. Cabinet solidarity allows frank discussions while a matter is under consideration, and permits the government to act as a single unit once a decision has been taken. It also provides the basis for the disciplined party system that gives fundamental shape to much of the constitution.

The most immediately visible aspect of Cabinet solidarity is the united face members present in public. If a government is held collectively responsible to the legislature, one cannot have individual ministers saying: 'Well, don't condemn me along with the rest of the Cabinet, because I disagree with that decision and argued all along that another course of action should be followed.' The prime facets of Cabinet solidarity are that ministers must not openly dispute decisions, and must vote in favour of all government policies. However, the ramifications of this solidarity produce various subsidiary rules. Eglington and Forsey have compiled a list of the rules flowing from Cabinet solidarity that have gained general acceptance:

1. Government advice to the Crown must be unanimous, even if arrived at after consideration of strongly held but opposed views.
2. A minister i) must loyally support and defend any cabinet decisions and not quaver by suggesting he was compromised or was reluctantly persuaded; ii) must be prepared not only to refrain from publicly criticizing other ministers but also to defend them publicly; iii) must not announce a new policy or change in policy without prior cabinet consent—if he does so cabinet may adopt the policy and save him from resignation, but if it does not, he must resign; iv) must not express private views on government policies; v) must not speak about or otherwise become involved in a colleague's portfolio without first consulting him and gaining his approval and probably that of the prime minister; vi) must not make speeches or do acts which may appear to implicate the government, and must not express personal opinions about future policy except after consultation; vii) must carry out the policy decided upon by cabinet so far as it affects his own portfolio; viii) must vote with the government, whether it is in danger or not; ix) must speak in defence of the government and any of its policies if the prime minister insists.[59]

Responsibility for punishing a breach of these rules lies with the Prime Minister, as the head of the Cabinet, with expulsion awaiting the worst offenders. A measure of a Prime Minister's control over his Cabinet is the degree to which the public façade of unanimity is maintained. Many of these rules act mainly to protect the ruling party from Opposition attacks that would erupt if divisions were perceived in Cabinet. Thus the degree of latitude allowed ministers will depend on the Prime Minister's assessment of potential political embarrassment.

Grave breaches of Cabinet solidarity have been very rare in Canada. Indeed, to cite examples one has to reach back to 1916 for Robert Borden's dismissal of Sir Sam Hughes for insubordination; or even further, to 1902 when Sir Wilfrid Laurier fired Israel Tarte for publicly disagreeing with the government's tariff policies.[60] Resignations because a minister can no longer agree with the government's policies are more frequent, but they are still few and far between. Forsey and Eglington could list only six instances in Canadian federal politics, but Lucien Bouchard's 1990 resignation over the Meech Lake negotiations should be added to this number.[61] Some resignations can be found in provincial politics, as when three anglophone ministers quit the Quebec cabinet in late 1988 over the use of the 'notwithstanding clause' to exclude a language bill from the Charter of Rights.

British politics provide a far more lively scene; Alderman and Cross list 49 resignations over policy disagreements by British cabinet ministers prior to 1967.[62] In addition, Harold Wilson twice had to deal with ministers who voted against government policies in the Labour Party's National

Executive Committee; in 1969 James Callaghan was shuffled to another ministry, while in 1974 three other ministers were reprimanded and threatened with dismissal if they ever voted against government policy again.[63] Britain has also witnessed three occasions when cabinet solidarity has been formally suspended in order to allow cabinet ministers to campaign or vote against a measure the majority of the cabinet supported: in 1932 over preferential tariffs, in 1975 in the EEC referendum campaign, and in 1977 in the Commons vote on the form of European Parliament elections.

Apparent suspensions of Cabinet solidarity in Canadian political history came in the free votes on capital punishment in 1967, 1976, and 1987. In 1967, however, only one Cabinet minister voted against the government abolition bill in each of the second and third readings; in 1976 not one dissented; in the 1987 vote all but four Cabinet ministers voted for abolition. In the two earlier votes at least there appears to have been pressure exerted to present a united front, despite the public position that the whips were 'off' the Cabinet.[64] The most recent suspension of solidarity for a Canadian parliamentary vote occurred in 1988, when nine Cabinet ministers voted against a government-sponsored resolution on abortion. After first coming to power, Pierre Trudeau experimented with a relaxation of Cabinet solidarity for a few months by encouraging his ministers to debate publicly the pros and cons of policies before a decision had been reached in Cabinet. But he soon abandoned this position after too much political embarrassment arose from the public dissent among Cabinet members.[65]

The maintenance of solidarity also relates to the responsibility of the whole Cabinet for decisions taken in its standing and *ad hoc* committees, where a large portion of its work takes place.[66] The structure and functions of these committees have varied over the years. The single most powerful one is the Priorities and Planning Committee, which now has a membership of 19 and is chaired by the Prime Minister. After the reorganization of Cabinet in January 1989, a government background paper described the 13 other Cabinet committees as having been 'placed under the Cabinet Committee of Priorities and Planning'.[67] This major committee essentially acts as an inner Cabinet, a title it held during the Clark government, and often takes final decisions on important government policies. The Treasury Board functions as a Cabinet committee, although it is constituted by statute as a separate committee of the Privy Council, and in the past has been responsible for major government expenditure plans; but it has been downgraded to maintaining control over day-to-day expenditures. Much of the Prime Minister's political control of the Cabinet is ensured by his or her direction of its committee system; membership and chairs of committees are all decided by the Prime Minister. While the most sensitive of policy decisions may still be discussed in full Cabinet, many issues never percolate above the committee level; or if they do, the policy choices have been so clearly delineated that ministers coming to the discussion at the full Cabinet level have few practical options. From an individual minister's perspective, Cabinet solidarity means that every member must loyally support all decisions made in the committees.

Cabinet Confidentiality

The confidentiality of Cabinet discussions and documents is essential to the maintenance of solidarity. Not only are fundamental state secrets protected in this manner, but so is the anonymity of ministers who took opposing views during the debates leading to a final decision. Furthermore, senior civil servants, whose views are apparent in departmental recommendations and whose competence may be discussed in Cabinet, are also protected from public debate and recrimination. It is thought that only with this blanket of confidentiality will free and open discussion be possible on sensitive political issues. This secrecy is protected in Canada by both positive law and convention. Legal protection at the federal level flows from the Canada Evidence Act, the Official Secrets Act, and the Privy Councillor's Oath. In general, however, Cabinet secrets may be disclosed when they become of only historic interest; many, but not all, Cabinet documents are made public after a thirty-year period. When ministers resign from the Cabinet over policy difference, they are permitted to make a brief statement about the matters that have led to their decision; but these disclosures seldom result in any great revelations beyond the obvious fact that there was a split in the Cabinet.[68] The necessity to retain Cabinet confidentiality extends to the protection of Cabinet documents from being used for partisan gain by new governments formed by another party. Joe Clark explained this rule to the Commons shortly after taking office as Prime Minister in 1979: 'There is an arrangement in place, as has been the case for some time now, in the event of a change of government where a senior official of the public service of Canada is custodian of documents and will refer back to the Prime Minister and senior ministers of the former government with regard to the release of any such documents.'[69]

An important court case arose in 1975 when the British government attempted to prevent Jonathan Cape Ltd from publishing the memoirs of a former cabinet minister, Richard Crossman.[70] This case is of particular interest for any examination of the boundary between law and convention, since Lord Widgery was prepared to use the convention of Cabinet confidentiality to extend 'the developing equitable doctrine that a man shall not profit from the wrongful publication of information received by him in confidence.'[71] Lord Widgery took quite a different approach to the role of constitutional conventions from that adopted by the three judges of the Ontario Court of Appeal who settled the *Stopforth* case; as it was noted earlier, the decision, written by Mr Justice Arthur Jessup, opined that a convention should not be permitted to extend the law of defamation.[72]

Lord Widgery set out the following principles that ought to be considered in an application to prohibit the publication of cabinet confidences:

> The Attorney-General must show (a) that such publication would be a breach of confidence; (b) that the public interest requires that the publication be restrained, and (c) that there are no other facts of the public interest contradictory to and more compelling than that relied on. Moreover, the court, when asked to restrain such a publication, must closely examine the extent to which relief is necessary to ensure that restrictions are not imposed beyond the strict requirement of public need.[73]

But in the end Lord Widgery refused to prevent the publication of Crossman's diaries because he felt that enough time had passed since the first events described in the book had occurred that nothing revealed in it 'would inhibit free discussion in the cabinet of today, even though the individuals are the same, and the national problems have a distressing similarity with those of a decade ago.'[74] Another aspect of this decision that has gone relatively unnoticed was the judge's refusal to grant protection to the conventional confidentiality between ministers and their senior civil servants; he concluded: 'I can see no ground in law . . . for saying that either the Crown or the individual civil servant has an enforceable right to have the advice which he gives treated as confidential for all time.'[75]

The *Jonathan Cape* case has apparently had the effect of eroding the obligation felt by former British ministers, and several revealing memoirs have since been published.[76] Philip Norton has argued that the convention of Cabinet solidarity has been weakened as a result.[77] It is interesting to note that few former Cabinet ministers in Canada have published memoirs that reveal Cabinet discussions or materials; indeed, the lack of revealing memoirs has been bemoaned, because a political scientist's insight is incomplete without them.[78]

Jonathan Cape marked a turning-point in judicial opinion, since previous judicial rulings had tended to protect Cabinet documents from exposure in court proceedings. But a series of decisions in the late seventies and the 1980s has led to a constriction of the protection that courts will afford to Cabinet documents: a consensus—shared among the appellate courts of Great Britain[79], New Zealand[80], Australia[81], and Canada's Supreme Court—that the Crown cannot claim immunity from presenting documents in court proceedings purely on the basis that they are Cabinet documents and should all remain confidential.

The most recent case from the Supreme Court of Canada that involved this issue, *Carey v. The Queen in Right of Ontario*, took place in 1986.[82] The decision here was built on the judgement of a 1982 case in that court,

Smallwood v. Sparling,[83] in ruling that 'Cabinet documents like other evidence must be disclosed unless such disclosure would interfere with the public interest.'[84] Thus the Court refused to grant an immunity to Cabinet documents as a class. In deciding that the documents should be revealed, Mr Justice Gerard La Forest considered that the case involved only a specific transaction to implement a relatively minor policy consideration, tourism, which had occurred twelve years previously; as a consequence, the public interest would not be harmed by revealing the details. Furthermore, La Forest underlined that this civil case was initiated because of alleged wrongdoing:

> The appellant here alleges unconscionable behaviour on the part of the government. As I see it, it is important that this question be aired not only in the interests of the administration of justice but also for the purpose for which it is sought to withhold the documents, namely, the proper functioning of the executive branch of government. For if there has been harsh or improper conduct in the dealings of the executive with the citizen, it ought to be revealed. The purpose of secrecy in government is to promote its proper functioning, not to facilitate improper conduct by the government.[85]

The traditional supremacy of law over convention was upheld in 1985 when Chief Justice James Jerome of the Federal Court of Canada ruled that the Crown could not claim any privilege based on the convention of Cabinet confidentiality in refusing to release documents requested by the Auditor General that related to Petro-Canada's takeover of PetroFina.[86] In reaching this decision, Jerome relied on the very broad statutory rights of access to documents granted to the Auditor General in the course of fulfilling his duties; he held that conventional rules could not be granted precedence over clear statutory provisions to the contrary. However, when this decision was taken to the Federal Court of Appeal and the Supreme Court of Canada, both courts settled the case without reference to conventions.[87]

The Nova Scotia government fought battles, over the confidentiality of cabinet discussions, with the Royal Commission it set up to inquire into the wrongful imprisonment of Donald Marshall. The Appeal Division of the Nova Scotia Supreme Court ruled that cabinet ministers could be compelled to testify before the Commission, but only about the general course of discussions held in cabinet concerning Donald Marshall.[88] This was the third instance where a court compelled the disclosure of discussions that had taken place in a cabinet meeting.[89]

Perhaps the greatest pressure Cabinet confidentiality faces is the anonymous leaking by ministers of information about discussions and decisions. But Patrick Gordon Walker, a former cabinet minister in Britain, has argued strongly that the 'unattributable leak' is an essential safety-valve that permits the evolution of cabinet solidarity.[90] Arthur Siegel has described how accepted ministerial leaks to the media have become in Canada: leaks are often used as 'trial balloons' in order to test public opinion, or by ministers to rally support for a position they are arguing for in Cabinet. Nevertheless, he adds that definite limits appear to be observed about what may be leaked:

> ... all government secrets are not of the same order; some matters can be leaked, others not. In practice, a distinction can be made between ordinary leaks and disclosures of true state secrets. The best examples of state secrets are security matters, decisions on altering the value of the Canadian dollar vis-à-vis other currencies and the budget.[91]

In Canadian political practice Cabinet solidarity appears to be generally respected because there are very few times when ministers have publicly spoken out against decided government policies, or broken confidences in any attributable fashion. Deviations have occurred, mainly through unattributable leaks; but leaks are possibly the only means for a group of ministers to maintain a public façade of unity.

Confidence

Although seldom invoked, the most important rule of our parliamentary system holds that a government must resign or call for an election when it loses the confidence of the legislature. It is this principle that gives parliamentary government its most essential character: the political executive is theoretically exposed to the continual threat of removal by the legislature. The confidence rule forms the very foundation of responsible government, but remains entirely in the realm of convention. Indeed, the start of responsible government in British North America was marked simply by the passage of a non-confidence motion in the Nova Scotia Legislative Assembly in 1848, and the subsequent resignation of the Executive Council.

The modern notions of responsible government arose from the frequent resignations of governments in England during the period between the two Reform Acts of 1832 and 1867. After the first extension of the franchise through the Reform Act of 1832, the British House of Commons gained enough political authority to force a change in ministries if the government lost the confidence of the elected Members of Parliament. Between 1832 and 1867 no government served out a full term in office; ten governments in that period either resigned or advised an election after a parliamentary defeat.[92] The passage of the Reform Act of 1867, however, resulted in the crystallization of political parties in order to organize election campaigns among such a vastly increased electorate. As a consequence, the political parties came to act in a disciplined manner in the House and to vote in blocks. Since 1868 only six British governments have ended because they lost the confidence of parliament.

The operation of strict party discipline on matters of confidence has meant that a government elected with a majority of MPs is generally safe from censure by the public's elected representatives in the legislature. As A.H. Birch has written: 'A crisis which would have brought down a government a hundred years ago now acts as an opportunity for its Parliamentary supporters to give an impressive display of party loyalty.'[93] The possibility of losing confidence most clearly exists in a minority situation. But one must bear in mind that a lost-confidence motion can conceivably result from internal party rebellion; forced changes in premiership in South Africa in 1939 and in Queensland in 1987 illustrate that majority governments do not enjoy guaranteed tenure in office.

The existence, ever since Confederation, of increasingly disciplined parties in the Canadian parliament has meant that there have been few instances of a government's formally losing the confidence of the House of Commons. The defeat of the Clark government in 1979 was only the fifth time a federal government had resigned or called an election after losing the confidence of the House. However, the fact that five of the seven parliaments that supported minority governments came to an end because the government lost the confidence of the House indicates the real threat the confidence convention poses to a minority government.

While it is universally agreed that a government that has lost the confidence of the legislature must either resign or advise an election, there is some uncertainty about what constitutes a loss of confidence. During the middle decades of the twentieth century political observers were led, by the congruence of two-party domination and strict party discipline, to conclude that any defeat of a government motion involved a loss of confidence. However, this sweeping view of the range of matters to be covered by the confidence convention has been substantially altered as a new consensus has emerged to support a more flexible rule to accommodate the operation of less-disciplined multi-party legislatures. Both Canadian and British governments have suffered a number of legislative defeats over the years, most recently since the early 1970s, without treating them as losses of confidence. For example, the British governments that held office between April 1972 and April 1979 were defeated a total of 65 times, while Trudeau's minority government in 1972-4 lost eight votes in the Commons.[94] Some of the British defeats even involved government MPs voting against government measures. One is thus inclined to ask: what sort of defeat constitutes a loss of confidence?

There is general agreement that a government has absolutely no option but to resign, or advise an election, if it loses a clearly worded motion of non-confidence. Also, a government would have no choice but to resign or call an election if it were defeated on an issue it had previously declared to be a matter of confidence. These two categories of confidence votes have been expressly recognized by the 1985 Special Committee on Reform of the Canadian House of Commons,[95] by the 1982 Australian Constitutional Convention,[96] as well as by many constitutional observers.[97] In these two types of defeat the government has no discretion to ignore the vote. The government must either resign, advise an election, or eventually face removal by the governor.

An element of discretion does arise, however, when other government measures are either amended or defeated. There has been strong traditional support for the idea that certain votes necessarily imply a test of the legislature's confidence in the government. The late NDP leader David Lewis summed up these types of implicit confidence motions as involving

> most particularly a defeat centring on financial matters, defeat on the Budget or tax measures, and a defeat on the Throne Speech motion. There is a logical reason for defeats on the Budget or Throne Speech being taken as a lack of confidence. The Throne Speech contains plans for the whole session, while the Budget contains the government's plans for fiscal policy.[98]

Both the McGrath Committee and the Australian Constitutional Convention have listed a defeat on Supply as demonstrating a loss of confidence.[99] However, Canadian parliamentary experience demonstrates that this traditional view has not always been respected. Several amendments to government motions, both in Supply and in address in reply to the Speech from the Throne, have been passed without the government's resigning or calling for an election. After subamendments softened the wording, amendments to motions of address in reply were passed in 1869 and 1951. Two Supply motions were defeated in 1869 and 1870. Supply motions were amended in 1946, 1951, and 1953.[100] Most recently a Supply vote for Information Canada was defeated in 1973; since an express no-confidence motion had been defeated twenty minutes earlier that evening, the government continued with its business and proceeded with the main vote on Interim Supply, which passed. In most of these cases, however, either the motion itself or the amendment made was minor in terms relative to broad government policy. None of these incidents involved the actual defeat of a main motion on Supply, or address in reply, or an amendment expressly stating that the House had lost confidence in the government.

The government can also choose, if it wishes, to treat other votes as expressions of no confidence. Eugene Forsey has said: 'Except in the case of a clear no-confidence motion, or a defeat of a measure the government has previously declared to be a matter of confidence, anything else is up to the government to decide.'[101]

It has also been suggested that a legislative defeat on one of the government's central policies throws into question whether the government has lost the confidence of the legislature. As the McGrath Committee's Final Report stated: 'The government in this case can either seek an explicit vote of confidence from the House, or resign, or request a dissolution.'[102] However, this notion is attacked by other constitutional authorities. Geoffrey Marshall has argued: 'In the 1960s and 1970s ... governments seem to have been following a new rule, according to which only votes specifically stated by the Government to be matters of confidence, or votes of no confidence by the Opposition are allowed to count.'[103]

Prime Minister Lester Pearson's refusal to resign immediately or call for an election after a tax bill was defeated in 1968 is often cited as a precedent that eroded the inflexible traditional view that confidence is involved in any supply or tax measure. Pearson claimed that since the government had not previously declared the bill to be a matter of confidence, he was not obliged to resign. Instead he secured the adjournment of the House for a couple of days and then returned to introduce a motion of confidence, which was carried. While there was an outcry from the Opposition benches at Pearson's manoeuvring, there were previous precedents of governments' introducing a motion in order to test the confidence of the legislature after legislative defeats. Prime Minister Louis St Laurent had introduced a new supply motion as a test of confidence in 1951 after the original one had been amended. In Britain, a new address in reply to the Speech from the Throne was introduced and passed in 1894, after the first address had been amended; an amendment to a bill in 1944 was reversed after Churchill made the matter a question of clear confidence.[104] Subsequent to the Pearson incident, two other government defeats have been followed by confidence motions as well; in 1976 the British Labour government successfully passed a confidence motion after its White Paper on Expenditure had been defeated, and in the same year the Ontario government survived a defeat in a similar fashion.

It appears from these incidents, then, that a government defeat on a major item calls into question confidence in the government. In order to settle the matter, governments have responded with a motion to test the confidence of their legislatures.

There have been several attempts over the years to introduce measures that would eliminate the uncertainty about what constitutes a loss of confidence. In 1923, during a time of minority government in Ottawa, a Progressive Party MP introduced a motion that the government should not resign after a defeat unless a no-confidence motion was subsequently passed. However, Prime Minister Mackenzie King refused to allow that survival after defeat was anything but the rarest exception, even when a government was in a minority position.[105] But in 1924 the British Prime Minister, Ramsay MacDonald, passed a motion in the House that allowed his government to survive defeats on matters that had not been previously declared to be a matter of confidence. Also, in 1972 the Special Joint Committee on the Constitution of Canada included a recommendation, which was never implemented, to limit losses of confidence to actual votes of censure and to votes the government had previously made clear would be a test of confidence.[106]

The most novel attempt to deal with the problem posed by the confidence convention came after the 1985 election in Ontario, with the accord between the Liberal and New Democratic parties. When the results of the election revealed that no single party could form a majority government, the NDP began negotiations with the two larger parties. Eventually the NDP came to an agreement with the Liberals and concluded their deal with a public ceremony in which a document was solemnly signed by the two party leaders. Apart from provisions detailing what policies should be pursued by a Liberal government, the pact included an apparent suspension of the tests of confidence. The most relevant sections of the agreement read:

> Should the Lieutenant Governor invite the leader of the Liberal Party to form a government, this agreement will be for two years from the day that the leader of the Liberal Party assumes the office of premier. It is understood that the traditions, practices and precedents of the Ontario Legislature are that individual bills are not considered matters of confidence unless so designated by the government.
> We undertake the following:
> • The leader of the Liberal Party will not request a dissolution of the Legislature during the term of this agreement, except following defeat on a specifically framed motion of non-confidence.
> • The New Democratic Party will neither move nor vote non-confidence during the term of this agreement.
> • While individual bills, including budget bills, will not be treated or designated as matters of confidence, the over-all budgetary policy of the government, including votes on supply, will be treated as a matter of confidence.[107]

The announcement of this agreement drew strong criticism from the Conservative premier, Frank Miller, who still remained in office. He declared that the accord would sound 'the death knell of our form of democratic government' and establish a congressional system.[108] There was some misunderstanding of the terms of the agreement, and several constitutional authorities denounced it as improperly removing any possibility of the legislature's exercising its right to censure the government or force an election for two years.[109] However, a careful reading of the terms of the agreement reveals that the NDP could well abstain on a vote of confidence, which would allow the larger Conservative party to outvote the governing Liberals and thus force an election. Indeed, when questioned at a news conference about the pact, Liberal leader David Peterson specifically refused to rule out the possibility of an election during the two-year agreement.[110] Furthermore, the defeats that the pact specifically declared would not be taken as matters of confidence belong to the group of measures a government might normally follow with an express confidence motion, in order to determine whether the government has in fact lost the support of the legislature.

Perhaps one of the most interesting reactions to this accord was the manner in which legal opinions were widely sought, even though the agreement related to the operation of a constitutional convention. Lieutenant Governor Aird mentioned publicly that he had sought the advice of J.J. Robinette, a prominent constitutional lawyer;[111] the Conservative government apparently considered referring the matter to the Court of Appeal; and press reports quoted some prominent lawyers who cast doubt on the legality of the accord and strongly suggested a reference case to settle the matter.[112] In the end the Lieutenant Governor was moved to issue a statement in which he said:

> On the advice of counsel with whose opinion I agree, I have advised Mr Peterson that the agreement between the Liberal Party and the New Democratic Party . . . has no legal force or effect and that it should be considered solely as a joint political statement of intent and that the agreement cannot affect or impair the powers or privileges of the Lieutenant Governor of Ontario nor members of the Legislative Assembly.[113]

Such a document could theoretically create legal obligations only if it were a court-enforceable contract. But it appears that this particular accord did not constitute a legal contract because the parties did not intend to create legal obligations by signing the document. As a noted authority on Canadian contract law, S.M. Waddams, has written: '. . . where it is stated either expressly or by implication, that no obligation is assumed, there will be no legally enforceable contract.'[114] Although the document signed by the two party leaders does not contain such a disclaimer, there were clear indications at the time that the parties did not view the agreement as a legal contract. The lack of legal intention was evident when Ian Scott, one of the Liberal negotiators who was later appointed Attorney General, told the press: 'It's an agreement between two parliamentary parties. A court . . . is not going to deal with that in the sense to declare that enforceable. . . .'[115]

However, any agreement to suspend the right to advise an election, or to vote no confidence in the government, would also apparently fail to constitute a court-enforceable contract, regardless of the intention of the parties. There are very strong indications that the courts would refuse to enforce the agreement on the grounds that it offends the public policy that entrusts the first minister with the discretion to advise an election, and bestows on the legislature the discretion to vote no confidence in the government. The agreement would fall foul of several decisions by British

and Canadian courts that have overturned contracts limiting the fundamental discretion of a legislative body or that of a minister.[116] In a particularly germane passage in one decision, Mr Justice Newcombe of the
Supreme Court of Canada once said:

> A Minister cannot, by agreement, deprive himself of a power which is
> committed to him to be exercised from time to time as occasion may require
> in the public interest, or validly covenant to refrain from the use of that
> power when it may be requisite, or expedient in his discretion, upon
> grounds of public policy to execute it. . . . [117]

Thus it would appear that no first minister can legally bind him- or herself,
in an agreement with another party, to refrain from advising an election.
Furthermore, the leaders of a political party do not appear to be able to
sign away their discretion to vote no confidence in a government. Therefore neither the NDP-Liberal pact, nor any other like it, could be enforced
in the courts. If a court were ever to deal with such an issue, it would
appear that the refusal to enforce the pact would amount to a common-law
recognition, in the public-policy doctrine, of these conventional rights to
call or force an election at any time.

CONCLUSIONS

The conventions relating to cabinet government are particularly crucial,
since they fill a legal vacuum in the Canadian constitution. These rules
have been altered and added to considerably over the years, permitting an
evolution in the constitution without the need for formal amendment.

Individual ministerial responsibility has clearly changed since it was
thought that ministers should be held personally responsible for all the
actions of their officials. This notion has given way to the view that the
culpability laid at the feet of a minister will relate only to those actions that
he or she could have been aware of; even in these cases, ministers appear
to be held culpable only for their personal lapse in supervising their
subordinates, rather than for the particular action of the official. The
concept of individual responsibility is also evolving away from the idea
that a department is accountable only to the legislature through the minister. Senior officials are appearing more often before legislative committees, and there is a trend towards making deputy ministers personally
accountable for administrative matters in their departments. Both these
changes in individual ministerial responsibility have developed because
the increasing size and complexity of modern government departments
render previous notions impracticable. Perhaps the most fundamental
evolutions in the practical operation of the principle of individual ministerial responsibility have arisen because of the rigid party discipline that has
emerged during the twentieth century; the sanctions for wrongdoing on

the part of individual ministers now reside with the Prime Minister rather than with the legislature.

The confidence convention has clearly evolved from the notion that any government defeat signifies a loss of confidence. There is unanimous agreement that a defeat on an expressly worded no-confidence motion, or on a matter previously declared to be a matter of confidence, must entail either the resignation of the government or the calling of an election. There is some controversy over whether other defeats necessarily involve the loss of confidence; as mentioned earlier, some authorities believe that the response to them can be left to the discretion of the government. However, other political actors and observers support the practice revealed in precedents from the last couple of decades that a defeat on a central item of government policy casts sufficient doubt on the government's support in the legislature that an express confidence vote should follow. On the defeat of minor items, it appears that confidence is not involved.

The conventions that govern cabinet government have been the subject of discussion in a number of court cases. The relationship between law and convention is highlighted in such contrasting decisions as the *Jonathan Cape* and *Stopforth* cases. In *Jonathan Cape* the judge was prepared to extend a common-law rule through the application of the convention of cabinet confidentiality. The trial judge in *Stopforth* was prepared to use the rule of civil-servant anonymity inherent in the principle of individual ministerial responsibility in order to dismiss a common-law defence against defamation, but the Ontario Court of Appeal overturned this decision and ruled that conventions should not be used to extend a common-law rule. The convention of cabinet confidentiality has also been the subject of much discussion in a series of cases dealing with Crown privilege; here the principles of cabinet confidentiality were examined in some detail in order to determine what range of cabinet documentation ought to be excluded from public exposure in court cases or in investigations by the Auditor General. The Supreme Court of Canada also clearly relied on the conventional relationship between the Cabinet and the legislature in reaching its decisions in *Arseneau* and *Blaikie* (No.2). Thus the courts have come to recognize, and in some instances protect, the conventional rules regulating the operation of cabinet government. Perhaps this recognition is not surprising in the light of the fundamental nature of the principles of responsible government to which these conventions give force.

4

The Legislatures

The formal provisions of the Canadian constitution are curiously silent on the operation of the national and provincial legislatures. Although the 1867 Constitution Act gives lists of the legislative jurisdictions of the two levels of government, the manner in which the legislatures go about enacting laws has been left largely undetermined in law. There is no indication in positive law of the primacy of the executive in proposing legislative measures and the means by which it secures the passage of the vast portion of those proposals. Furthermore, the subordination of the appointed Senate to the elected House of Commons is a matter ruled by convention. But the most important exclusion from the formal constitution lies in the rules of party discipline that support the principle of party government upon which our parliamentary system is built.

The actual operation of the legislative branch of government is determined by an amalgam of a few provisions of positive law fleshed out by usage, binding convention, and what has come to be called the 'law and custom of Parliament'. The positive laws relating to Canadian legislatures, however, bear little on their operation. The matters raised in the 1867 Constitution Act and other ordinary statutes deal almost exclusively with the manner of electing individual members, the number of members to be elected, their salaries, quorum, research grants to party caucuses, and the provision for the existence of a Speaker and the table officers of the House; a number of jurisdictions also have statutory measures to regulate conflicts of interests. Some case law also deals with other aspects of the legislatures. For example, it was decided in *Gallant v. The King*[1] that a bill could be presented to the Lieutenant Governor for assent only during the session in which it passed.

Perhaps the most coherent aspect of Canadian legislatures to be covered by positive law lies in their 'parliamentary privileges'.[2] These combine case law with some statute law and have determined the bounds of the internal matters legislatures are generally free to regulate without judicial interference. For example, the fundamental freedom of speech of members in Canadian legislatures is protected from legal suit, as is the reporting of legislative deliberations. Furthermore, the power to compel witnesses to testify under oath is given to Parliament by statute.[3] The legislatures also have the legal power to imprison individuals for contempt of the legislature.

The procedural rules of our legislatures are found in the first instance in their standing orders. These rules are formally drawn up by each legislative body and detail the manner in which bills are introduced, the number of readings, how debate on each measure is to be divided or limited, and the provision of days of debate to be directed by the Opposition. The formal standing orders are buttressed by a plethora of Speakers' rulings, which form the basis of the everyday conduct of business in the legislatures.[4] However, a common element among the several definitions of constitutional conventions is the exclusion of standing orders and rulings enforced by the officers of Parliament. The corollary was underlined when Speaker John Fraser reminded the House of Commons in 1988: 'The Speaker of the House of Commons by tradition does not rule on constitutional matters.'[5] Although Speakers enforce only procedural rules, and give findings on matters of parliamentary privilege, it is not always clear where conventional rules and the 'laws and customs' of Parliament begin and end. For instance, Fraser ostensibly refused comment on the constitutional powers of the Senate to divide in two a bill already passed by the Commons, but he did rule that such action was a breach of the privileges of the Commons. Although his ruling dealt strictly with the privileges of the two Houses, it is virtually impossible to separate that issue of privilege from the question of whether the Senate had a conventional right to act in such a manner. It may seem that the substantive difference between the laws and customs of parliament and conventions is not important, but the distinction might be significant in its relation to how a rule may be enforced.

The significance of the informal rules dealing with the legislatures cannot be underestimated. The general acceptance of the broad principles of parliamentary government ensures that both Government and Opposition have a respect for each other's basic rights, and co-operate in the normal conduct of legislative affairs. Although there are many disputes in any legislature about the opportunities afforded to the Opposition to debate policies and legislation, these conflicts occur within the context of an overall acceptance that both sides of the House have legitimate functions to fulfil. Only rarely do governments resort to the wide range of procedural devices at their disposal to force bills through a legislature, and opposition parties seldom try to obstruct the government totally. For instance, the passage of the Free Trade bill in late 1988 was only the third time in Canadian history when a federal government has invoked closure on each stage of consideration of a bill in the House of Commons.[6] And the fifteen-day bell-ringing affair in 1982 that arose from protests over the Government's omnibus energy bill is the only occasion when a federal Opposition has completely boycotted parliamentary proceedings for any substantial period.[7]

Much of the smooth functioning of the legislatures depends on the Speaker's presiding neutrally over the proceedings, ensuring that both Government and Opposition respect the rules of debate and questioning. The editors of *Beauchesne* have succinctly described some of the major rules that ensure the Speaker's neutrality in the House of Commons:

> The Speaker takes no part in debate in the House, and votes only when the voices are equal, and then only in accordance with rules which preclude an expression of opinion upon the merits of a question. .... In order to ensure complete impartiality the Speaker has usually relinquished all affiliation with any parliamentary party. The Speaker does not attend the party caucus nor take part in any outside partisan political activity.[8]

The most basic characteristic of Canadian political systems is that the Cabinet directs the legislative process. The government is able to secure the passage of the bulk of its proposed bills, though only a minute fraction of bills proposed by individual members are enacted. This dominance by the government of the day is ensured to a large extent by the standing orders of each legislature that set aside large amounts of time for consideration of government business and only a very restricted period of each week to private members' business. The basis for this control lies in the Cabinet's ability to command the loyalty of its back-benchers in formal votes.

In all Canadian jurisdictions, the Cabinet's control of the legislature is reflected in the virtual absence from the statute books of bills introduced by private members. The extent of this domination is clearly demonstrated at the national level. During Trudeau's last four years in office, 1980 to 1984, only 21 of 559 private member's bills were passed, and the vast bulk of successful bills changed electoral boundaries; Mulroney's parliament of 1984-8 saw only 7 of 623 private member's bills enacted. In contrast, 177 of 229 government bills from the Commons were enacted in 1980-4 and 244 of 285 during 1984-8.[9]

PARTY GOVERNMENT

A fundamental principle of the Canadian constitution is that our form of parliamentary democracy operates through political parties. The essence of modern Canadian democracy is the competition between parties for office. Only through political parties does the election of hundreds of people across the country translate into the election of a cohesive government. Political parties play a vital continuing role by acting collectively as the channel through which the government can ensure the enactment of its policies.

The party system is so pervasive in the legislative system that meticulous efforts are made to ensure that the rough party balance in the legislature as a whole is maintained in its daily operation. A method known as 'pairing' has long operated, whereby a member who will be absent from the legislature pairs with a member from the other side of the House, who will not vote in any proceedings. In this way votes in the legislature are kept roughly proportionate to the overall party standings. MPs are under a moral obligation to respect their commitment to remain paired and abstain in a vote. From time to time, however, pairs are broken, usually inadvertently; but sometimes the temptation to catch the opposing side off-guard is too strong. A notorious example occurred in the 1926 vote of no confidence, where the single vote from a broken pair tipped the balance to bring down the short-lived Meighen government.[10]

The notion of party government also pervades the operation of legislative committees in Canada. All committees have representation from as many parties as they can practically include; in this manner the committees provide a platform for all the parties in a legislature. (A party with a very small caucus may sometimes choose to sit on only a few committees in order to avoid exhausting its members.) However, the governing party maintains a majority on each committee, even if it is in a minority in the legislature as a whole. Generally a government member is chosen to chair every committee except the one overseeing public accounts, which is traditionally chaired by an Opposition member; at the federal level the Joint Committee on Scrutiny of Regulations also has an Opposition Co-Chair.

PARTY DISCIPLINE

The whole shape and tenor of Canadian legislatures is forged by the operation of disciplined parties. Canadian political scientists are so used to the idea of party discipline that it rarely receives any detailed study.[11] Often it is noted by scholars only when party discipline enables the Cabinet to push legislation through a parliament almost unhindered.

Crucial to the character of the Canadian political system is the general requirement for elected members to vote according to the policies of their parties. Without this rule the government of the day would be left bargaining with free-forming coalitions of MPs for each bill it wished to enact. But occasional breaches may be tolerated because, as Martin Westmacott puts it: 'There seems to be a well-established convention within all three parties that permits members to dissociate themselves from the party position if the decision of the caucus conflicts with a member's moral or religious beliefs or if the party position places a member in direct conflict with the interests of his constituents.'[12] But accepted deviations from the party line are not permitted on matters of confidence. Party discipline concentrates political accountability on the party leadership. This focusing of responsibility is a key characteristic of our form of parliamentary government, as John Stewart underlines:

> We emphasize primarily, not agreement or disagreement on each issue, but confidence—or lack of it—in the men and women who constitute the ministry. We want a government with a high sense of responsibility. To cultivate such a sense of responsibility we concentrate power . . . in the hands of the prime minister and his ministerial colleagues. By concentrating power we make responsibility difficult to evade. And then to assure those who have power are held responsible we require them to submit their activities to hostile scrutiny in the House of Commons.[13]

Party loyalty is a fundamental characteristic of Canadian legislators. Quantitative studies of their individual voting behaviour are unfortunately few and far between, but what evidence exists points to a fierce loyalty within parties. Between 1945 and 1960 not a single contrary vote was cast by a member of the government caucus in the Quebec National Assembly.[14] A study of the 1963-5 Canadian Parliament found that fully 80.3 per cent of the MPs never voted against their parties' policies. Indeed, out of all the possible votes cast in recorded divisions during that Parliament, only 0.56 per cent were cast against party lines.[15] During the 1981-5 Ontario Assembly, 95 per cent of all divisions were held without a single MPP voting outside the party blocs.[16]

The level of party discipline in Canadian legislatures is generally perceived to be much higher than in the contemporary British Parliament. The British used to maintain staunch party cohesiveness; during the 1950s between 97 and 98 per cent of all votes occurred without any crossing of party lines. But a relative relaxation of party discipline has since arisen, with roughly a quarter of all recorded divisions in the 1970s witnessing dissenting votes.[17] Despite this frequency of cross-party voting, however, British party discipline remains quite firm. Richard Rose has pointed out that even the MP who most often voted against his party's position during 1974-9 still recorded loyal votes in 90 per cent of the divisions.[18]

A considerable amount of cynicism has arisen about party discipline. As MP David Kilgour has written: 'The experience suggests the various party leaders could just as well cast a proxy vote on behalf of all their followers without bothering to have them physically present for votes.'[19] A former MP, René Matte, voiced similar frustration to the House: 'Il n'y a rien de plus stupide dans notre système que cette non-liberté de vote. . . .'[20] Indeed, party practice in the British Parliament indicates that relatively more freedom could be given to individual MPs without endangering the party system.

There is a gathering momentum to relax the grip of party discipline. The McGrath Committee report in 1985 suggested that a more restricted view of which votes constitute votes of confidence in the House of Commons would allow individual MPs a greater freedom to vote according to their own particular views and interests.[21] A political conundrum exists for party leaders in dealing with this issue, since they are roundly pummelled in the media when any measure of disagreement emerges within a caucus on an issue. At the same time it is clear that many Canadians wish to see their individual MPs freer to represent their constituency's interests. A Gallup poll in 1983 found that only 7.9 per cent of the respondents believed that MPs should just vote according to their party lines. A little under 50 per cent believed that MPs should vote as their constituents' views dictated, while 38.3 per cent felt that MPs should vote as their own judgement led them.[22] In balance, however, it seems that Canadian political leaders believe there is more to be gained by keeping party policy in clear focus, which can best be done by maintaining rigid party discipline.

There is a real reluctance among party leaders to permit more free votes in legislatures. Although generally in support of more free votes, Robert Stanfield has pointed out: 'The government runs the risk of appearing weak, while the opposition runs the risk of appearing divided.'[23] As a result, free votes are rare occurrences in Canadian legislatures. In the last three decades the only issues on which they have been held federally were on the flag debate in 1965, on capital punishment (in a series of votes), on measures relating to the salaries and benefits of MPs, and on the 1988 abortion resolutions.

Party discipline is enforced through the combined efforts of party whips and house leaders. These two positions are recognized in federal law only in so far as remuneration is provided by statute for whips and house leaders of parties with twelve or more MPs.[24] The functions and powers of these members have been left entirely to informal development and unwritten rules. The house leader is responsible for organizing the strategy of a party's participation in the daily work of the legislature, and along with the whip can schedule which members will appear on the party's list of speakers. In addition, house leaders may prepare the initial assignments to the legislature's committees.[25]

The party whips bear primary responsibility for maintaining loyalty among a party's legislative ranks. They are appointed by the party leader in the federal Conservative and Liberal parties, while the national NDP caucus elects its whip. The whips are responsible for keeping records on each MP's attendance and voting record in the House and committees. They are also charged with trying to convince individual members to vote with the caucus, or at worst abstain when they have a fundamental disagreement with the party's policy. Members can usually be persuaded to follow the party line through the whip's control of many matters affecting the interests of each MP. Martin Westmacott provides an insight into the inducements at the whip's disposal in his list of the whip's functions, which include the assignment of office space among a party's caucus, the designation of MPs to fill positions on parliamentary committees, the selection of speakers for debates and questions in the House, the granting of permission to leave Ottawa during a session, the arranging of pairing to allow an MP to leave, and the recommendation of MPs to be included on parliamentary groups travelling across the country or abroad.[26]

Perhaps the most effective form of sanction available to the whip is removal from the lists of MPs for the Speaker to draw on during question period or debate. Speakers have come to rely almost exclusively on these party lists in choosing whom to recognize to speak. As C.E.S. Franks has written: 'To this extent, the speaker has become a perhaps unwitting instrument for keeping the individual members under the discipline of party, rather than what the speaker's role in England originally was, a safeguard to ensure that the individual representative could without penalty exercise his abilities to follow his conscience in speaking freely in parliament. . . . '[27]

The whips in Canada have a more limited function than their British counterparts, who combine the functions of house leaders and whips. Although the chief government whip in Britain is always a member of the Cabinet, the Canadian whips are not; the government house leader in Canada, however, holds a Cabinet post in order to participate in the planning of the government's legislative strategy. The British discipline system is also more formally developed, with the whips in all parties circulating to members a list of the day's votes, which also indicates the degree of freedom an MP has in deciding how to vote by means of lines on the page, ranging from one to three, opposite each motion or bill. In contrast, Canadian whips expect virtually the same degree of solidarity on every vote.

The disciplinary role of the whip, however, should not be exaggerated. The former whip of the Liberal party, Jean-Robert Gauthier, has pointed out that the whip must try to rely on persuasion instead of sanctions in most dealings with wayward members: 'One has to appeal to their intelligence. I cannot treat these people as seals who follow any strategy or accept any tactic.'[28] Alan Kornberg has also concluded that party discipline results more from peer pressure among caucus members than from any enforcement attempted by the whip.[29]

THE PARTY CAUCUS

The caucus of each party's elected members has come to play an informal but crucial role in the Canadian legislative system.[30] Each party has regular caucus meetings of its members in order to discuss the direction of party strategy and policy. Parties usually set up committees of caucus to oversee general policy areas or to investigate particular issues. In Ottawa the Conservatives and Liberals hold regional caucus meetings each Wednesday morning prior to the weekly meeting of the national caucus. In the governing party, caucus and its committees can have an influential role in refining both legislation in the House and Cabinet proposals that have not yet been tabled. Some governing parties routinely permit their caucus to scrutinize proposed bills prior to their introduction in the legislature, and strong reactions in caucus can prove fatal to a bill. For instance, the Nova Scotia Tory caucus vetoed a draft bill in 1989 that would have amended the province's Human Rights Act to prohibit discrimination based on sexual orientation.[31]

It is in caucus that the Cabinet is able to gauge the level of backbenchers' support for a policy. Although the influence of caucus varies among parties and with issues, it is clear that the government caucus can insist on amendments to government policies and occasionally even force the withdrawal of a legislative proposal.[32] In this arena vociferous debate can rage among members, and ministers can face extremely hostile questioning. As Conservative MP Albert Cooper put it:

> Caucus is the one place where you take off the gloves and fight for everything you're worth because that's the forum, the spot where decisions are ultimately made and you win or lose usually in caucus. It is probably the most serious debating forum in Parliament.[33]

It has long been traditional that the discussions in caucus meetings are totally confidential to allow such frank debates to be held without damaging the party's public image, but leaks do occasionally occur.

There has been some criticism of caucus members' meeting in secret, outside the public legislative chamber, and increasingly influencing the course of legislation. However, Philip Norton has underlined the positive aspects of the growth of party caucuses: 'By establishing party forums within Parliament, MPs were, to some limited degree, regaining a slight measure of influence which they had clearly lost in the nineteenth century.'[34]

Once a consensus has been reached in caucus on the party's position on an issue, a member will publicly oppose that position at her or his own peril. Party discipline is enforced at rare times by suspending or even permanently expelling from caucus a member who remains too outspoken a critic of the party's policies. For instance, David Kilgour and Alex Kindy were expelled from the Tory caucus in 1990 for voting against the Goods and Services Tax (GST) bill. Another MP, Suzanne Blais-Grenier, was expelled from the same caucus in September 1988 after persisting in unsubstantiated claims about corruption in the government.

The tremendous cohesion among legislative parties in Canada is achieved without the benefit of any written rule, and is not referred to in the parties' internal constitutions. This situation contrasts with the requirement of the New Zealand and Australian Labour parties, which insist that their MPs sign a promise to vote according to the party line. All candidates for the New Zealand Labour party must sign a pledge that says, 'If elected I will vote on all questions in accord with the decisions of the caucus of the Parliamentary Labour Party. . . . '[35]

Several tangible inducements for caucus loyalty may be used by Canadian party leaders. The Prime Minister can use Cabinet appointments and committee chairs to keep ambitious backbenchers in line. Opposition party leaders may use their power to choose a 'shadow cabinet' to maintain discipline in the caucus. For instance, David Berger was fired by John Turner in May 1987 from his position as Liberal science-and-technology critic because of his views on the Meech Lake Accord; a few days before, the Liberal caucus had decided that there should be no further public dissension about the party's stand on the Accord.[36]

The final measure left to ensure party discipline is the threat or use of the party leader's power under the Elections Act to refuse to endorse a member as a party candidate in the next election. However, this power has rarely been used, and the most recent instances were not examples of the enforcement of discipline within a caucus. When Prime Minister Mulroney warned Sinclair Stevens in 1988 that party affiliation would be refused him in the election, this was the result of Stevens' conflicts of interests as a minister rather than of any dissent from policy. And when Robert Stanfield refused to endorse Leonard Jones as a Conservative candidate in 1974 because of his extreme views against bilingualism, Jones was not a sitting member at the time.

PARTY GOVERNMENT, LEGISLATURES, AND THE CHARTER OF RIGHTS

It is surprising, given the fundamental importance of the principle of party government, that political parties remain very much creatures of the informal constitution composed of conventions and usages. For the most part the recognition of political parties in federal law is limited to the registration of parties for the inscription of party names on election ballots, the division of free-time political broadcasts, the reimbursement of election expenses, the allocation of research funds to legislative caucuses, as well as the provision of extra stipends for party leaders, whips, and house leaders.[37] The rules of party discipline that give our political system its most basic character are left entirely to convention. Indeed, several court cases have affirmed that political parties are simply not legal entities.[38] As a result there is some debate about whether the Charter of Rights applies to the internal workings of the legislatures and to the operation of political parties.

One private citizen, Douglas McKinney, has twice sought a court order to declare that party discipline contravenes his right of freedom of thought and expression under the Charter of Rights. McKinney claimed that his MP was generally precluded by party discipline from voting according to either conscience or the wishes of the constituents. But Mr Justice Patrick Gravely pointed out in the first of McKinney's suits that s.32(1)(a) states that the Charter applies only to 'the Parliament and Government of Canada'. He went on to decide that

> the Charter is intended to apply only to the relationship between the state and its citizens. It deals with the rights and liabilities as between subjects and their government and not between private people or organizations.
>
> Can it be said that the alleged acts of the defendant political parties are the acts of Parliament of the Government of Canada?
>
> In my opinion the exercise of party discipline is not a government act but only the act of an unincorporated private association and cannot be regulated by the Charter.[39]

This conclusion was reached because the judge had earlier found that 'At common law, political parties, like trade unions, have no legal existence', and they 'do not have the capacity to be sued'.[40] Even though he declared that the Charter does not apply to political parties, he did concede that 'Party discipline has a long tradition in our Westminster-style parliamentary system, a system recognized in the Preamble to the British North America Act, 1867.'[41]

It seems difficult in the extreme, however, to maintain that the activities of political parties are not an integral part of Canadian 'Parliament and Government'. The common law may well assert that political parties are merely unincorporated private associations, as are university debating clubs. But political parties are so fundamental to the functioning of both the legislature and the executive that their total absence would alter Canada's 'Parliament and Government' almost beyond recognition. The internal, informal rules of party discipline are as essential to the workings of legislatures as are the standing orders of those bodies. Indeed, in most instances the product of the legislative process is the product of the party system. In practice the legislatures are composed as much (or more) of parties as of individual members. Because political parties are an essential element of Canadian legislatures, it might seem reasonable to suggest that their activities within their legislatures are indeed subject to the Charter.

By the same token one could assert that the standing orders and Speakers' rulings are subject to the Charter as well. It would be incongruous to maintain that the laws enacted by a legislature must not offend the provisions of the Charter, but that the rules dealing with the passage and enactment of those laws may offend the Charter with impunity.*

But the rules affecting the internal functioning of Canadian legislatures could possibly be excluded from court scrutiny for Charter infractions. A firm and historic principle of the common law is that the internal workings of Parliament are a matter of parliamentary privilege, and as such are not generally a matter for judicial determination. As the Supreme Court of Canada said in the *Patriation Reference* concerning the privilege of Parliament to adopt any sort of resolution without judicial interference: 'Reference may appropriately be made to art. 9 of the *Bill of Rights* of 1689, undoubtedly in force as part of the law in Canada, which provides that "Proceedings in Parliament ought not to be impeached or questioned in any Court or Place out of Parliament".'[42] The privileges of Parliament have additional protection in the formal Constitution with their recognition in s.18 of the 1867 Constitution Act, and are provided for in the 1875 Parliament of Canada Act. This constitutional recognition is relevant, since the Supreme Court of Canada has ruled that the Charter cannot be used to invalidate other provisions of the constitution, or legislation passed to give them force.[43] Furthermore, Mr Justice William McIntyre dealt with the application of the Charter in his majority decision in *Dolphin Delivery*, and said *in obiter*: 'It would seem that legislation is the only way in which a legislature may infringe a guaranteed right or freedom.'[44]

Admittedly a corollary rule about parliamentary privilege has also been enforced, with the courts allowing themselves the freedom to determine whether a matter is truly an issue of privilege that should be left to the legislatures to regulate.[45] Thus it could be held that the privileges of a legislature cannot include the freedom to adopt rules that infringe on the rights entrenched in the Charter.

Nevertheless it seems preferable that the internal workings of the Canadian legislatures should not be reviewable by the courts under the Charter of Rights.[46] Indeed, the alternative would open a Pandora's box of political and judicial horrors, not the least of which would be trying to decide whether any of these informal rules relating to legislatures constitute 'law'. Since limitations on the rights in the Charter can be saved only under s.1 if they are 'prescribed by law'; rules that are not 'law' could not be saved under s.1 of the Charter no matter how reasonable or demonstrably justified they may otherwise be. One possible way in which informal rules of the legislature might be saved under s.1 lies in the Supreme Court

---

*The Trial Division of the Nova Scotia Supreme Court has ruled that the Charter does not apply to the workings of legislatures. This decision came in a challenge to the provincial legislature's prohibition against television cameras covering its proceedings. *New Brunswick Broadcasting Co. et al. v. Donahoe et al.* (1990), 97 NSR (2d) 365. At the time of writing, the Speaker had indicated that he would appeal this decision.

of Canada's findings that measures that are 'operating requirements' of statutory or regulatory provisions can be included as permissible limitations of the Charter.[47] Some manner of recognizing the force of the conventions and standing orders seems essential if the Charter is to apply without severely disrupting the fundamental character of Canadian legislatures.

RELATIONS BETWEEN THE SENATE AND THE HOUSE OF COMMONS

The manner in which the two Houses of the Canadian parliament interact is determined almost wholly by informal rules. The formal Constitution provides no guidelines with which to assess the relative positions of the Senate and the House of Commons. Few distinctions are drawn between the two chambers in the positive laws of the constitution. The only restriction on the legislative activities of the Senate lies in section 53 of the 1867 Constitution Act, which stipulates that money bills must be first introduced in the Commons. As a matter of strict law the Senate enjoys a total freedom to amend, delay, or reject outright any bill or motion, including money bills. The only legal provision the House of Commons may use to override the Senate relates to the passage of motions to authorize an amendment to the formal Constitution. Section 47 of the 1982 Constitution Act empowers the House of Commons to circumvent the need for Senate approval of a resolution to amend the Constitution by repassing it six months after initial approval by the Commons.

The vast legal powers of the Canadian Senate are in direct contrast to those of the British House of Lords. After confrontations between the House of Commons and the House of Lords, the powers of the Lords were severely limited by legislative constraints. Acts were passed in 1911 and 1949 to allow bills to be given royal assent even though the Lords had not passed them. Currently a money bill may receive royal assent one month after its passage in the Commons, and most other ordinary bills can be presented for assent after a year if they have been reintroduced and passed by the Commons in a second session.[48] Despite these curbs on the legislative powers of the Lords, they have been far more active in amending and delaying legislation already passed by the House of Commons than has the Canadian Senate with its unlimited legal powers. Between 1974 and 1977 and 1979 and 1986, the House of Lords amended 59.8 per cent of the Commons bills that came before it, for a total of 8,234 individual amendments. During the same period the Canadian Senate made only 174 amendments to 3.8 per cent of legislation coming up from the Lower House.[49]

The advent of Brian Mulroney's first Conservative majority government in 1984 marked the beginning of a number of fierce controversies over the Senate's ability to obstruct or reject measures passed by the House of Commons. During the course of the 1984-8 parliament the Liberal-dominated Senate amended 18 bills sent to it from the Commons, delayed a money bill for several weeks (which forced the government to pay millions of dollars extra in interest payments), altered the Commons' resolution to amend the constitution according to the Meech Lake Accord, and agreed to John Turner's request to delay passage of legislation implementing the Free Trade Agreement until the matter had been put to the vote in an election.

Condemnation of the Senate's obstreperousness in this period came from many quarters. The Mulroney government even introduced a motion in the Commons to amend the Constitution so that the Senate could delay money bills for only 15 days and other bills for 45 days, after which time the bills could be given royal assent.[50] However, this motion appears to have been meant as merely a warning message and it never came to a vote.

Although the criticism of the Senate's behaviour became fairly generalized, it is not entirely clear that the Senate had in most instances acted contrary to the previously existing conventions. An examination of the rules and principles governing the Senate's exercise of power reveals that support may be readily found for much of its activities during 1984-8. The historical record of the Senate's treatment of measures passed by the House of Commons indicates that the Senate had not acted much differently in the late 1980s than it did in the previous several decades. The recent incidents, however, illustrate that the consensus regarding these rules and principles governing the exercise of the Senate's powers has been eroding, and that any future protracted obstruction of measures approved by the Commons would generate deep controversy.

It should be stressed that the level of amendments made by the Senate during 1984-8 was somewhat inflated because the new Liberal Senate leader, Allan MacEachen, discouraged the Senate committees from reporting on the subject matter of bills still before the House of Commons. This was a practice first initiated by Senator Salter Hayden to allow the Senate Finance and Banking Committee to devote sufficient time to the study of complex bills; too often major bills were sent to the Upper House when there was only a short time remaining in the session. Under the so-called Hayden Formula, Senate committees conduct their examination of particular bills while they are still in the Commons. In this way the Senate can make recommendations on bills and try to convince the government of the need for certain amendments before the bills even reach the Senate. Past governments have often agreed to the Senate's proposals, which were made as government amendments during committee stage in the House of Commons. Occasionally a bill was even withdrawn and a new bill introduced in the Commons incorporating the Senate suggestions; thus Trudeau replaced the 1975 Bankruptcy Bill with a new one that included most of the 139 recommendations made by the Senate committee.[51] However, Allan MacEachen discouraged this practice during the 1984-8 parliament. He believed that the pre-study of bills diminished the Senate's revising role, turning it into an advisory role, and that revisions suggested by the Senate should be made in a visible manner.[52]

THE SENATE AND BILLS PASSED BY THE HOUSE OF COMMONS

A review of the Senate's treatment of legislation forwarded to it by the House of Commons demonstrates that Canada's Upper House has continuously played a fairly active but declining role in refining bills before they receive royal assent. An analysis of the Senate's early legislative activities by Robert MacKay reveals that the proportion of public bills amended by the Senate varied within a range of 17.2 to 25.2 per cent between 1867 and 1943. However, a significant drop in Senate amendments has occurred since then. Between 1943 and 1957 the Senate amended only 13.1 per cent of the bills sent up from the Commons.[53] This rate has since dropped even further, to just 4.4 per cent in the period 1957 to 1988.[54] The main reason for this decline has generally been attributed to better drafting of legislation prior to its original introduction.[55] But it must be stressed that a substantial proportion of all amendments made by the Senate are technical improvements.

The reaction of the House of Commons to the amendments made by the Senate reveals that a basic amending role is clearly accepted. F.A. Kunz has found that, of the 289 bills amended by the Senate between 1925 and 1963, 253 were readily endorsed by the Commons in their altered form; of the remaining 36 bills, only three were lost because no compromise could be reached.[56] Since 1963 there have been 45 Commons bills amended by the Senate and 36 of those were promptly accepted by the Commons; none of the others failed to pass in the end.[57] Even during the controversial first four years of Mulroney's government, the Commons accepted in the first instance the revisions made in 12 of the 18 bills amended by the Senate.

A brief examination of the Senate's treatment of Commons legislation during the last three decades is helpful in putting into perspective its behaviour during the first Mulroney government. Although there have been fluctuations in the number of bills amended by the Senate, the 1984-8 period does not appear to be very much out of step.

It is instructive to note that the Liberal-dominated Senate amended a roughly similar percentage of bills during Pierre Trudeau's first four years in office (1968-72) as during Mulroney's first term (1984-8). A great deal was made by Mulroney of the fact that a Liberal Senate was acting against a Conservative government. Quite plainly partisan interests did motivate a good deal of the Senate's actions, but it is by no means clear that parti-

TREATMENT OF COMMONS BILLS IN THE SENATE, 1957–88

Parliament	# Commons Bills	# Bills Amended by Senate	% Bills Amended by Senate	# of Amendments	# Amended Bills Concurred in by Commons	# Not Concurred in by Commons	# Bills Further Amended or Insisted on by Senate
1984–88	248	18	7.3	83	12	6	2
1980–84	202	1	0.5	6	1	–	–
1979	7	–	0.0	–	–	–	–
1974–79	221	7	3.2	85	7	–	–
1972–74	64	1	1.6	1	–	1	–
1968–72	178	11	6.2	54	10	1	1
1965–68	113	5	4.1	9	5	–	–
1963–65	92	3	3.3	9	2	1	–
1962–63	18	–	0.0	–	–	–	–
1958–62	211	15*	7.1	34*	11	4*	1
1957–58	26	1	3.8	1	1	–	–

SOURCE: *Senate Debates*, 1957–88.

* These figures include a motion that Bill C-114, the Bank of Canada Bill, be not proceeded with; the bill became moot after the Governor of the Bank's resignation.

sanship is the primary or even a sufficient explanation of the total number of amendments made to Mulroney's legislation.

All the detailed analyses that have been made of various periods of the Senate's legislative activities up to 1963 have concluded firmly that partisanship has not been a major explanatory factor for the level of amendments made by the Senate. When the Senate and Commons were controlled by different parties, very little variation was found to occur in the proportion of Commons bills amended compared with periods when both Houses had majorities from the same party.[58]

An examination of the Senate's activities during the last three decades also provides evidence that partisanship may not be the main explanation for the number of amendments made. Multiple-regression analysis was performed to determine the relative correlations between the number of Commons bills amended by the Senate during the life of a parliament and the number of seats held by each party, the size of the government majority, and the number of Commons bills dealt with by the Senate (this last variable was included to allow for the variations due to short-lived parliaments where little legislation actually reached the Senate). The size of the government majority emerged as the single variable, with a significant positive correlation to the number of bills amended. There were also strong correlations between the size of each party's caucus, indicating partisan influence in Senate activity; but coefficients for both parties were negative, which would suggest some degree of cancellation of partisanship. The fact that both parties produce negative coefficients reinforces the conclusion that the size of the governing party's caucus, regardless of political stripe, is the most important variable related to the level of Senate activity.[59]

Although there can be no disputing the observation that partisan considerations have indeed prompted particular actions by the Senate, the statistical analysis indicates that one must strongly consider the pre-eminence of the over-arching role the Senate plays in constraining majority governments. This observation could be explained by the hypothesis that governments with large majorities in the House of Commons are less likely to include amendments sought by the Opposition during the passage of their legislative program through the House. The link between the ease of passage of a federal government's legislative program and the size of its caucus was demonstrated by Jackson's and Atkinson's finding that between 1945 and 1974 minority governments spent an average of 3.4 days considering each bill, while majority governments devoted only 2.2 days.[60] This constraining role of the Senate would help explain why the most secure majority government presided over by Trudeau saw such a large portion of its legislation amended, even though the Liberals controlled the Senate. Because Opposition interests may not be as widely accommodated in the bills that emerge from a House of Commons dominated by a large government caucus, there may at times be substantial political support in the general political community for particular amendments attempted by the Senate.

There is considerable ambiguity about what consensus may exist to support the Senate's right to amend Commons legislation. Many modern academic commentaries on the Senate's legislative activities have consistently supported the desirability of the Senate's performing a limited but substantive revising function,[61] although other writers have implied that the Senate should make only technical corrections.[62] Polling evidence indicates that the Senate's power to turn back legislation from the Commons is a fairly controversial matter with the public. When asked if the Senate should continue to have this general power, 46 per cent in 1987 and 41 per cent in 1988 said it should; however, 38 per cent in 1987 and 39 per cent in 1988 felt the Senate should not have this power.[63] The federal political leaders appear split on this issue as well. Liberal leader John Turner staunchly defended the Senate's right to amend Commons legislation.[64] Despite the negative rhetoric of the Conservative government, their ready acceptance of three-quarters of the individual Senate amendments made during 1984-8 implies an acceptance of at least a limited revising role for the Senate; also, during their period in opposition in the 1970s and 1980s, the Tories gave their approval to a number of Senate amendments.[65] Only the NDP denounces any role for the Senate, which they would prefer to abolish outright.

A consensus on the Senate's amending powers is further obscured because of the difficulty in finding principled justifications offered by the Senate for its amendments. A reading of the Senate *Debates* interestingly brings to light only rare mentions of such justifications. For the most part the Senators' comments are centred on the merits of the specific changes in the interests of the best administration of the policy contained in the bill, rather on the right of the Senate to make the amendments being discussed.

One of the main motivations for the creation of the Senate at the time of Confederation was apparently to allow the expression of provincial and regional interests. However, Robert MacKay and Colin Campbell conclude that few instances can be found of the Senate's amending legislation from the House of Commons in order to protect provincial interests.[66] F.A. Kunz is more generous in his review of the Senate's record of defending provincial rights, but his description only serves to underline how seldom Senate amendments have been motivated by federalist concerns.[67] The Senate's Legal and Constitutional Affairs Committee issued a report in 1980 on its powers, in which it claimed the Senate had indeed been a defender of provincial or regional interests. However, it did allow that the Senate's representational role had been minimized by the work of regional representatives in Cabinet.[68]

There is increasing evidence that the Senate will try to amend Commons legislation where the rights of individuals or minorities are endangered. Although MacKay was skeptical when he wrote in 1963,[69] Kunz argued two years later that one of the main tasks of the Senate has been 'to see to it that in the course of legislation the interests and rights of the ordinary person were not brushed aside to any unreasonable degree.'[70] There has been speculation that the Senate has begun to assume the mantle of 'champion of the little guy' in amending Commons legislation. Indeed, on the two occasions during the first Mulroney government when the Senate insisted on its amendments, in the face of Commons demands that the Senate drop them, it did so on bills where ordinary or disadvantaged individuals were seen to be losing ground to either the government (in the case of refugee legislation) or to big business (in the case of the Drug Patent Bill).

The Senate occasionally makes a stand on principles of parliamentary government, but these usually meet with little if any public support. Thus the Senate was roundly criticized for delaying an appropriation bill in 1985 because it (quite properly) said that parliament should not approve funds for which the government had not presented any spending plans;[71] and in 1988 the Senate earned a strenuous rebuke from the Speaker of the House of Commons for splitting up one large bill (which the Senate said dealt with separate issues).[72] In both instances the general reaction was that the particular principles raised by the Senate were by no means as important as the principle that the elected House should prevail.

Colin Campbell claims that one of the main activities of the Senate is 'business review', where the Senate acts as a conduit for further amendments to legislation desired by affected business interests.[73] In this respect the Senate may continue to fill in modern form one of its original functions of protecting property interests. However, Campbell's evidence is too sketchy to establish that this is a persistent trend in the Senate's amendments to Commons legislation. Much of the activity Campbell refers to occurs in the Senate's Banking and National Finance Committees, whose major activities have often been centred on the study of the subject-matter of bills still before the Commons under the Hayden Formula, through which so many of the Senate's proposals have in fact been formally incorporated in the Commons. Also, not all amendments the Senate might make in response to corporate lobbying may be fairly classified only as business review. For example, the Senate generated much controversy in 1961 when it insisted on an amendment to a Customs bill in order to provide a court review of determinations made by the minister; that amendment might be described with equal accuracy both as a defence of civil rights and as a response to business interests.

The search for a pattern in the Senate's amending activities is further complicated because the Senate may sometimes be the tool of a government thankfully exploiting the opportunity to make amendments that it either overlooked or considered impolitic while the bill was before the House. The government also sometimes agrees in advance to allow some Opposition amendments to be passed in the Senate in return for co-operation on particular issues in the House.[74] Trudeau even enlisted the Senate to try to overcome amendments to wiretap legislation that had been made in the House by the Opposition parties during his period of minority government.

One area in which the Senate now appears to be constrained from acting is the passage of money bills. Although it used to amend money bills quite frequently, no money bill has been amended since 1961. The furor in 1985 caused by the Senate's merely delaying passage of the appropriation bill demonstrated that the Commons has finally crystallized support for a rule it has propounded since Confederation, that the Senate may not insist on altering the financial provisions of money bills.[75] The Senate's pressing of its claim to substantial and costly changes to the Unemployment Insurance Bill in 1990 thus appears to contradict a modern convention. The reason for this convention is that essential control over the spending and raising of taxes must rest with the elected House because these matters lie at the heart of the government's responsibility to the Commons. In the light of this, the Senate's move in late September 1990 to veto the Goods and Services Tax Bill, which involved a major restructuring of the government's taxation policies, appears to have gone well beyond the bounds of acceptable revising activity.* A good lesson for the Senate on this point lies in the fate of the House of Lords after it opposed the passage of a tax bill in 1909, a move that precipitated the first of the Parliament Acts that have left the British Upper House with only a power of delay rather than a veto.

My conclusion is that there is no accepted set of issues, such as provincial or civil rights, upon which substantive amendments by the Senate are especially justified. However, there does appear to be a general principle underlying the Senate's amending activities: it should not act to frustrate

---

*In September 1990 the Senate Finance Committee decided to recommend that the GST Bill be rejected. Before the Senate could adopt the Committee's report, Prime Minister Mulroney responded by invoking s.26 of the 1867 Constitution Act and advised the Queen and the Governor General to appoint eight extra senators, who thereupon allowed the Tories to defeat the Liberal motion to concur in the Committee's report. Had this motion carried, the GST Bill would have been dead, and a replacement bill could not have been introduced by the government until a new session of parliament had been convened. The Senate has never vetoed a tax bill, although it has made minor amendments in the past. Section 26 was put into the Constitution to allow the Commons to overcome fundamental Senate obstruction, and Mulroney's decision to implement this measure was the only use made of it since 1873, when Prime Minister Alexander Mackenzie was refused a request for extra senators by the British government on the grounds that they were not required to break any deadlock between the two Houses.

the general thrust of Commons legislation put before it. The very low rate of Senate amendments in recent decades is clear evidence that a firm consensus exists on a rule to require the Senate to act usually in such a way as to pass Commons legislation unchanged. This rule would be based on the principle of the pre-eminence to be given to the elected Lower House by an appointed Upper House in a modern democracy.

Even so, this general prohibitive rule may sometimes be set aside with subsidiary rules that justify Senate amendments in certain situations. Assuredly the Senate may pass any amendment that it knows will be agreed to by the Lower House. Thus technical amendments that harmonize French and English translations, or ensure the consistency of dates, figures, or procedures set out in a bill are readily made by the Senate and accepted by the Commons. Substantive amendments that are made with the knowledge and support of the government are also quite permissible. In both these cases the Senate would be acting consistently with the general principle mentioned above.

I suggest, however, that there is considerable support for a further empowering convention that permits the Senate to make substantive amendments on the rare occasions when the government has no clear support from the majority of Canadians to implement a policy that adversely affects some individuals or groups; there must be vocal support from the concerned public for such changes envisioned by the Senate. In this event the Senate may force the government to reconsider legislation that has passed through the House without accommodating the major points of resistance raised in opposition both outside Parliament and within the House. The Senate would then be acting in its classic role of forcing 'sober second thoughts' upon a government. But the pre-eminence of the elected chamber should be respected by the Senate's giving way after the Commons has passed a motion rebuffing the changes made by the Upper House.

There does not seem to be any particular reason for the Senate to make more than one attempt to force a government to reconsider a bill. Depending on the speed with which the Senate considers a bill, a significant impediment can be placed in the path of a government merely by the passage of one set of amendments by the Senate. During 1984-8 the delays averaged 69 days between the original third reading given a bill in the Commons and the day when the Commons considered the Senate's initial amendments; these delays were stretched to 104 days on the Copyright Bill, 111 days on C-55, and 243 days on C-84—both Immigration Bills. Some of the most heated controversy generated by the Senate during 1984-8 arose when it made second assaults and stated an insistence on its amendments to the Drug Patent Bill and the refugee legislation after the Commons had rejected them. What support the Senate has among the general political community for forcing sober second thoughts does not extend to its continued obstruction by not accepting the Commons' response to Senate amendments.

Some might suggest that on extremely rare occasions the rule empowering substantive Senate amendments might be led to its ultimate conclusion when the Senate refuses to pass legislation to enact fundamental changes to the Canadian society or economy for which the government had no clear political mandate from the electorate but that would not offend the Charter in any way. Such a refusal, however, would be conditional only until the measure had been put before the electorate. This suggested convention would justify the action taken by the Senate in July 1988, on Liberal leader John Turner's request, to delay the passage of legislation implementing the Free Trade Agreement until there had been an opportunity for the Canadian public to vote on the issue.

Considerable controversy was generated in the media over this action, but only for a short period. Editorial reaction was swift and vociferously negative. Commentaries in thirteen daily newspapers—in St John's, Halifax, Saint John, Montreal, Ottawa, Toronto, Winnipeg, Regina, Calgary, and Vancouver—almost universally condemned Turner's use of the Senate; only the *Toronto Star* defended Turner.[76] The general theme of these commentaries was that an appointed body should never be able to dictate important matters to the elected officials of the country; since the House of Commons had approved the bill, the Senate had no option but eventually to acquiesce and pass the measure.

However, there was not such a united front among academics who dealt publicly with the Free Trade issue. Reg Whitaker forcefully defended the Senate;[77] Desmond Morton said the Senate had 'a perfect constitutional right' to delay the free-trade legislation;[78] Jack Granatstein allowed that the Senate's action was objectionable but 'as long as the Senate exists, it is understandable';[79] while William Christian unreservedly castigated the Senate.[80] Gordon Robertson also ridiculed the Senate's forcing of an election, terming it 'pious hypocrisy'.[81] However, former Senator Eugene Forsey steadfastly maintained that the Senate had acted within its proper rights: 'The Senate has a power that can be invoked, only in particular circumstances, a reserve power of the Senate. There is no doubt of its legitimacy.'[82] Among defences of the Senate's action, the common theme was that Mulroney's government had received no electoral mandate for such a drastic change to our relationship with the United States, and that the Senate was not absolutely vetoing the will of the Commons but ensuring that the matter be decided democratically; in short, the Senate's actions were aimed at defending our democratic values.

The controversy raged for a short while in the media, but gave way within a few weeks to a quieter acquiescence as the public's reaction became known. An Angus Reid poll, released about ten days after the Senate's announcement, indicated that 58 per cent of Canadians supported Turner's appeal to the Senate and 34 per cent were opposed. A Gallup poll conducted a little later revealed that 52 per cent believed that Turner was justified, while only 30 per cent did not.[83] Thus there was solid support among a majority of Canadians for the Senate's forcing of an election on such a major issue. Clearly most of the public did not share the views of the editorial writers on the subject. The campaign in the subsequent election also demonstrated that the majority of Canadians were glad to have the chance to vote on the matter. Neither the Tories nor the NDP were able to develop the Senate's action into a campaign issue.

The deep division of opinion immediately following Turner's announcement that the Senate would delay passage of the Free Trade Bill might suggest that there was no firm consensus in July 1988 on a rule either empowering or prohibiting the Senate from trying to force an election. Certainly there had been support in the only previous Canadian precedent, when there was no public outcry to the Senate's refusal in 1913 to pass a naval bill without an election on the issue; but that had occurred long ago and had been little discussed in academic literature, let alone in public debates on the powers of the Senate. The generally positive public reaction to the Senate's actions in 1988, however, indicates that public opinion crystallized in favour of allowing the Senate to delay passage of legislation on a crucial matter that the public had not had an opportunity to vote upon. It was also made clear that once an issue had been put to the electorate—as this one was in 1988—the Senate had no option but to pass the measure.

This episode is interesting in underlining our uncertainty about trying to determine what level of agreement is required for the creation of a continuing rule. The polling evidence and the lack of controversy in the election over the Senate's action demonstrated that there was much more support for, than opposition to, the Senate's acting in such a manner. It is not certain, however, that the consensus of opinion is sufficiently strong, broadly based, or durable to indicate conclusively that a convention now exists empowering the Senate to block the Commons and indirectly force an election in rare circumstances. In order to believe that the consensus that emerged during a particular constitutional precedent indicated the existence of a convention, one needs to be generally assured that a consensus would exist for a similar incident in the present. But it is doubtful if the 1988 election can be said to have definitely settled the issue in this manner. Perhaps in the end the balance should come down against the existence of an actual rule empowering the Senate to refuse to pass a major bill that lacks an electoral endorsement, because profound controversy would likely erupt again if the Senate ever tried to force another election. Furthermore, the public became disillusioned with the 1988 election as a vehicle to settle a single policy, such as the free-trade issue. A poll conducted in the middle of the campaign revealed that 65 per cent of Canadians had decided that they would like to have a referendum on the free-trade issue after the election.[84] This attitude implies that most Canadians might not again be so warm to the Senate's forcing an election.

It is no longer open to the Senate to exercise its legal power to veto a bill absolutely, without hope of future passage. The advent of the Charter of Rights has led to a consensus that any bill that is offensive enough to be prohibited should be struck down by the courts and not by the partisan appointees of the Senate. The range of matters covered by the Charter, however, is very restricted.

THE REQUIREMENT OF IDENTICAL BILLS

Only by convention is it required that a bill presented for royal assent must have been approved in identical form by both Houses of Parliament. Section 91 of the Constitution Act, 1867, says only that 'It shall be lawful for the Queen, by and with the advice and consent of the Senate and House of Commons, to make laws. . . . ' Thus it seems that there is at least a legal requirement that the Senate approve a bill in some manner. The unerring practice has been to ensure that if the second chamber amends a bill, the House where the bill was first passed must adopt a motion agreeing to the alterations before royal assent can be given. Canada has always operated with a conventional rule, first evolved in British parliamentary practice, that a bill must be approved in identical form by both the Senate and the House of Commons prior to royal assent. But what is the legal validity of a bill that receives royal assent without having been approved in identical form, or that has failed to complete every stage of consideration in both Houses?

The editors of *Beauchesne* rather confidently state: 'If a bill should receive royal assent and be afterwards discovered not to have passed its proper stages in both Houses or be otherwise not in conformity with the constitutional procedure, it is in such cases so much scrap paper.'[85] However, the situation does not appear that clear at all to the British editor of *Erskine May's Treatise on the Law, Privilege, Proceedings and Usage of Parliament*, who said: 'The point has never been directly determined in a court of law, but judgments delivered in modern cases have maintained that no attack should be permitted in the courts upon the validity of the enacting provisions of an Act of Parliament.'[86] There are a few British historical precedents in which a later Act was passed in order to correct the procedural defects of a bill or to give it unqualified validity. In the most recent cases, however, the Lords' amendments to a bill in 1972, and to another bill in 1976, were inadvertently not included in the final bills assented to; in the 1972 incident some of the Lords' amendments had not even been finally considered by the Commons. In each case later legislation effected the missing amendments, but both original Acts were assumed to be valid.[87] In a 1974 judgement of the House of Lords, Lord Reid stated that the courts could not look into the procedural history of a bill before its assent:

> The function of the court is to construe and apply the enactments of Parliament. The court has no concern with the manner in which Parliament or its officers carrying out its Standing Orders perform these functions.[88]

This ruling would be of particular interest if a Canadian government rejected a clause the Senate had added to a bill, and the government nevertheless presented for assent a bill that contained all provisions except the additional clause. It could then be said quite accurately that both the House of Commons and the Senate had approved all of the text presented for assent. A more contentious move would be the presenting of a Commons bill for assent in the form that had received approval in principle from the Senate in its second reading.

The general enabling phrase of s.91 of the 1867 Constitution Act may provide Canadian courts with a legal justification, lacking in Britain, to enquire into the procedural history of a bill that has been assented to. The courts could conceivably hold that they had the legal power to ensure that the bill assented to had in fact been 'advised and consented to by the Senate'.[89] But they would have to rely on the informal rules governing parliamentary procedure in order to complete this determination.

CONCLUSIONS

Although the positive law of the constitution provides such details as the manner of election and number of members, the existence of the Speaker and other officers, and certain privileges of Canadian legislatures, the most important aspects concerning the actual working of the legislative process have been left to the operation of informal rules. Canadian parliamentary democracy is fundamentally shaped by the principles of party and Cabinet government. Yet party discipline, which supports these principles, is determined entirely by constitutional convention. The vast legal powers of the Senate have also been thoroughly constrained by convention.

So far the interaction between the courts and the informal rules of the Canadian legislatures has been minimal indeed. But if judicial attention were turned to the operation of the legislative branch of government, it would have to tread lightly. The presently accepted doctrine of parliamentary privilege, whereby the courts give a wide berth to the internal workings of legislatures, appears to be a necessary policy to pursue. Any deeper inquiry, such as one under the Charter of Rights, would require the courts to re-evaluate the nature of the boundaries between law, convention, and the laws and customs of parliament. Any application of the Charter to the internal workings of the legislatures may be disastrous if it is not mindful of the profound transformation effected by informal constitutional rules.

5

Federalism

A fundamental principle of the Canadian Constitution is the federal division of governmental power. But the original Constitution Act, 1867 provided the national government and Parliament with several overriding powers, which led K.C. Wheare to argue that Canada has only a 'quasi-federal' Constitution.[1] The imprint of the national level of government is stamped in provincial jurisdictions by several provisions of the 1867 Act, but especially by those that allow for the reservation and disallowance of provincial legislation, the appointment of Lieutenant Governors by the national executive, and the declaratory power of Parliament to rule that certain local works are to be regulated nationally. Other provisions are found in the federal government's power to appoint and set the salary of all superior court judges in a province, and in Parliament's power to pass national legislation with respect to the educational rights of Protestants and Catholics in Quebec and Ontario. Indeed, in many respects Canada did not possess a fully federal system of government for several decades after Confederation.

Political practice since Confederation has given birth to usages and binding conventions that have neutralized the federal government's power to intrude into the provincial legislative process. Although reservation and disallowance were commonplace in the nineteenth and early twentieth centuries, these powers have since atrophied. The declaratory power was invoked by Parliament at least 470 times in earlier decades but has not been resorted to since 1961.[2] And Parliament has never passed educational legislation under s.93 of the 1867 Constitution Act.

The legal framework of the Canadian Constitution provides a misleading image of the nature and operation of federalism in Canada. Apart from the neutralization of the national government's supervisory powers, developments in political practice have altered in other ways the division of powers laid out in the various Constitution Acts. The character of Canadian federalism has been significantly shaped by a web of intergovernmental diplomacy that sees many policies implemented by one level of government only after extensive consultations with, and even the express agreement of, the other. In addition, a strong tradition has always existed to require that the appointments to a great many institutions of the national government be made on a provincial or regional basis; this principle has had a fundamental impact in shaping the role and function of the national Cabinet. In order to understand something of the manner in which Canadian federalism actually functions, one must appreciate the degree to which political practice has forged an informal transformation of the legal division of jurisdictions between the national and provincial levels of government.

In regulating the amending process prior to the enactment of the Canada Act in 1982, the Supreme Court of Canada recognized that constitutional convention used to play a crucial role. In the Patriation Reference the Court declared that a 'substantial degree of provincial consent' was required for any request by the federal authorities that the British Parliament amend the constitutional Acts relating to the powers of the provincial governments and legislatures. Although the ambiguous formulation of this convention has been criticized, the Court's justification for it was widely agreed upon. A majority of the Court declared that the federal character of Canada would be greatly changed if the federal government could unilaterally alter the powers of the provincial governments through the amendment originally proposed.[3] Other conventions that define the federal nature of the contemporary Canadian constitution may be equally deserving of judicial protection should a similar occasion arise.

RESERVATION AND DISALLOWANCE OF PROVINCIAL LEGISLATION

One major element of Canada's original constitutional framework that acted against full autonomy for provincial governments lay in the reservation and disallowance of provincial legislation. Even though s.92 of the Constitution Act, 1867 purported to convey to provincial legislatures the right to 'exclusively make laws' on certain subjects, that same Act also provided a means for federal control to be exerted over the provincial legislative process. Under s.90 the measures relating to the reservation and disallowance of federal legislation were applied to the provinces. Thus, just as the imperial government in London could ensure that enactments of the Canadian Parliament did not infringe on imperial policies, so too was the federal government able to veto provincial measures that impinged on national interests. When a bill is presented to Lieutenant Governors for assent, they have the option to grant assent, refuse it, or reserve the bill 'for the signification of the Governor General's Pleasure'—

in which case the federal Cabinet then decides whether or not to grant assent to the reserved bill; and the federal government may issue instructions to the Lieutenant Governors on all these powers. The Governor General in Council may also disallow any provincial bill within one year of its receiving assent from the Lieutenant Governor.

Right up until the Second World War fairly active use was made of Lieutenant Governors' ability to reserve a provincial bill, and of the federal Cabinet's ability to veto any provincial Act. The federal government had disallowed 112 provincial Acts by 1943, the year of the last case of disallowance. Lieutenant Governors had reserved 69 bills by the end of 1937; only one more bill has since been reserved—in 1961. Of these 70 reserved bills, only 14 were assented to by the Governor General.[4] Thus provincial legislatures have been prevented from acting fully autonomously in the passage of 182 bills since 1867. Such a broad intrusion into the provincial legislative process by the central government might have cast considerable doubt on the federal character of the Canadian constitution. However, the decades since the last war have seen the development of a widely based consensus against the use of either reservation or disallowance. Firm conventions appear to have fully nullified both these powers, and one can conclude that the provinces are protected from any further interference in their jurisdictions.

Constitutional opinion appears to have changed considerably since the late 1940s, when both Eugene Forsey and F.R. Scott wrote spirited defences of reservation and disallowance.[5] Scott declared: 'We know that the Fathers of Confederation did not intend the provinces to have the power to act detrimentally to the nation as a whole, and entrusted the national executive with the duty of protecting the national interest against abuses of provincial jurisdiction.'[6] Scott was particularly concerned that the federal government should be able to disallow provincial statutes that infringed on basic human rights.[7]

However, official proposals to abolish reservation and disallowance were made by the premiers of Alberta, Saskatchewan, Manitoba, and Quebec at the 1950 Dominion-Provincial conference. J.R. Mallory notes that although no action was taken on these suggestions, neither was there any opposition raised.[8]

The last case of reservation in 1961 was occasioned by the objections of the Lieutenant Governor of Saskatchewan to a bill dealing with mineral rights.[9] Prime Minister Diefenbaker objected strenuously, but it appears that his condemnation was aroused principally because the Lieutenant Governor had acted on his own initiative rather on instructions from the federal government. Diefenbaker failed to condemn this power generally, as he made the qualified statement that 'if legislation is within the legislative competence of the provinces, except constitutionally in extraordinary circumstances, there should be no interference with provincial jurisdiction.'[10] Indeed, he castigated Pierre Trudeau in 1972 for failing to instruct the Lieutenant Governor of Quebec to reserve a bill abolishing the oath of allegiance to the Queen previously taken by members of the National Assembly.[11]

The years of Trudeau's prime ministership, however, were characterized by a growing expression of opinion against disallowance and reservation. Prior to coming to office Trudeau had already concluded that these powers were obsolete.[12] When pressed by Diefenbaker in 1972, Trudeau called reservation a 'paternalistic and undemocratic method'; if a provincial law was unconstitutional, Trudeau argued, it should be left to the courts to rule on the matter.[13] Although when Trudeau refused to act on Quebec's language bill in 1975, he did not completely rule out a future use of the power of disallowance. He called disallowance '... une exception au principe général qui veut que les parlements fédéral et provinciaux soient autonomes dans leur champs de compétence législative réspectifs et endossent la résponsabilité pleine et entière des mesures qu'ils ratifient.'[14] Trudeau's one permissible area for disallowance appears to have been in the protection of human rights, as two major constitutional proposals he authored during the seventies make clear. The 1971 Victoria Charter would have abolished reservation and disallowance because it included an entrenched bill of rights; and the ill-fated Bill C-60 of 1978 would have progressively abolished these powers with respect to any province that ratified the bill of rights it contained.

Reservation and disallowance have come under strong criticism in the reports of official committees examining the constitution. The Molgat-MacGuigan Commission recommended the abolition of these powers in 1972, and so did the Pépin-Robarts report in 1979, after noting that they 'now are considered dormant'.[15] A Senate committee report also concluded in 1980: 'The powers of reservation and disallowance have become obsolete. They are incompatible with a genuine federation'.[16]

Academic opinion greatly coalesced during the 1980s, with the preponderant view holding that reservation and disallowance had been effectively extinguished. This view is embraced in unqualified terms by Beaudoin, by Brun and Tremblay, by Cheffins and Johnson, by Hogg, by Stevenson, and by Van Loon and Whittington.[17] More tentative conclusions have been reached by Chevrette and Marx, by Mallory, and by Ward.[18] Only two scholars have proposed that these powers might still be exercised: Paul Weiler has argued that the federal government could disallow provincial legislation enacted under the notwithstanding clause of the Charter of Rights, and Eugene Forsey believes that the fact that these powers were not abolished with the 1982 Constitution Act means the federal government was not willing to accept that they were defunct.[19] Given the overwhelming body of opinion against the exercise of these powers, however, the failure of the provinces to call for the abolition of reservation and disallowance in the 1982 Constitution Act is more likely a testimony to the strength of the conventions nullifying them.

The conventional rules concerning reservation and disallowance appear to stand in stark contrast to the legal rules of the constitution. There is no question that the relevant sections of the 1867 Constitution Act still remain in the statutebooks. Although a series of judicial decisions had previously made mention *in obiter* of various practical restraints on these powers, the Supreme Court of Canada declared in 1938 that reservation and disallowance remained fully extant in law.[20]

With its recent willingness to deal with conventional questions touching on 'constitutionality and legitimacy', the Supreme Court of Canada would now in all likelihood state that the powers of reservation and disallowance have been neutered by convention.[21] This would contrast with the 1938 decision of the Court, when it was asked whether there were any limitations on these powers. Chief Justice Lyman Duff declared: 'We are not concerned with constitutional usage. We are only concerned with questions of law.'[22] As a result, the Court held that the powers found in the 1867 Constitution Act remained in full force. Since the Patriation Reference, it is unlikely that the Court would hide so deeply within the folds of formalism if asked again about the limitations on reservation and disallowance. Indeed, in the Patriation Reference the court said *in obiter* that 'reservation and disallowance of provincial legislation, although in law still open, have, for all intents and purposes, fallen into disuse.'[23]

Clear and broadly accepted conventions have arisen to nullify the powers of disallowance and reservation. Only a stalwart few would now propose that the federal government could ever play a supervisory role, overseeing the provincial legislative process. Canadian federalism has evolved tremendously since this view was prevalent. The past couple of decades have seen opinion consolidating around the claim that the provincial legislatures cannot be subordinated to the federal executive. Widespread agreement on the principles of provincial autonomy, as well as of democratic government, now provide the foundation for rules preventing the Lieutenant Governors and the federal cabinet from reserving or disallowing provincial legislation.

THE POSITION OF LIEUTENANT GOVERNORS

Another aspect of Canada's constitutional framework that originally eroded the autonomy of provincial governments relates to the position of Lieutenant Governors. Under the 1867 Constitution Act the Lieutenant Governors are appointed by the Governor General in Council (s.58), have their salaries set by the national Parliament (s.60), and are subject to instructions from the Governor General (read federal Cabinet) on matters relating to the assent, veto, or reservation of bills passed by their provincial legislatures (ss.55 & 90). As a result, the Lieutenant Governors were viewed for several decades after Confederation very much as governors acting for the national government—much in the same way as the Governor General was an agent of the Imperial government.[24]

However, the legal position of Lieutenant Governors has since been clarified in several judicial decisions that have downplayed the significance of their appointment by the federal government. Perhaps the most important ruling came from the Judicial Committee of the Privy Council in 1892, when Lord Watson declared that a Lieutenant Governor is an agent of the Crown, not of the national government:

> The act of the Governor General and his Council in making the appointment is, within the meaning of the statute, the act of the Crown; and a Lieutenant Governor, when appointed, is as much a representative of Her Majesty for all purposes of provincial government as the Governor General is for all purposes of Dominion Government.[25]

This decision was buttressed by one of the Supreme Court of Canada in 1948, in which it was held that a Lieutenant Governor holds an office of the provincial government, not of the government of Canada.[26] These rulings have ensured that in law at least, the Lieutenant Governors and the Governor General are equal and distinct representatives of the Queen. This equality of position, however, is tempered with a broader base of functional powers given to Governors General in the 1947 and 1988 Letters Patent.

A substantive change in the relative positions of the Lieutenant Governors and Governor General was made with the enactment of the Constitution Act, 1982. Section 41 provides that amendments to the offices of Queen, Governor General, and Lieutenant Governor can be achieved only by unanimous consent of the federal and provincial legislatures. The previous arrangements under the 1867 Constitution Act barred the provincial legislatures from amending the office of Lieutenant Governor.[27] But no express mention was made of amendments affecting either the Queen or the Governor General. As result, the federal government was able to secure important changes in the powers of the Governor General through the fiat of Letters Patent in 1947, issued solely on the advice of the federal Cabinet. This method of changing the powers of the Governor General is all the more remarkable, since the 1947 Letters Patent conveyed all of the monarch's powers to the Governor General. The powers of the Lieutenant Governors were not expressly protected from federal legislation. F.R. Scott underlined that the placing of Lieutenant Governors outside the legislative reach of the provinces was intended to ensure the supervisory role of the national level of government.[28] Thus the change brought about in 1982 removed another legal impediment to equality between the two levels of government, since all the monarchic offices are now amendable only by both levels of government acting in concert.

With these several changes effecting a greater legal equality between the Governor General and Lieutenant Governors, it is rather unusual that the positions of the two officers have not evolved into such equality in constitutional practice. For instance, a Governor General is addressed as 'Your Excellency', while Lieutenant Governors bear the comparatively lowly title of 'Your Honour'.

A more significant measure of the political subordination of Lieutenant Governors lies in the conventional rule that generally bars them from initiating direct communications with the Queen. The Supreme Court of Canada has mentioned *in obiter* the convention that continues to follow the pattern set at Confederation, whereby provincial dealings with the Queen are usually channelled through the Governor General.[29] This situation contrasts with that of state Governors in Australia, who are appointed by the Queen personally and who may communicate directly with Buckingham Palace. But this lack of free and direct dealings between Lieutenant Governors and the Queen could have practical implications only if the Governor General were advised by the federal Cabinet to refuse to relay a province's message to the Queen; in such an extraordinary situation, however, the provincial premier might claim a right of direct communication with the Queen.

An anachronistic vestige of provincial subordination lies in the appointment of Lieutenant Governors solely on the Prime Minister's advice to the Governor General. A convention has never arisen to require the Prime Minister to consult with or act on the recommendation of the provincial government concerned. Prime Ministers have on occasion consulted with premiers of their own party affiliation, but this has not been a generally observed practice. Little attention in constitutional negotiations has been given to the method of appointing Lieutenant Governors. Perhaps the fact that provincial governments have not demanded control over their own vice-regal appointments is the surest indication of how completely Lieutenant Governors have been stripped of any substantive role as agents of the national government. Indeed, it was the perception that Governors General continued to act as imperial officers that led Dominion governments to demand control of the appointment of their governors. The fact that Lieutenant Governors are chosen by the Prime Minister has no practical importance to the operation of federalism beyond the control of a patronage appointment.

The subordination of provincial governments that had occurred through their Lieutenant Governors has been erased by significant changes in both the legal and conventional rules of the Canadian constitution. The appointment of Lieutenant Governors, their acting on the federal government's instructions, and their ability to enforce the federal government's will through the reservation of provincial bills had all acted in the early decades of Confederation to place provincial governments in a position much inferior to the national government. However, so much of this has since changed that there is now little if anything at all in the powers or position of Lieutenant Governors that points to the practical subordination of the provincial level of government to the national one.

FEDERALISM IN CENTRAL INSTITUTIONS

An important way in which informal rules have transformed the actual operation of the Canadian constitution lies in the manner in which the federal principle manifests itself within the institutions of the central government. Increasing attention has been paid to what is now called 'intrastate federalism', which sees the informal inclusion of regional or provincial representatives in virtually all the important institutions of the national government.[30] In most instances this representation is both symbolic and functional in spreading patronage appointments across the country. However, in certain positions these provincial or regional appointees have a substantive role as advocates of the interests of their area in the decision-making process of the body concerned.

Perhaps the most fundamental expression of intrastate federalism in Canada is found in the conventional requirement that the federal Cabinet be composed representatively. As Dawson put it when referring to cabinet formation: 'The first requisite to be met is that every province must have, if at all possible, at least one representative in the cabinet'; he went on to call provincial representation 'a rigid convention of the constitution'.[31] Several other scholars have also identified the obligation prime ministers are under to include ministers from as many provinces as possible in their Cabinet.[32] When the vagaries of the electoral system have left governing parties without enough MPs to respect the principle of provincial representation, senators have sometimes been appointed to the Cabinet instead; thus Joe Clark included three Quebec senators in his Cabinet in 1979.[33] As Leader of the Opposition at the time, Pierre Trudeau commented mildly: 'It is important that every province have representatives in cabinet, and if they cannot be elected I have no strong objection to their being appointed.'[34] Indeed, following the election in 1980, Trudeau included in his Cabinet a senator from each of the three western provinces where the Liberals had failed to win seats. David Smith argues that the appointment of these senators 'is evidence of the strength of the convention that Cabinet must encompass representation from all the provinces.'[35]

As a result of this representational principle, ministers are expected to act as advocates for their provinces in Cabinet discussions.[36] Dawson points out that ministers may also act as the political 'boss' in their provinces, settling intraparty disputes and doling out patronage plums.[37] Particular ministers can develop into a sort of super-minister, overseeing federal government activities across several departments in a larger region; for example, Lloyd Axworthy and Allan MacEachen filled such roles in Trudeau's government, while John Crosbie, Elmer MacKay, and Don Mazankowski have championed their regions in Mulroney's Cabinet. It is a testimony to the vigour with which ministers act as regional advocates that the Cabinet has acted as the primary arena for the accommodation of competing provincial claims at the national level. Indeed, a major reason for the failure of the Senate to act as an effective forum for regional interests is that the Cabinet has an effective representational function.[38] Although changes in the decision-making structures of Cabinet have diffused somewhat the influence of regional ministers, they continue to play a vital role.[39]

The Supreme Court of Canada has also been composed on a regional basis since its inception. The Supreme Court Act has always required that at first two, and now three, judges be appointed from the Quebec bar or benches. This stipulation ensures that appeals under Quebec's civil code can be heard by a panel of judges whose majority are experienced in the code. There has also been an informal division of the remaining appointments among the other regions of the country. Although it was not until 1903 that the first judge was appointed from the West, the expansion of the Court to nine judges in 1949 has provided ample room for the accommodation of appointees from each region. Since 1949 the Court has been composed of 3 judges from Quebec, 1 from the Atlantic provinces, either 2 or 3 from Ontario, and either 2 or 3 from the Western provinces.[40]

A question might be raised about whether this requirement of regional appointments is actually an obligatory constitutional convention or just a custom of preferred practice. Certainly if the justification for them is purely symbolic, one could suggest that they are only matters of usage. However, there are other practical reasons, beyond the symbolism, that can justify these regional appointments. Peter Russell claims that they are a necessary measure to ensure the loyalty of provincial élites.[41] W.R. Lederman has also argued that it is invaluable to have the Court composed of experienced jurists who are familiar with the background issues and concerns of each of the nation's regions.[42] In an era when an important aspect of the Court's work involves the resolution of disputes between federal and provincial governments, this may be significant. Since reasoned foundations for these regional appointments can be identified, Russell appears correct in concluding that a binding convention is involved.[43]

The political importance of regional appointees to the Supreme Court is underlined by the proposed Meech Lake Accord, which would have seen new appointments to the Court being made by the federal government on the recommendation of provincial governments. It is interesting that conventions would have had to continue to play a large role in determining which provinces non-Quebec judges would be drawn from, as the particular distribution of judgeships among the provinces was not specified in the Accord.

The constitutional amendment proposed by the Meech Lake Accord would have seen the formal inclusion of provincial nominations for appointments to both the Senate and the Supreme Court. The Accord also stipulated that while legislative ratification was being pursued, the federal government would make appointments to the Senate only in accordance with the procedure contained in the proposed amendment. Indeed, between the signing of the Accord and its demise, Mulroney made appointments to the Senate only after seeking a list of nominees from the relevant provincial government. Four Senators from Quebec and one from Newfoundland were appointed from lists of nominees submitted by the two provincial governments. Ontario, however, stalled by saying that the Meech Lake Accord should be formally entrenched first.[44] The Alberta legislature went so far as to pass the Senatorial Selection Act, and a province-wide election was held in October 1989 to elect nominees for the government to submit to Ottawa to fill a vacancy in that province. But the federal government refused for many months to consider appointing the winner, Stan Waters, on the grounds that the election was unconstitutional; he was eventually appointed in 1990.

FEDERAL-PROVINCIAL CONFERENCES

An extremely important aspect in the development of Canadian federalism has been the use of intergovernmental meetings as forums for dealings between the two levels of government. Meetings of ministers and officials of the two levels of government have played a key role in coordinating and developing policies that overflow the formal division of powers found in the 1867 Constitution Act.[45] The most visible of these meetings is the Federal-Provincial First Ministers' Conference: at least 61 formal conferences of Prime Ministers and Premiers have been convened between the first one in 1906 and early 1988. Conferences are also organized on a regular basis among all the federal and provincial ministers responsible for particular policy areas; between 1973 and 1983 there were 254 separate meetings of federal-provincial ministers. The work conducted at these meetings is often prepared for and followed up by meetings organized between the relevant senior government officials of the two levels of government; 417 such meetings were held from 1973 to 1988.[46] These figures illustrate the degree to which the division of jurisdictions provided in the legal framework of the Constitution has been modified by governmental bodies created informally through political practice.

Discussions at Federal-Provincial First Ministers' Conferences, which have become a fundamental institution of the Canadian constitution, have focused primarily on large issues of constitutional amendment, the economy, fiscal arrangements, and, more recently, aboriginal rights. Formal conferences of first ministers are substantial events, with the number of delegates and advisers totalling as many as 487 for the 1984 meeting on aboriginal rights.[47] At least one meeting a year has been held since 1963, and it would appear that an obligation now exists to hold one each year. This seems to be justifiable in the light of these meetings' importance to the functioning of modern federalism, with its emphasis on negotiation and consultation between the two levels of government.

As important as these conferences have been, they had existed almost entirely outside of the positive law of the constitution until the 1980s. The Constitution Act, 1982 recognized their existence in its requirement in s.37 that the Prime Minister convene a First Ministers' Conference on aboriginal rights within a year of the Act's coming into force, and in the further stipulation in s.49 that such a conference had to discuss the amending formula by 1997. The only amendment made to the 1982 Act—the Constitutional Amendment Proclamation, 1983—added another stipulation in s.37.1 that two further conferences be held on aboriginal rights by 1987. The constitutional resolution of the Meech Lake Accord would have entrenched First Ministers' Conferences with its requirement in s.50 that they be held on an annual basis; the formal Constitution would thus have been amended to reflect an already established pattern.

Despite recognition in law, the actual workings of First Ministers' Conferences remain governed by informal rules. For instance, they are convened only on the federal government's invitation, the sessions are chaired by the Prime Minister, and the agenda is set by the federal government (although consultations are held with provincial governments).[48] Other crucial matters such as who may speak, how often and in what order, and the nature of the agreements made during these conferences are left entirely to political practice.

First Ministers' Conferences have become an essential step towards any formal amendment of the constitution that affects the nation as a whole. The process of constitutional amendment in Canada has been exclusively led by negotiations among the provincial and federal executives. Even though formal amendments must now be approved by the legislatures that are relevant to the topic of the amendment, these legislatures are presented with a resolution approved by the first ministers on a take-it-or-leave-it basis.

First Ministers' Conferences, supplemented by meetings of finance ministers, have conducted negotiations for the five-year Fiscal Arrangements determining the division among the provinces of tax income collected by the federal government. In this forum a consensus is usually sought, though not always successfully, and when it is achieved it forms the basis of the political acceptability of the relative shares each province receives. (It should be noted that the 1967-72 Fiscal Arrangement was not approved by a conference.[49]) Before implementing these arragements, an obligation appears to exist requiring the federal government to discuss any upcoming financial transfers arrangement with the provincial governments in a First Ministers' Conference. This requirement is founded on the profound importance of fiscal arrangements to the operations of provincial governments. It is difficult to say, however, whether this obligation stems from a convention on the subject or merely flows from considerations of practical policy implementation in an area where co-operation between the two levels of government is vital. Furthermore, the checkered history of negotiations on this issue indicates that federal governments have not considered it necessary to seek the provinces' actual approval of their plans.

Although definite agreements are not often formulated at the conclusion of First Ministers' Conferences, some meetings—such as those on the constitution in 1981, 1983 and 1987—do result in signing ceremonies of formal agreements. The nature of these agreements is unfortunately difficult to characterize. As Mackenzie King mentioned at the conclusion of the 1935 conference:

> A Dominion-provincial conference is neither a cabinet nor a parliament. It is an institution which enables representatives of the Government of the Dominion of Canada and the governments of the provinces of Canada to confer together, exchange information and opinions, and formulate proposals, in respect to Dominion provincial co-operation, which can be represented to the governments concerned and to the Parliament of Canada and legislatures of the provinces.[50]

While a First Ministers' Conference is not an executive or legislative body found in the formal constitution, it has arguably become an informal institution for intergovernmental deliberation whose decisions, when reached, are expected to be acted upon. Any undertaking that is agreed to at a First Ministers' Conference has a special significance, both because it has been reached by the first ministers—who are in a position to implement their commitments—and because of the general perception that the agreements announced publicly at these conferences will be implemented.

FEDERAL-PROVINCIAL CONSULTATIONS AND AGREEMENTS

The meetings of formal federal-provincial conferences actually constitute only a small segment of the complex web of negotiation and consultation that develops between the various governments in Canada. For instance Gordon Robertson has estimated that during the 1970s federal-provincial meetings of ministers or senior officials occurred at an average of about 500 times each year.[51] This high level of interaction is necessitated by the large degree to which the jurisdictions of the two levels of government overlap. Harmonious government activity requires considerable efforts to co-ordinate federal and provincial polices on aspects of the same subject.

A growing bureaucratic structure has evolved to deal with these inter-governmental relations. Quebec initiated this development in 1961 when it created a Ministry of Federal-Provincial Relations. Separate depart-ments for intergovernmental relations were later set up by Alberta, New-foundland, Ontario, British Columbia, and Saskatchewan (since aban-doned).[52] In 1975 the federal government established the Federal-Provincial Relations Office as a separate entity under the Privy Council Office's umbrella. The governments in Ottawa, British Columbia, Alberta, and Quebec each have ministers of intergovernmental relations, while the other provinces leave this responsibility to their premiers. An agreement reached at the First Ministers' Conference in May 1973 saw the creation of the Canadian Intergovernmental Conference Secretariat to service meet-ings of federal and provincial ministers and officials. The CICS not only serves federal-provincial and interprovincial conferences but has orga-nized certain international meetings, such as the 1988 Francophone Sum-mit and the 1989 meeting of New England Governors and Eastern Canadian Premiers. Although it was designated as a federal department by Order-in-Council later in 1973, the CICS actually operates on a jointly funded basis, with Ottawa paying half the costs and the provinces sharing the other half according to their population.[53] It epitomizes the continuing institutionalization and essentially co-operative character of federal-provincial relations in Canada.[54]

One area that especially demands co-operation between provincial and federal governments is the enforcement of criminal law and the adminis-tration of justice. Fundamental policy changes in the Criminal Code or the Young Offenders Act have almost always been preceded by consultations between the two levels of government. Uniform resistance among the provinces to federal proposals in these areas can be enough to scuttle an initiative by the federal government. For instance, in the late 1970s a federal Minister of Health and Welfare suggested to a meeting of federal and provincial justice ministers that the simple possession of cannabis be decriminalized. Although the federal justice minister supported this mea-sure, the unanimous and vociferous condemnation of this proposal by the provincial justice ministers caused the initiative to die an unpublicized death. The Minister of Health told the meeting that he could not proceed on this matter in the face of united provincial opposition.

Justice is one of a number of areas where overlapping jurisdiction requires co-ordination of policies between the two levels of government. Transportation, economic planning, agricultural policies, the environment, and health care are just a few areas where one government needs to consult with others before implementing major innovations to its policies. Certain issues are sometimes best dealt with by a joint federal-provincial program, which presupposes an agreement on policy objectives between the two levels of government.

The Macdonald Commission of 1982-5 on economic union and development prospects for Canada concluded that there are several patterns of policy-making within the federal division of jurisdiction in Canada that belie the simple division of jurisdictions between two levels of government:

> At one end of the continuum, policy making is completely independent: governments take action without consulting others or considering their interests. Under this arrangement, other jurisdictions adjust independently. . . .
>
> The second level of interaction is characterized by consultation. On this level, each government recognizes the effect of its actions on other jurisdictions and the fact that all are acting in the same areas and/or in closely related areas. Here it is important to provide the means for governments to keep one another informed and to provide opportunities for persuasion, pressure and influence. . . .
>
> The third level of governmental relations involves efforts to achieve co-ordination. Here, governments will try to develop commonly acceptable policies and objectives which they will then implement within their own jurisdiction. . . .
>
> Finally, there is joint decision making, which requires that federal and provincial governments act together, committing themselves to particular courses of action and standards of conduct. Shared cost arrangements take this form.[55]

Thus it appears that the legal division of jurisdiction in the constitution is overlaid with informal categories that allow varying degrees of unilateral freedom of action for any one government, federal-provincial consultation, co-ordination, or joint decision-making. It is beyond the scope of this study to suggest which policies fall within which category; these categories may well prove ambiguous in any search for their limits. I believe, however, that we need to recognize the strength of the informal requirement that certain policy decisions should not be implemented simply unilaterally. Indeed, a considerable amount of intergovernmental friction centres on arguments that particular polices should be subject to joint consideration or approval. As the consensus on the relative bounds of these categories of policy-making builds or erodes, J.R. Mallory's 'faces of Canadian federalism' might interchange .[56] The volatile political fallout when federal-provincial consultation fails—as it did with the 1984 Canada Health Act and the Free Trade Agreement—is an indication of how important intergovernmental co-ordination is to the Canadian constitution.

Perhaps the bulk of federal-provincial consultations between the federal government and that of a particular province occur bilaterally. Individual bilateral agreements cover many subjects, ranging from the creation, renewal, or amendment of cost-shared programs, through agreements on the substance of regulations of the two governments on a subject of overlapping jurisdiction, to the conclusion of formal accords to implement particular pieces of legislation. However, few of these types of agreements would appear to fulfil the requirements of a legal contract, discussed in Chapter 3; they lack an intention to create a legally binding contract, and often the subject-matter would fail to become a contract on the grounds of the public-policy doctrine: legislators must remain free to enact any measure they wish. Many federal-provincial agreements are later incorporated in legal form through regulations or legislation, but until that stage they remain informal agreements and are not legally enforceable. However, a small number of federal-provincial agreements are concluded within a particular legislative framework that either gives legal effect to the agreement itself or requires the agreement to give effect to a formal legal instrument.

Illustrations of the rich variety of federal-provincial agreements are found in the separate offshore-development agreements concluded by the federal government with the Nova Scotia and Newfoundland governments. Initial accords were reached with each provincial government by which the governments pledged to introduce legislation in an agreed form to implement a complicated regime for joint federal-provincial management of offshore petroleum resources. At that stage neither accord was a legally enforceable document and either party could have failed to implement the legislation without legal sanction. In the end, the federal and provincial legislatures enacted bills to give effect to the two schemes.[57] The two original accords were both incorporated into the new legislation through stipulations that the joint boards created to administer the offshore developments would fill these functions and pass such bylaws as both the Acts and the accords provided. The Canada-Nova Scotia Act also provided specifically that the first ministers, or other designates, could make further amendments to the accord.

These amendments, achieved through regular executive agreements, could in turn have legal force under the legislation if they related to the functions or bylaws of the joint board. Both the Canada-Nova Scotia Act and the Canada-Newfoundland Act also require the relevant federal minister to obtain the approval of the provincial minister before passing regulations on certain issues; in these circumstances the signification of the provincial minister's consent would have legal force in determining the legality of any federal regulations. The preamble to the Canada-Newfoundland Act also declares that both governments had agreed that 'neither Government will introduce amendments to this Act or any regulation thereunder without the consent of both Governments.' Although preambles have only limited use in statutory construction, the recognition of this informal undertaking could have possible consequences in a court's assessment of the validity of the unique method of interdelegation by which the joint board was created, in identical federal and provincial legislation, or of the validity of an Act that tried to amend unilaterally the legislative scheme.

There are not many cases of governments' reneging on formal agreements reached with other governments before they have begun to be implemented. The few examples appear to be limited to high constitutional matters: Quebec's Premier Bourassa withdrew his support from the Victoria Charter in 1971 after facing strong opposition from his cabinet, and two provinces withdrew their support for the Meech Lake Accord after changes of government. But qualifications must be placed on both, since Bourassa made it clear in 1971 that his agreement to the Charter was conditional on his cabinet's support, and both the New Brunswick and Manitoba governments partially fulfilled the technical obligation found in the 1987 Accord by presenting a resolution to their legislatures. Perhaps more examples can be found of unilateral reductions of spending or the imposition of new restrictions on previously agreed cost-shared programs—notably the federal government's banning of extra-billing in the 1984 Canada Health Act.

The binding nature of the Canada Assistance Plan was the subject of a reference case sent to the British Columbia Court of Appeal in 1990, after the federal government acted unilaterally to change the disbursement of funds under the Plan. The governments of Ontario, Manitoba, and Alberta joined the British Columbia government in this case, in which the court found that the provincial governments had a 'legitimate expectation' that the Plan would be protected from unilateral federal amendment.[58]

One is left with the general impression that Canadian governments respect an overwhelming majority of the large number of agreements reached each year between the two levels of governments. There appears to be a firm expectation that a government will observe its intergovernmental commitments. I would suggest that there is an important constitutional convention regulating federal-provincial negotiations that is analogous to one of the basic rules of international law and diplomacy: *pacta sunt servanda*, agreements are kept. As with the international equivalent, there may well be some permitted exceptions to this general rule, such as the coming to power of a new government opposed to the policies of the previous administration, or a change of circumstances that erode the basic presuppositions of the agreement. A strong argument could also be made that this rule might be occasionally breached when a government believes it needs the freedom to pursue effective government policies in its jurisdiction. But the stable conduct of federal-provincial relations requires certain performance of intergovernmental agreements just as much as international relations do.

CONCLUSIONS

Political practice has played a vital role in transforming the legal framework of the federal division of powers provided in the Constitution. The reservation and disallowance of provincial legislation were at one time frequently exercised powers that fundamentally eroded the federal principle in Canada. These powers, however, have been nullified by firm constitutional conventions that now deprive the federal government completely of any supervisory intervention in the provincial legislative process. And the federal division of the country has had a significant impact within the national level of government through the requirement that the Cabinet be composed of provincial representatives. The tremendous increase in informal consultation and co-ordination between federal and provincial governments has been a key element in the evolution of modern federalism in Canada. The growth in volume and importance of intergovernmental relations has been reflected in the institutionalization of First Ministers' Conferences and in the references to these conferences in each of the major constitutional amendments achieved or proposed in the 1980s. Overlapping jurisdictions and the growth of cost-shared programs have led to a vast array of federal-provincial meetings of both ministers and senior officials. Broad and informal categories overlaying the formal division of jurisdictions may have evolved that distinguish between those matters a government may implement unilaterally and those that should first be the subject of consultations with, or even the consent of, the other level of government.

Federalism is one of the fundamental principles of the Canadian constitution, and an understanding of its operation can be gained only through an appreciation of the constitutional conventions that have arisen as the political community has struggled to establish an acceptable balance of the relative powers of the two levels of government. In many ways this balance is a constantly shifting chimera, but the range of the variation has substantially altered since Confederation. Since the legal foundation was laid in 1867, a broad consensus has emerged that favours much stronger and more autonomous provincial governments, free from such interventions by the national government as reservation and disallowance. A profound crisis of political legitimacy could be provoked by any national government or court that tried to enforce these utterly obsolete legal provisions remaining in the Constitution.

6

Judicial Independence

An independent judiciary is a fundamental element of liberal democracy. The rule of law necessary to democracy is obtainable only through a judiciary that is free from overt political pressures and remains neutral and impartial between parties and issues.[1] With the federal division of powers the Canadian courts must also play an essential role as umpire in disputes of jurisdiction between the national and provincial governments. As Chief Justice Brian Dickson has pointed out, this role 'requires that the umpire be autonomous and completely independent of the parties involved in federal-provincial disputes.'[2] It is crucial that the judiciary be viewed, both individually and collectively, as impartial in resolving disputes that come to the courts for resolution. In essence this independence is ensured by protecting the judiciary from direction by any level of government, and by preventing the off-bench excursion of judges into political debates.

The independence of the Canadian judiciary was achieved through a mixture of positive law and constitutional convention. The basis of judicial independence has existed in England since the Act of Settlement in 1701 and was gradually applied to colonial judges in British North America.[3] This protection was formally embodied in s.99(1) of the Constitution Act, 1867, which provides that judges hold office during 'good behaviour'. For the most part, however, the independence of the judiciary has been assured in Canada by the respect that has been accorded to the constitutional conventions prohibiting the executive from interfering in judicial decisions, as well as to those limiting the activities of judges. But as Mr Justice Gerald Le Dain wrote in an 1985 decision of the Supreme Court of Canada, '... while tradition reinforced by public opinion may operate as a restraint upon the exercise of power in a manner that interferes with judicial independence, it cannot supply essential conditions of independence for which specific provision of law is necessary.'[4] Since 1968 statutory measures have introduced across the country the progressive institution of judicial councils, created to remove the executive from the initial investigation of complaints against judges. At present a national Canadian Judicial Council exists, as well as eleven other provincial and territorial councils; only Prince Edward Island has yet to create a council.

The Quebec provincial Charter of Human Rights and Freedoms, enacted in 1975, added a further statutory guarantee of judicial independence. Article 23 provides: 'Every person has the right to a full and equal, public and fair hearing by an independent and impartial tribunal, for the determination of his rights and obligations or of the merits of any charge brought against him.'[5]

A broad declaration of judicial independence would have been included in the Constitution Act, 1982 had the ill-fated Bill C-60 been enacted after its introduction by the Trudeau government in 1978. Section 100 of that Bill stated: 'The principle of the independence of the judiciary under the rule of law and in consonance with the supremacy of law is a fundamental principle of the Constitution of Canada.'

The range of constitutional protection was extended much further during the 1980s. In the 1982 Constitution Act, the Charter of Rights and Freedoms declared in s.11(d) that anyone charged with an offence has the right 'to be presumed innocent until proven guilty according to law in a fair and public hearing by an independent and impartial tribunal.' In *Valente v. The Queen*, where a provincial court judge refused to hear a case on the grounds that he could not act independently of the executive, the Supreme Court of Canada interpreted this section and outlined three elements constituting 'a standard that reflects what is common to, or at least at the heart of, the various approaches to the essential conditions of judicial independence in Canada.'[6] In the unanimous judgement of the Court, Mr Justice Le Dain wrote that the first element of this independence lies in security of tenure, 'whether until an age of retirement, for a fixed term, or for a specific adjudicative task, that is secure against interference by the executive or other appointing authority in a discretionary or arbitrary manner.'[7] Financial security was declared to be the second essential condition of judicial independence. And as Le Dain wrote: 'The essence of such security is that the right to salary and pension should be established by law and not subject to arbitrary interference by the executive in a manner that could affect judicial independence.'[8] The judgement then went on to state that the administrative independence of the courts comprises the third essential element. This independence is satisfied by judicial control over 'the assignment of judges, sittings of the courts and court lists—as well as matters of allocation of rooms and direction of the administrative staff engaged in carrying out these functions. . . .'[9]

The most important manner in which the independence of the judiciary is achieved lies in the freedom of judges to decide the outcome of individual cases without any pressure from outside the courts. It is inherent in the rule of law that a case be decided on its particular merits, according to the law that applies to the situation at hand.[10] Judges must be able to make their decisions without fear that they will be sued, dismissed, demoted, removed from the court roster, or have their pay reduced. As long as judges fulfil their duties, act within the law, and do not behave in some fashion that brings the courts into fundamental disrepute, they should have no concern for retribution because of the disposition of a case. Furthermore, the independence of the judiciary has to be protected from attempts by either the legislature, the executive, or private parties to direct the outcome of a case.

It must be noted that the rights enumerated in s.11 of the Charter of Rights, where the guarantee of judicial independence lies, have been found by the Supreme Court to apply only to offences of a criminal or quasi-criminal nature with penal consequences.[11] This protection is sufficient to protect the independence of many courts, however, since most courts dealing with civil issues also handle criminal offences (small-claims courts are one exception that would not be covered at all). Furthermore, through s.7 of the national Charter of Rights the guarantee of judicial independence might possibly be given a wider application to other courts and tribunals.[12]

Gilles Pépin has pointed out that the guarantees in the Canadian Charter of Rights are subject to both the reasonable limitations mentioned in s.1 and the notwithstanding clause, s.33, and could in theory be dispensed with by simple statute.[13] It may be, however, that the convention that limits the general use of this clause would prevent its application to judicial independence. Given the fundamental importance of the principle of an independent judiciary, there is good reason to suggest that s.11(d) must never be overridden.

The provision for judicial independence in the Quebec provincial Charter is quite far-reaching, at least in description. The Quebec Charter's guarantee of judicial independence also includes 'a coroner, a fire investigation commissioner, an inquiry commission, and any person or agency exercising quasi-judicial functions.'[14] But this provincial Charter can also be explicitly overridden by an express statement in any statute under article 52.

In a 1986 decision the Supreme Court of Canada gave renewed emphasis to the provisions of the Constitution Act of 1867 that protect judicial independence. A majority opinion written by Chief Justice Dickson declared that judicial independence is 'the lifeblood of constitutionalism in democratic societies'.[15] He held that the preamble of the 1867 Act had given additional constitutional protection in Canada to the principles of judicial independence originating in the United Kingdom.[16] The power of parliament under s.100 of that Act to set the salaries of federally appointed judges 'is not unlimited', according to Dickson. He continued: 'If there were any hint that a federal law dealing with these matters was enacted for an improper or colourable purpose, or if there was discriminatory treatment of judges vis-à-vis other citizens, then serious issues relating to judicial independence would arise and the law might be held to be ultra vires s.100 of the Constitution Act, 1867.'[17]

REMOVAL OF JUDGES

As Mr Justice Le Dain declared in *Valente*, security of tenure is the first requirement of an independent judiciary. The most blunt pressure the executive or legislature can exert on the judiciary is to remove a judge who makes a decision contrary to their interests. Since the Act of Settlement was passed in 1701, English judges have enjoyed statutory protection from arbitrary removal, and this security of tenure has since been extended to the Canadian judiciary. This protection was embodied in s.99(1) of the Constitution Act, 1867, which provides that 'the Judges of the Superior Courts shall hold office during good behaviour, but shall be removable by the Governor General on Address of the Senate and House of Commons.' There is some question about whether this provision creates two methods of removal: one by executive action for misbehaviour, and another by parliamentary resolution for any reason.[18] However, it is generally assumed by contemporary Canadian authorities that s.99(1) creates only one method of removal: by parliamentary resolution for misbehaviour.[19] William R. Lederman has cited the English method of removing judges for misbehaviour by the Crown's applying to a Queen's Bench judge for dismissal by writ of *scire facias*, but this common-law means of removal seems to have been superseded in Canada by statutory provisions, as it is no longer mentioned by any authority.[20]

The protection afforded by s.99(1) of the 1867 Constitution Act, however, extends only to superior court judges; it does not embrace county or provincial court judges. Under the federal Judges Act, county court judges are removable by the Governor in Council after a recommendation to do so from the Canadian Judicial Council. The statutory provisions relating to provincially appointed judges vary from province to province. Nevertheless, almost all judges are covered by the guarantees of secure tenure, which Le Dain declared to be an essential feature of judicial independence under s.11(d) of the Charter: '. . . that the judge be removable only for cause and that cause be subject to independent review and determination by a process at which the judge is afforded a full opportunity to be heard.'[21] Thus most Canadian judges are protected from ever being summarily removed by the government of the day.

Although judges should be shielded from removal simply because the politicians or public disagree with the policies enforced by the judge, there must always be some mechanism to remove individuals from the bench who behave in such an unacceptable manner that the judiciary is brought into disrepute. It would be fair to paraphrase the Supreme Court of Canada's ruling on cabinet secrecy[22] in terms that apply to the independence of the judiciary: '. . . the purpose of judicial independence is to promote its proper functioning, not to facilitate improper conduct by the judges.' In order to ensure that the misbehaviour for which judges may be constitutionally removed does not simply comprise going against government policy, every Canadian jurisdiction except Prince Edward Island has set up judicial councils to deal with complaints raised against individual judges and to recommend whether they should be removed; several provinces also provide that a judicial hearing may either replace or supplement the judicial council's inquiry. In PEI a judge of the Supreme Court conducts a formal investigation of complaints against a provincial court judge.[23]

Considering the number of people who have held judicial office, a surprising few have actually been removed from the bench. Not one member of a superior court has actually been formally dismissed, although four recommendations for removal have reached at least the stage of a parliamentary petition; on two of these occasions, however, the judges resigned.[24] Only four judges from county and district courts have been removed since Confederation.[25] Unfortunately no comprehensive historical figures are available for provincially appointed judges, but there do not appear to have been many instances of removal before the early 1980s.[26]

There does, however, seem to have been increasing attention paid to the behaviour of judges in the 1980s. Perhaps the advent of the Charter of Rights heightened the public awareness of judicial behaviour in response to the added responsibilities of the courts. Judge Paul Thériault, of the New Brunswick Provincial Court, was removed in 1989 after pleading guilty to refusing the breathalyzer.[27] In 1988 the Chief Justice of the Manitoba Provincial Court, Harold Gyles, lost that position, while remaining as an ordinary judge of that court, after being acquitted of criminal charges in a traffic-ticket-fixing scandal; two other judges were given suspended sentences and resigned in this same affair.[28] Judge Raymond Barlett, of the Nova Scotia Family Court, was fired in 1987—a first in that province—after upbraiding women who appeared before him for not being subservient to their husbands, as he declared the Bible required.[29] Several provincial court judges have resigned either after their removal has been recommended or in anticipation of a judicial council investigation. Judge Llyod Henriksen, of the Ontario Provincial Court, resigned in 1985 after being recommended for dismissal, as did Judge Ronald MacDonald in Nova

Scotia in 1989. One Quebec and two Ontario provincial court judges resigned during 1989-90 before formal investigations were held by their respective judicial councils.

Some judicial councils may also recommend disciplinary action short of removal.[30] Judge William Ross, of the Ontario Provincial Court, was suspended indefinitely in 1989 in order to receive treatment for stress that had resulted in bizarre incidents where the judge had ordered spectators to be held in jail simply for trying to leave the courtroom. Judge Frank Allen, of the Manitoba Provincial Court, was reprimanded by that province's judicial council in 1989 for helping two friends get parking tickets cancelled.[31] In 1988, Judge Jack S. Climans, of the Ontario Provincial Court, was required to apologize to a group of Sri Lankans for derogatory remarks.[32] A Quebec Sessions Court judge, André Chaloux, was strongly criticized for 'uncouth' comments he had made about another judge during a trial.[33]

There is some controversy surrounding how much latitude the law gives provincial executives in removing their judges. While British Columbia ensures that the government must remove a judge when recommended to do so by the judicial council of that province, other provinces allow the governor-in-council discretion in acting on a report from the judicial council. A special concern was voiced by Jules Deschênes that some governments have the legal power to remove a judge who has been exonerated by a judicial council's investigation.[34] However, common-law principles of natural justice might allow that judge to make further representations of some sort before a cabinet moved to discipline him or her. On the other hand, Russell has argued that some discretion should remain because 'judges inquiring into complaints about fellow judges might be too lenient and prevent responsible ministers from doing anything about judges who are woefully intemperate or neglectful of their duties.'[35]

There is also concern about the legal latitude afforded some provincial governments in the grounds to remove a judge. For example, both Russell and Deschênes are highly critical of Nova Scotia's law that permits a judge to be removed for acting 'in a manner contrary to the public interest'.[36] The one-year probationary period for newly appointed provincial court judges in Nova Scotia and Newfoundland was removed from the statute books after the Newfoundland provision was struck down for offending s.11(d) of the Charter. In his decision, Mr Justice Noel Goodridge recognized that the Newfoundland government had always respected the conventions of judicial independence. But he added that under the Charter, conventional protection is insufficient:

> If a court were to rely upon the traditions now so firmly entrenched in the judicial system, there would be little hesitancy in finding that the Provincial Court judiciary is, in fact, independent. The tradition of independence has and will continue to serve the justice system, hopefully, forever. A tradition, however, has no force of law.[37]

Goodridge's decision reflects an increasing trend to establish legal barriers around judicial independence in place of the informal rules that have previously operated.

Several scholars have offered suggestions about what constitutes misbehaviour for which judges may be legitimately removed from office, but these are far from conclusive. For example, Dawson has argued that 'bribery, gross partiality, and criminal proclivities are probably the only offences which would lead to certain removal.'[38] Both Gall and Russell imply that acceptable justifications for removal may well range more widely, in an unfortunately indeterminate manner.[39] The federal Judges Act was amended in 1971 to include references to judges' becoming 'incapacitated or disabled from the due execution' of their offices for age or infirmity, to 'misconduct', failing 'in the due execution' of the office, or 'having been placed, by his conduct or otherwise, in a position incompatible with the due execution of his office.'[40] Again unfortunately, most of these phrases are fraught with ambiguity. Russell tried to place some limit on the removal of judges by contending that 'It would be a breach of constitutional convention to initiate removal proceedings against a judge because the government regarded a judge's decisions as being in error or at odds with its policies.'[41] This formulation also presents difficulties, however, since a policy pursued by most governments is the impartial administration of justice and the eradication of various forms of prejudice and discrimination. It is instructive, though not reassuring, to note that not even a conviction on a serious offence has always led to an automatic removal from the bench. In 1986 a member of the Saskatchewan Court of Appeal, Mr Justice Nicholas Sherstobitoff, was fined $400 after pleading guilty to impaired driving, but continues to sit on that court.[42]

Perhaps a principled justification might be offered that judges are removable when their conduct compromises the fundamental requirements of judicial independence and impartiality. The rule of law implies respect for the laws by all members of society, and thus a judge who pleads guilty to, or is convicted of, a serious breach of law, such as a criminal offence, should be removed; respect for the courts cannot be maintained when a person with a criminal record sits in judgement. The Nova Scotia Judicial Council clearly stated in 1989 that Judge Ronald MacDonald, who had pleaded guilty to an assault on his wife, could not deal impartially with similar cases in his court. Furthermore, it dismissed the notion that the judge could remain on the bench provided he not hear similar cases: '. . . he must be a judge for all purposes or not at all.'[43] Judicial impartiality demands that all members of society are assumed to have equal claims to justice when litigating an issue, so any judges who compromise their adjudicative impartiality—by portraying a fundamental predisposition in favour of, or against, particular individuals, groups, or issues—might be removed. However, this ground for removal does not prevent a judge from feeling sympathetic or compassionate towards an issue or the plight of a litigant; the bias must be such that judges are demonstrably perceived as being unwilling or unable to decide a case other than in accordance with their prejudices. Judges must maintain an impartiality between litigants to the extent that the public can have full confidence that suits are settled on the basis of the legal arguments presented in court rather than on the basis of who the parties are. Furthermore, since the resolution of legal suits has to be settled rationally, on the basis of the relevant law, judges who display a pattern of irrational or psychologically disturbed behaviour should be suspended or dismissed, depending on the cause. Finally, members of the bench must also be removed who degrade their judicial positions by dereliction or by acting in such a severe or abusive manner that they fundamentally undermine public respect for their ability to act judicially; this ground for removal must apply to off-bench behaviour as well as to courtroom activities. The essential motivation in all these justifications is that the public's faith in the independence, impartiality, and integrity of the judiciary must be protected.

It is necessary to have a clear consensus on the informal justifications for removal, since the relevant legal provisions still provide considerable discretion. Although positive legal rules have been extended in recent decades, the basic protection of judicial tenure continues to rely to a large extent on informal understandings of what constitutes sufficient misbehaviour to justify removal. These conventions are especially important in protecting provincially appointed judges.

JUDICIAL IMMUNITY

A considerable body of case law has arisen to define the legal immunities of judges. These assure the judiciary that they are free to decide individual cases without fear of suit for damages for wrongly decided cases. However, the rule of law continues to be respected through threads of the rules of immunity, which continue to ensure that 'no-one is above the law'. For example, judges are still liable for criminal activities and for personal wrongs committed off the bench.[44] Superior court judges in Canada have acquired through adoption the fundamental immunities of British superior court judges, who are said to enjoy 'absolute immunity'; but this is perhaps something of a misnomer, since there are indeed activities that are actionable if committed from the bench by any judge. Certainly in the normal course of judicial activity a judge is free from suit. Mr Justice Roger Chouinard drew upon British jurisprudence[45] in his 1985 judgement for the Supreme Court of Canada that suits are only permissible against a superior court judge '. . . who in bad faith did something which he knew he did not have the jurisdiction to do, or . . . who was not acting in the course of his judicial duties knowing that he had no jurisdiction to act.'[46]

Provincially appointed judges do not have such a wide immunity from suit, and a number of jurisdictions disclaim by statute any judicial immunity for malicious acts and for instances of excess or lack of jurisdiction.[47] In 1986 the New Brunswick court of Queen's Bench allowed a suit to proceed against a provincial judge who had ignored a Queen's Bench order to deal with a case. In permitting the action, Mr Justice John P. Barry declared: 'No one is above the law, judges included. In fact we take an oath to uphold the law, not defy it.'[48]

The inquiry by a Royal Commission in Nova Scotia into the wrongful conviction of Donald Marshall Jr for murder raised the broader question of whether judges can be required to explain their reasons for particular decisions. A five-judge panel of the provincial Court of Appeal had acquitted Marshall in a reference case in 1983; but the concluding paragraph of their decision mentioned that the miscarriage of justice was more apparent than real and that Marshall was the author of many of his own misfortunes. The Royal Commission attempted to compel these judges to testify at the hearings in order to explain their comments, and also to discover why Leonard Pace sat on the panel even though he had earlier dealt with the case as Attorney General at the time of Marshall's original conviction. However, these efforts were blocked by both levels of the Nova Scotia Supreme Court on the grounds that these judges were neither 'compellable nor competent' to testify, because judicial immunity would prevent any legal action on these issues and the commissioners could not exceed the regular powers of superior court judges in compelling witnesses and testimony.[49]

When this case reached the Supreme Court of Canada, the majority also shielded the judges, on the basis that the provincial executive could not set up an inquiry into either the adjudicative or the internal administrative processes of federally appointed judges.[50] Most members of the Supreme Court also stressed that judges have an immunity that normally protects them from being accountable for the mental process by which they reach their publicly stated reasons. These matters might conceivably only be broached in the context of a specially constituted disciplinary tribunal, such as a judicial council. In the end, the Attorney General requested the Canadian Judicial Council to hold a disciplinary hearing to investigate whether the Appeal Court panel who heard Marshall's case had acted properly.[51]

The implications of these decisions, however, reach far beyond this particular case. At stake is the range of inquiry that can be initiated by any government into the judicial system in its jurisdiction. The limitations of the restrictions espoused by the Nova Scotia courts are exhibited by the ongoing Manitoba inquiry into the treatment of aboriginals by that province's justice system; no judges have been publicly interviewed.

Although the principle of judicial independence must be maintained, there are solid grounds favouring inquiries that might include testimony from sitting judges; one such example would be a commission looking into systemic bias, pervasive interference, or corruption within the judiciary. Judicial independence is meant to facilitate and ensure the operation of an impartial judiciary. In such instances the inquiry would be aimed at restoring or protecting the fundamental independence of the judiciary. However, the bastion erected by the underlying principles of the Nova Scotia and Supreme Court of Canada decisions dealing with the Marshall inquiry would serve to protect a judiciary from an outside inquiry into any endemic bias or corruption within the judiciary. Many observers would strenuously contend that such matters should only be dealt with in proceedings against individual judges through investigations by the relevant judicial council. The difficulty with this position is that the judges themselves play such a large role in most judicial councils. The Canadian Judicial Council is exclusively composed of judges, and they fill at least half the positions on seven provincial councils.[52] It may be that public confidence in such an inquiry would only be ensured in some situations by a commission totally unconnected with the existing judiciary or with councils of a particular jurisdiction.

THIRD-PARTY INTERFERENCE IN ADJUDICATION

An important dimension of judicial independence is ensured through informal constitutional rules that protect the judges from outside pressure to resolve a particular case in a certain way. Some formal legal sanctions also exist in cases where an individual attempts corruptly to obstruct justice—by bribery, for example. However, the impartial adjudication of legal disputes can be ensured only if the judge trying a case is not subject to any argumentation or direction except in the course of the normal presentations by counsel representing the parties to the action. Thus no third party should be able to exert pressure on a judge through informal or private channels. A fundamental convention prohibits cabinet ministers from trying to interfere in a dispute and cajoling a judge to decide in the interest of the government or its supporters. Other informal rules protect the judiciary from pressure from the legislature. But not even other members of the bench should try to interfere in a judge's decision in a particular case.

An essential criterion of judicial independence is that ministers of the Crown do not use their positions to influence judges to make decisions favourable to the government or its supporters. Ministers should neither criticize a judge publicly nor make private representations to judges. As Wade and Bradley put it: 'The government may say that a judicial decision differs from the legal advice upon which it had acted or that it proposes to bring in amending legislation, but ministers are not expected to state that a court's decision is wrong.'[53]

Although this principle is generally respected, a number of incidents indicate that for some ministers the temptation is too strong to resist. The importance of preventing any appearance of informal pressure by cabinet ministers on decisions by judges was underlined by a series of incidents, revealed in 1976, that came to be known as 'the judges' affair'. Marc Lalonde, as Minister of Justice, had visited a judge on a Sunday morning in order to explain the political ramifications of a conviction of some Trinidadian students; Jean Chrétien telephoned a judge in order to find out when a decision would be brought down on a case involving a constituent of his; C.M. (Bud) Drury called a judge to see if an apology by another cabinet minister, André Ouellet, would be sufficient to have contempt charges dropped. Ouellet's charges had stemmed from public criticism he had made of a judge's decision to acquit some companies of price-fixing charges.[54] In the end, Drury offered an apology in the House of Commons for his behaviour and offered his resignation, although Trudeau declined to accept it.[55] Trudeau, however, did make a statement to the House that cabinet ministers should communicate with judges and officials of courts of record only through the Minister of Justice.[56] Two years later another minister in Trudeau's government, John Munro, resigned after it became known that he had phoned a judge just before the sentencing of a constituent. In 1978 Ontario Premier William Davis, after improper overtures by his Solicitor General on behalf of a constituent, issued a statement that only the Attorney General 'may communicate with members of the judiciary concerning any matter which they may have before them in their judicial capacity.'[57]

The sensitive nature of any ministerial contact with judges has been underlined by more recent events. In 1988 federal Transport Minister Benoit Bouchard came under fire for directly writing to a New Brunswick Provincial Court judge, on the judge's request, to clarify the powers of airport security personnel.[58] And federal Fitness and Amateur Sport Minister Jean Charest had to resign in 1990 after it was revealed that he phoned a judge to clarify some matters relating to a court case.[59]

A more problematic dimension of executive interference into the judicial process lies in the penchant of some Attorneys General for suggesting sentencing guidelines for judges in their jurisdiction. The tremendous disparity in sentences meted out for the same offence can be cause for concern. But if an Attorney General truly believes that more uniform or stringent sentences are required, these objectives should properly be achieved through legislative amendment. Judges should be free to exercise the discretion in sentencing given to them by law without pressure from the political executive.[60]

The judiciary should also be free to reach impartial decisions without interference from the legislature. To this end it has long been a convention that matters that are *sub judice* are not permitted to be discussed in the legislature. As the editors of *Beauchesne* explain:

> Members are expected to refrain from discussing matters that are before the courts or tribunals which are courts of record. The purpose of this sub-judice convention is to protect the parties in a case awaiting or undergoing trial and persons who stand to be affected by the outcome of a judicial inquiry. It is a voluntary restraint imposed by the House upon itself in the interest of justice and fair play.[61]

This convention is most stringently followed with respect to criminal offences and reference cases, but the practice has not been very consistent with respect to civil suits.[62]

The Quebec National Assembly has formalized this prohibition with the stipulation in rule 35(3) of its Rules of Procedure that no member may 'speak to a matter that is before a court of law or a quasi-judicial body, or under investigation, if the words uttered might cause prejudice to anyone.' Despite this prohibition, René Lévesque caused a furor in 1982 when he lashed out in the Assembly against the RCMP and the federal government over an earlier break-in to Parti québécois headquarters and the subsequent theft of party membership lists.[63] An RCMP officer was on trial at the time for this episode and Lévesque's outburst caused a mistrial; a second trial was cleared only after a Supreme Court of Canada ruling in 1988.[64]

Several unfortunate breaches of this convention also occurred in the New Zealand legislature in the late 1980s, when some MPs made several statements about on-going criminal cases; these incidents culminated in the naming of a person who had been charged with conspiracy to defraud, but whose identity had been protected from publication by an order of the court trying the case. In effect the MPs used their parliamentary privilege to allow the public reporting of issues that could not otherwise have been published because of the court order. The Public Issues Committee of the Aukland District Law Society in turn published a report that was highly critical of this abuse of convention:

> In constitutional terms, Parliament cannot, and in our view must not, be used, whether by Members of Parliament collectively or by an individual Member of Parliament, as a forum to accuse and in effect try citizens of criminal conduct. . . . What defiance of a name suppression order clearly does do is deprive the individual concerned of the benefit of an order which a judicial officer has seen as necessary in the interests of justice for the protection of the individual concerned or—and this needs to be stressed— for the protection of persons associated with him or her. . . . It permits the individual Member of Parliament concerned to frustrate and even override the functions of the Courts and the Judiciary.[65]

Another aspect of judicial independence is the desirability of a judge's being able to decide a case without pressures being exerted from within the judicial branch of government; unfortunately this topic is seldom discussed. Such pressure should come neither in the form of direct intervention by a judge on behalf of friends or family appearing before another judge, nor in the form of reduced court dockets or geographically remote sittings assigned by the Chief Justice because of policy disagreements. An unusual example of a breach of this aspect of judicial independence arose in 1988 when an Ontario Provincial Court judge, Robert Dnieper, appeared before another judge as an 'assisting adult' on behalf of a person charged under the Young Offenders Act.[66] In addition, judges should not comment publicly on matters that are currently the subject of legal proceedings, either in their own or another courtroom.[67]

More subtle problems are also raised by this issue, which involve the extent to which a judge, during informal discussions, may persuade another judge of a certain settlement. Judges occasionally discuss problematic aspects of cases with their colleagues, and it should be incumbent on them to carry out these discussions with great circumspection. Another difficulty arises with the dealings some judges have with law clerks or students in the preparation of a final decision on a case. It is not unheard of in some jurisdictions for a judge to read from a clerk's memo in delivering an oral judgement. But, as J.O. Wilson wrote on the role of a law clerk: 'It is certainly no part of his function to write all or any part of a judgment which must be in a judge's own words.'[68] The principle behind these concerns is that the independence of the judiciary and the rule of law are assured only when the public can be confident that a decision is that of the judge who heard the case, and that the decision has been based on the arguments heard during normal proceedings rather than on private argumentation by third parties.

LIMITATIONS ON THE ACTIVITIES OF JUDGES

An important dimension of judicial independence is ensured through rules that restrict the off-bench activities of judges. Just as it is crucial to independent and impartial courts that politicians be kept from interfering in the judicial process, so must judges be kept from compromising their perceived neutrality by intruding into the political process. In addition, one must be assured that judges do not have any private interests that could compromise their impartiality. Each jurisdiction has some statutory provisions to prevent judges from carrying on other businesses or occupations while serving as a judge; unfortunately some jurisdictions, such as Nova Scotia, permit these activities if they are approved by the Governor-in-Council.

Perhaps the most frustrating aspect of a judge's occupation stems from the severe limitations placed on his or her public, and even private, behaviour.[69] However, it is essential for the public perception, and operative substance, of judicial independence that judges do not engage in open debate on political issues. As a publication of the federal Department of Justice warns new appointees to the bench: 'The judge is not permitted to engage in public debate on any of his or her decisions, or to express personal opinions on major social issues, which might lead to an apprehension of bias when such issues come to be adjudicated by the court.'[70] Gall and Russell have each offered similar expressions of an obligation for judges to refrain from commenting on social issues, while Russell adds that one reason for this restraint is to protect the courts from reciprocal political interference in the judicial process.[71]

There are several examples in modern Canadian history of judges' wandering from this requirement to avoid political controversy. The best known of these incidents arose from public criticisms levelled by Thomas Berger in 1981, while he served on the British Columbia Supreme Court, against the constitutional agreement that led to the 1982 Constitution Act.[72] Berger attacked the accord for its exclusion of Quebec, and also for the minimal role give to aboriginal rights. Acting on a complaint from a Federal Court judge, the Canadian Judicial Council investigated Berger's utterances. The committee that initially looked into the affair concluded that this sort of behaviour generally warranted removal, but did not recommend it in this case. Although the full judicial council did not agree with the committee's general conclusion about the seriousness of the matter, it did also state: 'The Judicial Council is of the opinion that members of the Judiciary should avoid taking part in controversial political discussions except only in respect of matters that directly affect the operation of the courts.'[73] Amidst all the controversy his remarks caused, Berger resigned from the bench. Some commentators, however, have been critical of the curtailment of judges' freedom of speech that this precedent sets.[74]

But there does seem to be a general acceptance of judicial involvement in debates concerning the legal system, although Gall mentions that judges must never advocate that needed reforms would be best pursued by a particular party.[75] In this respect Canada appears to have inherited the British tolerance of judicial involvement in the formulation and passage of legislation dealing with the legal system. Not only does the Lord Chancellor play a large role in the preparation of such bills, but this is the one general area in which the Law Lords are permitted by convention to participate in the legislative process of the House of Lords.[76] However, the 1989 courtroom boycott by Quebec Court judges, in a dispute with government over their salaries, illustrates the potential dangers of unrestrained judicial criticisms of policies concerning the courts.

Since the controversy generated by Berger's outspoken attack on the

1981 constitutional accord, several other judges have also mistakenly wandered into the political arena. In 1985 the Chief Justice of Manitoba, Alfred Monnin, created a stir in 1985 with his signing of an anti-abortion petition; but a subsequent complaint about this was unsuccessful before the Canadian Judicial Council.

A Quebec Youth Court judge, Andrée Ruffo, caused a controversy in the late 1980s by her outspoken criticisms of the provincial social-services ministry. Her activities resulted in a judicial council investigation of 58 complaints laid by the department. She also was told by Chief Justice Albert Gobeil to cease her public speeches. However, she has responded to Gobeil's orders with a civil suit.[77]

The Chief Justice of the Supreme Court of Canada, Brian Dickson, also made a grave error of judgement in a speech he made when receiving an honorary degree from the University of British Columbia in May 1986. He strongly criticized the level of funding given to post-secondary education in Canada:

> Second-class funding of universities will inevitably lead to second-class teachers, second-class students and, ultimately, a second-class nation. It has been said by many people that education is too important to be left to educators. That may be true. But it is also true that education is too important to be left to Ministers of Finance.[78]

This speech raised a considerable clamour because Parliament was at that time considering the government's legislation on federal-provincial funding of post-secondary education. Dickson's speech was immediately latched onto and used by Opposition MPs in their condemnation of the government's bill. Sixteen Opposition speeches and questions made reference to the fact that the government's policy was being condemned by the Chief Justice. On the very first sitting day after Dickson's speech, Howard McCurdy made a statement in the Commons that typifies the use to which the Chief Justice's speech was put:

> The judge was speaking directly to the federal Minister of Finance who has taken over the post-secondary education portfolio and introduced legislation that will devastate the system. When a Chief Justice deems it necessary to speak out against Government policy the Government would do well to listen and, in response, provide the provinces with resources to post-secondary education commensurate with the key role they must play in ensuring Canada's economic, political and social future.[79]

This incident exemplifies exactly why judges should refrain from entering political debates. Not only will their comments be used for purely partisan ends, but public confidence in the impartiality of such judges could not be justified if the issue in question were ever to be litigated before them.[80]

There is certainly a general prohibition against judges' becoming involved in any overtly partisan activities after their appointment to the bench. An unfortunately large number of judges have active partisan backgrounds and it is important for the public to believe that they have been able to shed their political ties and can act impartially. This prohibition is left mostly to constitutional convention. The various elections Acts in force in Canada have also deprived judges of the vote, ostensibly to ensure their political neutrality. But the prohibition in the Canada Elections Act was struck down in 1988 by a challenge launched under the Charter of Rights by a couple of Federal Court judges.[81]

The conventional bar to political activities is important, but a disquieting pattern emerges from the lists of donors to federal political parties that is released each year by the Chief Electoral Officer. A careful reading of these lists reveals a number of people across the country who have continued to make donations to the PC Canada Fund even after their judicial appointments. One former Nova Scotia judge appears in these lists for five of his seven years on the bench. Perhaps more jurisdictions should adopt Manitoba's statutory provision that 'No judge or magistrate shall engage in any manner in partisan political activities.'[82]

Judges also need to be extremely circumspect about the private meetings they hold. Once again the concern is that they would be predisposed towards any groups they had met. There is also the necessity to avoid the impression that judges could be privately influenced in their decisions on pending cases. In 1988 a complaint was made to the Canadian Judicial Council about a private meeting held by the Chief Justice of the Supreme Court of Canada with representatives of the Canadian Advisory Council on the Status of Women.[83] REAL Women of Canada complained that this compromised the integrity of the court, since the CACSW was reportedly participating in four cases before the court at the time of the meeting. REAL Women took particular exception to the comment in the CACSW's 1986-7 Annual Report that this meeting had been held in part 'to convey the Council's concern on how the new equality rights would be interpreted by the judiciary.'[84] However, the Judicial Council of Canada dismissed the complaint, on the grounds that the essential purpose of the visit was to allow the Chief Justice to develop a proper approach to equality issues to be pursued by the Judge's Education Centre. REAL Women were informed by the Judicial Council of Canada: 'The fact that the Chief Justice of Canada in his capacity as Chairman of the Interim Management Board of the [Judge's Education] Centre was able to take the time in his onerous schedule to meet with the President and two executive members of the Canadian Advisory Council on the Status of Women is to be commended not criticized.'[85] Although this particular complaint was dismissed, it does underline the potential compromise of judicial independence if judges start meeting privately with interest groups. The judiciary open themselves to easy suspicions of favouritism and partiality if they hold private meetings with some but not all groups interested in particular issues.

One problem that may potentially jeopardize the independence of the judiciary is the tendency of governments across Canada to use judges to head up royal commissions or other inquiries. For many years judges have headed an array of *ad hoc* commissions of inquiry, ranging from the Gouzenko spy affair to the Dubin inquiry into drugs in sport. The 1985 report of the Canadian Bar Association's Committee on the Independence of the Judiciary argues against judges' serving in these capacities. The committee felt that not only does the judiciary suffer because of the loss of valuable time from a judge, but judicial independence is potentially eroded:

> A judge who sits on a commission of inquiry may lose or be perceived to have lost his independence and impartiality at least as regards the subject matters of the inquiry and other matter related to it. This may seem like a minor problem but commissions of inquiry often study very broad and potentially contentious issues. And moreover, the individual judge and the bench generally may well suffer a loss of independence in the eyes of the public. When judges are too frequently seen to be working with the government, even if merely as commissioners, there will be a natural tendency for the public to see judges as not completely independent of the government.[86]

The Committee did allow some exceptions for issues that could make 'the choice of a judge as commissioner particularly appropriate'.[87] Ontario's Attorney General, Ian Scott, once argued against judges' serving on public inquiries, labour boards, or police commissions; he felt they should resign from the bench if they wished to take up these positions. Scott's objections were based on the loss of manpower to the courts, rather than on the perceived loss of independence; but he did concede that occasionally judges could head an inquiry dealing with an issue of 'sufficiently broad public interest'.[88] Only fifteen days later Scott appointed Mr Justice John Osler, of the province's Supreme Court, to head an inquiry into how tainted wines had slipped past the Liquor Control Board's testing procedures.[89] Indeed, there does seem to be a fairly general acceptance of a role for judges as heads of commissions of inquiry.

THE APPOINTMENT OF JUDGES

A vital contribution to the independence of the judiciary is made in the initial selection and appointment of jurists to serve on the bench.[90] Given the security of tenure and wide immunities of serving judges, it is critical that careful choices are made in staffing the judiciary. The appointment procedures across the country have come under much criticism because of the wide latitude governments have had in choosing new judges.[91] The main concern has been the extent to which political patronage has influenced the selection of judges; in the Maritime Provinces particular problems have been seen with respect to both federal appointments and provincially appointed judges.[92] Patronage poses three obvious problems: there is concern that partisans will favour their former political colleagues; that unsuitable individuals can be appointed to the bench because of their political connections; and that well-qualified candidates may never be appointed because they support the wrong party. These objections are compounded when one party has been in office for an extended period. A study by Peter Russell and Jacob Ziegel of the appointments made by the Mulroney government during its first term in office has revealed an alarming degree of political overtones. They found that 48 per cent of all the judges appointed in this period were known Conservative Party supporters, while only 7.1 per cent were known Opposition party supporters. The portion of Tory supporters soared to over 70 per cent of the judges appointed in Saskatchewan, Manitoba, and the Maritimes.[93] In a study I have made of the 32 provincial judges appointed by the Nova Scotia Conservatives between 1978 and mid-1990, not one publicly identifiable Liberal was appointed and the only NDP partisan was an MLA who was appointed on the eve of a general election.

A related weakness could be perceived in the promotion of judges from one level of court to a higher bench. However, there appears to be little evidence that judges have tried to curry favour in order to be promoted, or that judges who have been elevated have favoured the government in their decisions. In fact there is merit in providing appellate courts with judges who have gained adjudicating experience in trial-level courts.[94] At present the federal government has an informal practice of consulting with both the Chief Justice and the Attorney General of the province involved before elevating any judge.[95] Unfortunately the research done by Russell and Ziegel casts an ominous shadow by revealing that 45.3 per cent of judges promoted by the first Mulroney government had once been Tory party supporters, while only 17.2 per cent had been known Opposition party supporters before their initial appointments to the bench.[96]

Fortunately there appears to be an increasing tendency among provincial governments to move to a more impartial selection process, which limits the discretion of the executive and establishes some means for assessing the professional qualifications of potential candidates. An important role has been given to the judicial councils in British Columbia, Alberta, Saskatchewan, Newfoundland, and the two Territories.[97] Since 1978 separate nominating committees have existed in Quebec to make an initial recommendation on candidates for judicial appointment, and a central nominating commission was also established in Ontario in 1988. Although few jurisdictions require it by statute, most appointments are now made only from lists of nominees approved by the judicial councils and nominating commissions.

The federal government has also changed its appointment procedures with the institution of committees in each province and territory to screen candidates and place them on a list of qualified persons from which the Minister of Justice will choose new appointees.[98] A similar procedure was also adopted in Nova Scotia in 1989, although that committee may also distinguish between qualified and highly qualified candidates. The difficulty with this arrangement is that the committees merely screen out the incompetent candidates and are unable to recommend which candidates are best suited to judicial careers. As a result, the ministers still have an unfettered discretion to choose, and there is no impediment to the continued play of partisan considerations in the actual selection of judges. The first six appointments made to the Nova Scotia Provincial Court under the new system all involved known government partisans; one person had not even been in the courtroom for twenty years before his appointment, and had practised real-estate law for much of this time.

Some developments in the appointment of judges, especially in Ontario, have gone a long way to promoting the institutional independence of the judiciary. It is to be hoped that the range of discretion remaining to the executive in other jurisdictions will be similarly restricted. Once the influence of partisan politics has been overcome, more attention can be focused on the experience, knowledge, and capabilities of candidates for judgeships. Too little attention has been paid to the attributes appointing authorities should look for in new judges, but an ability to approach issues with an open mind, and the self-discipline to examine competing claims dispassionately, are just two essential qualities. Judicial independence relies to a great extent on the personal qualities of those appointed to the bench.

JUDICIAL INDEPENDENCE REVIEWED

The independence of the Canadian judiciary relies increasingly on entrenched constitutional provisions as well as on statute and case law. Nevertheless constitutional conventions continue to play an important role in modifying these legal rules. Although basic procedures for the removal of judges—preventing the summary removal of most judges— now exist in all jurisdictions in Canada, the essential reasons justifying any removal are still largely determined by informal understandings of the substance of impermissible behaviour. Furthermore, the interference by the executive or legislature in the determination of specific cases before the courts is prohibited largely by convention. Finally, the restrictions placed on the private and public behaviour of judges that prevent their off-bench intrusion into the political arena are also determined by convention.

The entrenchment of the principle of judicial independence in the Charter of Rights, however, has provided the impetus for a further spread of positive law to regulate this important aspect of the Canadian constitution. With the Supreme Court of Canada's decisions in *Beauregard* and *Valente*, we have had clear signals that the judiciary are fully prepared to chart the course to be followed in ensuring their own independence. I believe that these decisions foreshadow a potential shift in the political role of the judiciary, especially with respect to what control the elected representatives of the public may have held over it.

The independence of the judiciary essentially evolved in Britain during the eighteenth and nineteenth centuries. Its essence lay in the legal security of tenure of judges, as well as in the conventional prohibition against executive interference in the resolution of cases before the bar. However, elected politicians still remained in overall control. The doctrine of the sovereignty of Parliament ensured that the legislature could amend or overturn any decisions that ran counter to the general will of the electorate. Furthermore, the whole body politic retained control, through Cabinet and Parliament, over the general level of financial and administrative resources to be allocated to the justice system.

In Canada, however, with the indication by the courts that their financial and administrative independence are essential ingredients of any judicial independence, there is now the potential for a political battle to emerge between the judiciary and the other branches of government over just what resources are to be made available to the courts. This danger is well illustrated by the Quebec judges who boycotted their courtrooms in 1989 over their salaries, and by those Ontario judges who previously threatened strike action. One can foresee that the courts may eventually decide that their independence can be assured only when the judges are in control over the full range of physical and human resources involved in the judicial process. As Judge François Beaudoin, president of the Conference des juges du Québec, said: 'When you are reduced to begging for a decent salary, how can you be truly independent?'[99]

A long-term difficulty lies in the complete freedom of judges to interpret as they wish provisions of the Constitution relating to judicial independence. In its interpretation of s.100 of the 1867 Constitution Act in *Beauregard*, the Supreme Court of Canada has already placed its own restrictions on the clear language giving Parliament the right to set salaries. The Court has also interpreted the Charter of Rights so that its provisions do not apply *in toto* to the judiciary—despite the fact that some sections make sense only if the courts are so included.[100] Furthermore, this freedom of interpretation with respect to the judicial function is seen in the Supreme Court of Canada's persistent willingness to restrict, for the benefit of the courts, the very clear language of legislation providing that 'any matter' may be put to the courts by executives as reference questions.[101]

The Canadian constitution has now effectively placed the courts as the ultimate definers of the requirements of judicial independence. And it is possible that the courts will gather to themselves, through constitutional interpretation, overall control of financial matters relating to the courts. But as a Vice-Chancellor of Britain has written:

> However important the system of justice may be, its demands have to be weighed against the competing demands of other public services. The question of how the available national resources are to be divided between the various functions of government is essentially a political question. Therefore, in the last resort, the amount of the total legal budget must be determined politically and controlled by Parliament.[102]

The essential protection against a judicial usurpation of the right of the legislative and executive branches of government to control the overall finances of the judiciary lies in the possibility of introducing amendments to the formal Constitution to overturn explicitly such interpretations made by the courts. Furthermore, s.33 of the 1982 Constitution Act provides the legislature with the legal, though fading, power to enact legislation notwithstanding the provisions in the Charter concerning judicial independence. Even so, politicians would face considerable political resistance in trying to overturn pronouncements by appellate courts relating to the requirements of judicial independence. Survey research has indicated a fundamental reverence of the judiciary among Canadians. A 1989 Gallup Poll revealed that 59 per cent of the respondents had either 'a great deal' or 'quite a lot' of confidence in the Supreme Court of Canada, while only 33 per cent felt the same about the House of Commons.[103] In addition, a national survey conducted on public attitudes towards the Charter of Rights in Canada has revealed that more than 60 per cent of Canadians prefer the courts to be the final arbiters, rather than the legislatures, when a law is found to offend the Charter.[104] Because of this veneration of the judiciary, it is extremely doubtful that a government would be able to exercise its ultimate legal option to overturn a court's declaration on judicial independence.

In the end, the independence of the judiciary and its place within the overall framework of Canadian government must depend on a respect for the constitutional conventions that modify the formal provisions of the constitution. So long as the executives and legislatures do not encroach on the courts in such a manner that the judiciary fear the loss of their essential independence in adjudication, the courts will no doubt continue to respect the rules that restrict their basic activities in resolving legal disputes. By the same token the judiciary must respect the rules that essentially limit judges to adjudication and exclude them from open political debate; if they do not, they risk the imposition of new laws that could restore the primacy of elected politicians over the appointed judicial branch of government. The Charter of Rights, however, has brought with it an increasingly political dimension to litigation that expands the reach of the judiciary.[105] It may become more important than ever in the future to appreciate the present conventions supporting judicial independence if judicial power ever challenges fundamentally the activities of the other branches of government.

7

The Variety and Character of Conventions

The bare bones of Canada's constitutional laws have been dramatically transformed by the informal rules arising out of political practice.[1] The powers of the governors, ministerial responsibility, the legislatures, federalism, and judicial independence are all aspects of the constitution that depend heavily on informal rules to modify, or fill voids in, the relevant rules of positive law. As important as these informal rules are, however, their nature and operation may not be fully appreciated.

Those rules generally grouped together as 'conventions' may actually contain several distinguishable classes of rules. If distinctions are drawn among conventions, it will be easier to ascertain which rule should prevail when several conventions conflict; the suitability of particular conventions for some sort of codification may become more apparent. Furthermore, a study of the role of conventions in the courtroom can also be undertaken from a firmer foundation. An understanding of why conventions vary and how they can be distinguished can lead us away from the traditional path of precedent-seeking to focus our attention instead on the role of the basic principles of our constitution.

VARIATIONS AMONG THE INFORMAL CONSTITUTIONAL RULES

The weaknesses in the prevailing views on the informal rules of the constitution may be traced back to inadequacies in the original theories posed by A.V. Dicey and Sir Ivor Jennings. A major problem is the general skepticism about the need to distinguish among these rules. Although Dicey drew lasting attention to the role informal rules play in transforming the constitutional laws, he failed to draw any substantive distinctions among the 'customs, practices, maxims, or precepts' composing the group of 'constitutional or political ethics' he termed conventions.[2] Several decades later, Jennings underlined the difference between binding conventions and non-obligatory usages or practices: conventions are supported by some constitutional reason or principle, but usages are not.[3] Despite the attention he drew to the differences between usage and convention, he continued to treat all conventions as if they were a homogeneous group of rules. This approach continues to characterize contemporary constitutional thought.

However, some reflection on the many informal rules at work in the constitution can produce illustrations of rules that vary according to acceptance, precision, observation, or importance. J.P. Mackintosh has remarked that different orders of constitutional conventions do appear to operate:

> ... conventions have different degrees of force. Some are fundamental in that to break them would overturn the basic principles of the constitution. . . . Some conventions are of considerable force but might conceivably have altered by the year 2000, without totally changing the nature of the constitution. . . . There are other conventions which are of less importance and merely indicate that certain usages are inadvisable or inappropriate.[4]

These three types of conventions can be easily illustrated. The first, fundamental sort of convention is found in the rule that a government that has clearly lost the confidence of the legislature must either resign or advise an election; this rule forms the very foundation of responsible parliamentary government. Another example of a fundamental convention is the related rule that a governor must appoint as prime minister the person who can command a majority in the legislature. Mackintosh used the responsibility of individual ministers for the actions of their subordinates as an example of the second variety of convention that can evolve, and has evolved, over time; another example would be the evolution of opinion over which votes in the legislature involve a test of confidence. A convention relating to inadvisable behaviour might be found in the notion that governors do not normally address their legislatures except to open or close a session, or to grant royal assent. However, this breakdown within constitutional conventions is not sufficient to explain how informal rules may range from mere usage to fundamental conventions. The problem is that Mackintosh has described only some of the differences between these rules without attempting any analytic explanation. If one can identify conventions of different importance or obligation, it seems essential that both the reasons for, and consequences of, those variations be understood.

A persisting tendency to downplay the division between usage and convention, as well as the pervasive trend to ignore distinctions among conventions, greatly weaken our understanding of the informal rules shaping the Canadian constitution. Most importantly, the lack of a means to distinguish among informal constitutional rules leaves us without guidance in a constitutional dilemma posed by conflicting rules. The choice of action would become much clearer if we could give a principled reason why a particular rule should prevail.

VARYING FACTORS OF CONVENTIONS

An examination of the different elements of informal rules reveals four interrelated factors that can vary in combination to produce distinct classes of rules. The first factor relates to the importance of the principle or reason that lies behind the rule. The second relates to the degree of agreement among political actors and constitutional observers on the principle behind the rule. The third has to do with the level of agreement on the specific terms of the rule. The fourth factor is how close the content of the rule comes to embodying the principle involved. Another element that might lead to distinctions among informal rules is the degree to which they are supported by existing precedents.

The principle behind a rule appears to be one of the most crucial factors that vary among the informal rules of the constitution. A distinction between usage and convention can be made on this ground alone: usages have no particular reason for existence beyond ceremony, habit, or convenience, while conventions may be supporting principles that define the essential characteristics of our constitution. Four absolutely fundamental groups of principles may be identified within the legal and conventional rules of the Canadian constitution: Canada is a self-governing independent nation; it is a liberal democracy; its government operates within a responsible parliamentary framework based on organized and disciplined parties; and it has a federal division of government. The fundamental importance of a principle should be measured by the degree to which the constitution would function differently in the absence of that principle. By this measurement another group of principles surrounding the monarchic element of the constitution does not appear as important as the other four groups of principles mentioned; the actual powers of the head of state are determined by the nature of parliamentary government and would remain much the same if Canada abolished its ties to the monarchy.

The second factor involves the degree of agreement among political actors, constitutional observers, and the general public concerning the principle that a rule supports. How much debate occurs about the existence of a convention often flows from the level of support for the principle involved. For example, there is unanimous support for the principle that a government must maintain the confidence of the legislature in order to remain in office. Thus there is also general agreement for the rule that a government that loses a vote of confidence must either resign or advise an election. However, there is considerable disagreement over the notion that a governor may act as some sort of umpire in order to protect the constitution from general abuses by a government. Consequently much controversy surrounds the idea that a governor may exercise prerogative powers in order to deal with gross improprieties and scandals committed by a government, as opposed to plainly unconstitutional actions.

The informal rules of the constitution may also vary in a third manner, according to the degree of agreement over their specific terms. There may be disagreement over even the most general formulation of a rule, such as when a minister should resign for administrative blunders. There may also be widespread support for a general rule, even though it is agreed that this rule can only be phrased in ambiguous terms. Thus it is not always clear how a governor may exercise Bagehot's formulation of the monarch's right to be consulted, to encourage, and to warn; certainly the opportunities for Canadian governors to exercise these rights have varied tremendously over the years. It can also be agreed that the details of a convention may vary within a certain range; thus a governor may refuse with propriety a second dissolution to a government only within a very short time after the first election—perhaps a month or two at most.[5] However, it would seem inaccurate to insist, as Marshall does, that all conventions are given to ambiguity or flexibility.[6] Despite the range of imprecision that can be found in a great many conventions, a number are capable of being formulated in clear, precise terms that would enjoy a wide base of support. For instance, it is unanimously agreed that individual ministers are appointed and removed only on the Prime Minister's advice, that the Governor General may not reserve bills for the Queen's pleasure, and that British ministers may not advise the Queen on the appointment of the Canadian Governor General.

The consensus that supports both the principle behind a convention and its details should not be restricted only to the political actors directly involved, but should also encompass the academic community, judges, and the concerned public. Constitutional authorities have played a major role in synthesizing precedent and politicians' beliefs as part of their task of determining where the consensus of opinion lies and what principles are at stake in a particular situation. During political disputes, politicians readily quote academics in support of their opinions of the terms of the constitutional rule at hand;[7] judges have also relied on academic authorities in reaching some declarations about specific conventions.[8] In order for conventions to operate most effectively as rules of critical morality—rather than as the internal, private mores of the particular politicians involved in a given incident—it appears that the consensus that supports a rule should be drawn from as wide a range of interested persons as possible.[9]

One should bear in mind that a convention does not have to be supported unanimously in order to be binding. A strong consensus, where the preponderance of opinion would favour the rule or principle, is sufficient for political actors to face an obligation to observe the convention.

The fourth factor—which may vary among the informal rules of the constitution—is how close the terms of the rule come to embodying the principle it supports. In other words, does the content of the rule directly contain a principle, or does it act as a subsidiary rule? An example of a rule that closely incorporates a constitutional principle is one that flows from the doctrine of individual ministerial responsibility: ministers are answerable to the legislature for their departmental officials. A subsidiary rule requires legislative committees to seek permission from ministers before their officials appear at committee hearings. Another subsidiary rule flowing from the same principle is that when civil servants do appear before legislative committees, they will steadfastly defend departmental policies. Both of these subsidiary rules are removed further from the original principle than the first example. Just how closely a rule comes to embodying a constitutional principle might be determined by considering how the operation of the principle could be affected by a variation in the particular terms of the rule. For example, the current view is that a Governor General's tenure should be limited to five years. However, there is no particular reason, except convenience, why the term should be five, seven, or ten years. Thus the specific terms of the rule can be varied quite considerably without having any effect on the operation of the principle that the office of Governor General should be a position of limited tenure.

Perhaps the most troublesome factor of informal rules involves letting historical precedents provide evidence of a rule's existence. Precedents may be positive, negative, contradictory, or entirely missing. Positive precedents involve direct action on the part of the actors to observe a particular rule; for example, every Canadian minister who did not hold a seat in the legislature at the time of his or her appointment to the Cabinet has tried to win a seat within a short period. Negative precedents involve actors abstaining from visible actions in supposed deference to a rule; no British monarch has refused to sign a bill since 1707. Precedents are most useful only when a consistent pattern of either positive or negative precedents emerges; thus it is generally accepted that the Queen cannot veto a bill and that all ministers must either have a seat in the legislature or obtain one. Grave difficulties arise when a contradictory series of incidents is found, because observers have tended to argue that the inconsistency simply demonstrates that no rule exists; the scattered history of ministerial resignations has greatly eroded rules of culpable ministerial responsibility to the point that many observers argue they no longer exist. However, contradictory incidents can be of use if the temptation is resisted to view them simply as marks on a score sheet.

The utility of historical precedents lies in what they reveal about the consensus of opinion on particular behaviour in a given circumstance. Attention should be focused not only on the statements made by the political actors involved, but also on the reaction to their behaviour—to the possibility that a lower rule had to give way to a more important convention and the relevance of the circumstances to modern conditions. Precedents really only provide an opportunity to assess the consensus at a given time on the constitutional principle involved, the agreement on the terms of the rule, and the importance of the rules involved. Precedents are not some independent entity that creates conventional rules. The rule is created only by the existence of a general consensus in the political community. The expression of that consensus may be crystallized by some historical incident, but the consensus itself may also exist prior to the precedent; the historical incident does not necessarily create the consensus. A consensus of opinion may exist on some behaviour that has not occurred—for example, that a Prime Minister must not recommend him- or herself to be appointed Governor General—and an obligation on political actors can thus arise without any prior historical precedent. I would argue, therefore, that precedents are not necessary to the existence of a constitutional convention; precedents serve only as useful means to gauge the consensus of opinion that actually creates a rule.

CATEGORIES OF CONVENTIONAL RULES

A reasoned basis for the different types of conventional rules observed by Mackintosh may be provided by the operation of these elements of conventional rules. These factors may vary in combination to produce quite different orders of rules. Individual labels are suggested here in order to facilitate discussions about the consequences of distinguishing among different types of informal rules.

Firstly, one group of rules is basic to the constitution and must be continuously respected; any breach or alteration of the terms of these rules would produce significant changes in the operation of the constitution. These rules closely embody or buttress vital constitutional principles and are supported by general agreement on the existence and value of the principle involved, as well as on the terms of the rule itself. These rules may be best described as *fundamental conventions*. Examples are found in the following requirements: governors must act on any constitutionally correct advice offered by their ministers; governors may exercise only their prerogative powers if an elected minister can be found to accept responsibility; the Cabinet must either resign or call an election if it loses a clear vote of confidence in the legislature; the federal government cannot disallow provincial legislation; and politicians must not try to influence judges in their deliberations on a case.

Secondly, there is a group of rules that must be observed in some form, but whose specific terms may be altered without any drastic change to the practical operation of the constitution. They ultimately protect widely accepted and important constitutional principles, but do not necessarily incorporate those principles closely. This second type might be termed *meso-conventions*, since they can be viewed as lying alongside fundamental conventions. Both meso-conventions and fundamental conventions share a basic characteristic in that their total absence would significantly alter the operation or character of the constitution. The terms of a meso-convention, however, may vary in two ways. The particular details of the rule may be quite clear but may also be replaced with other details. For instance, the rule that the Prime Minister nominates the person to be appointed Governor General could well be amended to include either the full federal Cabinet or even consultation with the provincial governments; the Prime Minister's prerogative to nominate the Lieutenant Governors could be similarly changed. Meso-conventions might also vary because the terms of the rule permit some flexibility. An example of this variation is found in the rule that cabinet ministers without seats must become members of the legislature within a reasonably short period after their appointment. While this rule must be obeyed in order to protect the responsible nature of cabinet government, there is no clear definition of just how quickly a minister must find a seat; the Canadian precedents have varied from Robert de Cotret's case, who was appointed to the Senate the day after he became a cabinet minister, to the nine-month period during which General McNaughton spent unsuccessfully trying to win by-elections for a seat in the House of Commons. Another example is the requirement that the federal Cabinet be composed of representation from each of the provinces if possible; just how many cabinet ministers each province should have is unclear, although the general rule is one of prime importance. Thus the particular details of a meso-convention may vary without detriment to the constitution, although the rule must be respected in its general formulation.

Thirdly, there are some rules that prescribe a desirable manner of behaviour, but may be occasionally disregarded without significant impact. These uneventful breaches may occur for either of two reasons: their terms are so far removed from the principle they support that their breach produces no significant change in the operation of the constitution, although the principle involved may itself be vital to it; or, the principle to which the rule is related does not have a significant role in the basic ordering of constitutional processes. Nevertheless there is still a general obligation to observe these rules in the normal course of events. This third variety of conventional rules might be termed *semi-conventions*: they are rather less than the other classes of conventional rules because the constitution is not significantly affected by their absence or breach. An example of a rule that only distantly supports a vital principle is found in the modern requirement that a Canadian be appointed Governor General. This rule ultimately supports the fundamental principle that Canada is a fully independent nation, although no one would say that Canada was not an independent nation in 1951 and only became one in 1952 with Massey's appointment. An illustration of a rule that supports a principle of relatively minor importance is found in Bagehot's classic formulation of the rights of the monarch: to be consulted, to encourage, and to warn. Although there is general agreement on these conventional rights, there are a number of cases where provincial premiers have denied their Lieutenant Governors the opportunity to exercise these rights without making any significant impact on the constitutional process.[10] The existence of precedents illustrating uneventful non-observance of these rules may be taken as an indication of their less-binding status.

Although distinctions may be drawn between these three types of conventions, they all share a common characteristic in the general level of agreement that supports them. These rules are true conventions, because they protect constitutional principles rather than traditions, and the consensus of informed opinion would currently hold that they should be obeyed.

There is also a fourth group of rules—proposals of behaviour is probably a better description—that lies outside the three groups just reviewed because these rules lack general acceptance. Their important characteristic is the lack of consensus preventing them from acting as definitive rules of critical morality that political actors are under a clear obligation to respect. Indeed, their existence may be hotly contested. These may be referred to as *infra-conventions*, because their controversial nature leaves them below the three classes of true convention. They may be supposed by some actors and authorities to be conventions, but in fact they cannot really be viewed objectively as binding rules since they lack sufficient consensual agreement on their existence. Opinion on this group can be deeply divided over the principles involved. A governor's ability to force an election is a matter of infra-convention, since there is a great division of opinion about the principle that the governors might act as general guardians of the constitution. There may also be strong disagreement over the specific terms or application of a rule that is accepted in some general formulation; thus the subsidiary rules governing individual ministerial culpability remain fairly contentious.

Some infra-conventions may well be embryonic rules that will go on to acquire enough support to be transformed into a higher class of convention: the present reluctance of most governments to utilize the notwithstanding clause of the Charter of Rights may develop into a binding convention. Similarly, a rule that had once been a firmly accepted convention could degenerate into infra-convention; the once widely held notion that a defeat of a major piece of government legislation constitutes a loss of confidence has lost virtually all its supporters. Such developments can occur because of a new consensus has solidified around the importance of the principle involved or the terms of the rule, or because the institutional circumstances in which a rule operates have changed.

A fifth type of informal rule lies below all classes of convention. *Usages* are patterns of behaviour that have no further compulsion for observance other than mere habit, convenience, or ceremonial symbolism. It should perhaps be noted that even usages have some aspect of obligation attached to them, since there are always expectations that certain processes will be followed when a regular pattern of behaviour has emerged. However, such an obligation is unlike that imposed by conventions, because it is not directly based on, or aimed at supporting, any particular constitutional reason or principle; the obligation is merely the pressure to conform to expected behaviour or ceremonies. There is no sanction if a usage is not respected, or if another new procedure is adopted, beyond the general opprobrium that might greet such an event.

Clear examples of usage abound. For example, when royal assent is given to a Bill in Parliament, the whole business of both Houses is interrupted and the Commons are summoned to assemble in the Senate by the Gentleman Usher of the Black Rod. The doors of the Commons are ceremoniously closed in the face of the Gentleman Usher, and he must knock on the door three times before he is permitted to enter and announce the summons to join the Senate. Such a usage may have had good meaning several centuries ago in Britain, when the Commons had a physical fear of the royal summons, but it has no merit today beyond pure pomp and ceremony. The actual gathering of both Houses before the Deputy Governor General for royal assent is another usage that has no reason beyond symbolic ceremony; royal assent could quite as easily be granted, as in Quebec and Australia, in the governor's office. These pure usages should be distinguished from other methods of procedure or behaviour that contain further elements of obligation based on some constitutional principle.

One criticism that might be made of any attempt to classify conventions is that conventional rules appear to be qualified in many ways, or are dependent on the circumstances of the occasion. However, some of these difficulties may be overcome by avoiding the temptation to view any one area of the constitution as though it were governed by a single rule. Many topics are governed by a complex of both general rules and sub-rules that apply to particular situations or act as qualifiers to the general rule. Within this complex quite clear statements may be made, while others may be indeterminate or controversial.

For example, the responsible nature of our system of government is upheld in general by the principle that a government must maintain the confidence of the legislature; if it loses that confidence, then it must either resign or advise an election. What precisely constitutes a loss of confidence is unclear, however, and real controversy surrounds the idea that a government should resign if a major element of its legislative program is defeated—a belief that is therefore an infra-convention. But very firm statements can also be made that would appear to be matters of fundamental convention, such as that a government must resign or call an election after a defeat on an expressly worded motion of no confidence, or on a vote that the government has previously declared to be test of confidence.

A rule's sensitivity to the context in which it must be applied is often a relational sensitivity to other rules that may conflict; thus the context may determine that one particular rule should give way to another. The fact that a rule might be overlooked on some occasions may indicate that one lower-order rule has given way to a higher rule, rather than that the lower rule is ambiguous or non-existent. The recognition of a hierarchy among conventions could help greatly in understanding why a rule was not followed in a particular situation.

It should be hastily added that these suggested classifications represent more of a continuum than precisely defined categories. Furthermore, this scheme for classifying conventions also poses its own controversies. There are many disagreements that could arise over the importance of the principle a rule supports and how significant would be the absence or breach of a rule. Nevertheless this ordering of informal constitutional rules may be useful in focusing constitutional debates on the principled basis for a rule, as well as on the importance, and level of acceptance, of a rule. This shift would allow for a more rigorous approach to constitutional rules than debates over who did what, said what, and got away with what action—which seem to cloud discussions that are based on precedent as the key to conventional rules.

The informal rules of the constitution do vary considerably. Some rules are more important, more widely accepted, more frequently observed, and more precisely formulated than others. The scheme proposed here is offered as a means of explaining these distinctions, and of beginning discussions on their consequences.

CLASSIFYING CONVENTIONS

In deciding how to characterize a rule, a pattern of behaviour, or a proposed action, one should direct the line of inquiry first towards the reason why certain behaviour should be followed. First one should ask, what reason could be given to justify an obligation to behave in a certain manner? If no other direct reason can be given apart from tradition, ceremony, convenience, or symbolism, then the matter is one of usage and no further questions need be posed. Infra-conventions arguably support some constitutional principle, but are characterized by fundamental controversy either over the principle involved or over the general formulation of their terms. Semi-conventions are rules that are generally agreed upon, and observed, and that would not significantly alter the constitutional process in their breach or absence; these rules may either closely embody a constitutional principle of minor importance or distantly support a more fundamental principle. Meso-conventions are constitutional rules that would be widely supported and relate closely to important constitutional principles; these rules must be respected in their general formulation, although the specific details may vary without consequence. Fundamental conventions have broad support and directly incorporate crucial constitutional principles; any breach or substantive alteration of their terms could have significant effects on constitutional processes.

In considering all these questions in a particular context or hypothetically, one can examine any relevant precedents, statements of political actors about either the general principles or the specific terms of the rule, the assessments of constitutional authorities about the principles involved and the outcome of the precedents reviewed, and the public reaction, if any, to the incidents. However, precedents should not be requisites for conventional rules. What is important to consider is the consensus that would presently exist regarding certain behaviour; such a consensus can be supported independently of whether historical precedents exist, or even in contradiction to them.

THE UTILITY OF DISTINCTIONS AMONG CONVENTIONAL RULES

If this suggested hierarchical classification of conventions is to be of much use, its value must be more than just as an intellectual exercise in constitutional taxonomy. The conceptual distinctions among different types of conventions have a practical value in helping to sort out which conventional rule should be given precedence when several rules conflict; they may also provide clarification in the emerging role conventions are coming to play in the courtroom, especially in Canada. Also, efforts to codify conventional rules could be greatly aided by an appreciation of which conventions are most suited for codification. Some manner of distinguishing among various informal rules, therefore, could be of immense use.

One value of the classifications suggested for conventions lies in offering a means of discerning the sort of obligation that should be attached to certain behaviour. If the matter simply involves a usage, then the behaviour would be acceptable only so long as the symbolism or convenience is valued. If an infra-convention is identified, then the slight obligation that might be found attaches only to those who believe in the existence of the rule; internal morality alone is involved. A semi-convention ought to be observed in the normal course of events, but may be disregarded temporarily if it conflicts with a higher rule. When a meso-convention is at work, the rule should always be obeyed in its general form, although some adjustments in detail may be made to suit the current circumstances. On the other hand, a fundamental convention must be faithfully observed or else significant changes would be affected in the constitution.

The identification of several classes of conventions is also helpful in efforts to codify the informal constitutional rules. In any contemplated codification, careful consideration must be given to maintaining the evolutionary potential that conventions convey. Conventional rules may be codified in one of two manners: either formally, through legislative enactment or constitutional entrenchment; or informally, as a definitive statement of rules or principles that is agreed to by the main political actors. The judicial protection formal codification may entail must be balanced against a possible loss of flexibility in the constitution and the increased power of the judiciary to regulate the activities of elected politicians.

In making these assessments, however, attention must be paid to the differences among the several types of conventional rules. In a paper prepared for the 1982 Australian Constitutional Convention, a body that undertook the codification of a number of the informal rules of the Australian constitution, Cheryl Saunders and Ewart Smith underlined the utility of distinguishing among conventions for their suitability for codification:

> Some conventions might appropriately be included in a written constitution, subject to enforcement in the courts; others might be included in the constitution as non-justiciable declarations of principle; others might be articulated outside the constitution by way of an informal agreement on the content of which is understood. Classification of conventions in this way might be a useful exercise in the future.[11]

However, the failure of the Australian Convention to draw up some method of distinguishing the different levels of constitutional conventions before beginning the codification efforts meant several years were wasted in controversial debates over which particular rules should be codified. In the event, the conventions that were first codified in 1983 were ones dealing with the appointment of the Governor General, the composition of the Executive Council, and the independence of the judiciary; almost all the particular rules could be described as fundamental or meso-conventions. Many of the rules that were codified at a later meeting of the Convention in 1985 involved varying degrees of controversy, ambiguity, or innovation.[12]

The best candidates for codification, especially formal codification by statute law or constitutional entrenchment, are fundamental and meso-conventions, since they are supported by a clear consensus and can be applied without controversy. Furthermore, their importance to the actual operation and character of the constitution might recommend the protection from abuse that formal codification can accord. When conventions are formally codified into positive law, they usually become fully justiciable and enforceable in the courts.[13] One criticism levelled against judicial enforcement of conventions is the possible rigidity that could be imparted by judicial formulation; this might become a particular problem for entrenched conventions. Thus formal codification is sometimes rejected on the grounds that the flexibility conventions convey to the constitution should be preserved.[14] Whether or not this might be a substantive problem for other conventions, it certainly would not be a concern when fundamental conventions are at issue. The nature of fundamental conventions is such that their terms must be faithfully respected or significant effects would result in the way the constitution functions; any rigidity that might result from a judicial enforcement would not be of any particular consequence.

Semi-conventions, on the other hand, possess a degree of flexibility that does not easily lend itself to formal codification. The circumstances in which these rules may be breached with propriety ought to be determined in the political arena rather than in any judicial setting. Only an informal codification of these rules, as a statement of preferred behaviour, would permit their flexible operation and evolution.

LAW AND CONVENTION REVISITED

It is also very important to make distinctions among conventional rules when examining the relationship between law and convention. When A.V. Dicey first wrote about conventions as an amorphous group of political ethics, he was content to dismiss all these informal rules as a subject that 'is not one of law but politics, and need trouble no lawyer or the class of any professor of law.'[15] Modern constitutional defenders of Dicey's rigid division between law and convention have continued to base their assumptions about the nature of conventions on observations of all informal rules lumped together. For example, both Hood Phillips and Colin Munro point to the ambiguity of many conventional rules in criticizing the notion that conventions can be properly justiciable in the courts.[16] In his denial of justiciability, Munro also asked rhetorically how one is supposed to measure the relative importance of different conventional rules. But the ability to distinguish among different classes of informal rule allows one to eliminate controversial, ambiguous, and rarely followed supposed rules and focus on the core of precise, accepted, and observed conventions. Fruitful discussion of the relationship between law and convention begins with the recognition that informal rules fall into various categories that have differing relationships to positive law.

Dicey's dichotomy between law and convention clearly needs rethinking in the light of judicial practice in the late twentieth century. Although the courts have not treated conventional rules exactly as they would rules of statutory or common law, it is quite evident that some conventions can be a fit subject for litigation. A wide range of cases has been discussed here, in the early chapters, where conventions were dealt with in some manner by Canadian courts. And there is great potential for judicial consideration of other conventions in future cases dealing with such matters as the legal immunities of governors, the application of the Charter to the internal workings of Parliament, judicial independence, the powers of reservation and disallowance, and the international competence of provincial governments. The relevant question to be posed in contemporary constitutional debates is not whether conventions are subject to judicial adjudication, because they have been many times. The more pressing question for Canadian constitutional jurisprudence is which conventions should be justiciable and in what manner.

If there is a place for conventions in the courtroom, it will apply to fundamental conventions and meso-conventions, because of their general acceptance and their crucial role in the practical operation of the constitution. In the total absence of specific rules belonging to these two classes of convention, the constitution would function in a significantly different manner. Any judicial decision based only on positive laws alone, and ignoring relevant fundamental or meso-conventions, would enforce a legal framework bearing little semblance to the actual character of the constitution. The courts could thus provoke a crisis of political legitimacy. A rigorous examination of the relationship between law and convention would be best approached by recognizing the distinctions to be drawn among conventional rules, and by excluding from the analysis semi-conventions, infra-conventions, and usages. With this approach we would be left to study what relationship judges should foster between the positive laws of the formal Constitution and only those conventional rules that are widely accepted, are fundamentally important to the structure and operation of the political system, and are capable of fairly clear formulation.

The main defence of Dicey's dichotomy between law and convention rests on an insistence that legal rules are judicially enforced while conventions are not. However, the particular uses to which judges put conventions have varied a great deal and may arguably amount to 'enforcement'. On the one extreme Sir Lyman Duff banished them completely from his consideration of any restrictions on the powers of reservation and disallowance;[17] Mr Justice James Jerome declared that explicit statutory provisions relating to the authority of the Auditor General must prevail over the conventions of Cabinet secrecy;[18] and a 1969 decision of the Judicial Committee of the Privy Council refused to consider that conventions could effect the legal power of the British Parliament to legislate for post-UDI Rhodesia.[19] These cases would support the rigid dichotomy proposed by Dicey.

There are other examples, however, of conventions receiving more favourable attention from the courts. The Australian High Court in 1958 explicitly referred to conventions in deciding that a British Act did not have effect in Australia;[20] in *Jonathan Cape* (1975)[21] the judge was prepared to use the cabinet-secrecy convention to extend the application of an existing common-law rule dealing with confidentiality; and the trial judge in *Stopforth* (1978) similarly employed a convention to extend a common-law defence against defamation.[22] In 1986 the Supreme Court of Canada referred to the conventions supporting the neutrality of the public service in upholding the dismissal of a federal official and in justifying the legitimacy of Ontario legislation limiting the political rights of civil servants.[23] Furthermore, the Supreme Court has twice used the conventions of responsible government as an interpretative guide to extend statutory provisions.[24] The terms of particular conventions have often been defined in *obiter dictum* passages of a decision.[25] The most direct adjudication of conventions came in the two reference cases heard by the Supreme Court over the amendment of the constitution. In the first case in 1981 the Court both recognized the existence of the convention requiring substantial provincial consent and commented on its terms, even though it considered them to be ambiguous; and in the Quebec Veto case (1982), the Court held that there had never been a convention giving Quebec a veto over constitutional amendments effecting provincial powers.[26]

These cases pose a strong challenge to Dicey's litmus test of court-enforceability. Although it is quite plain that some distinction between conventions and law ought to be maintained because formal legal sanctions may be provided by a court for the breach of most rules of positive law, this distinction is not clear-cut because the recognition and formulation of conventional rules in the course of a court decision may provide some manner of 'enforcement' in a broad sense. For instance, the Supreme Court's declaration in the 1981 Patriation Reference that unilateral amendment would breach existing conventions may have resulted in the enforcement of those conventions, since it has been widely credited with spurring political leaders on to reach an accord. As William Lederman has argued in his comments on this decision:

> In nearly all cases, the power authoritatively to identify and declare the terms of established conventions will be enough to extract voluntary compliance from the political actors. At the end of the day, if the prestige of the Supreme Court of Canada and the legitimacy of its power of judicial review in a federal country are widely accepted by the official political actors and by the people at large, the judicial declaration will induce willing compliance. If there is no such official and general acceptance of the role of the Court, what effective measures would be possible?[27]

Since the essence of enforcement of a rule by the courts is to ensure compliance with that rule, the courts may be 'enforcing' conventions even without formal legal sanctions. If this kind of enforcement of conventions is admitted, then Dicey's distinction between laws and convention wears quite thin. The dichotomy is further eroded in instances where conventions are used to extend the application of a statutory or common-law rule, because a formal court sanction may then be offered for the breach of convention. It seems rather pedantic to insist that the sanction is issued for the *legal* rule and that the convention is merely an interpretative guide; in the absence of the convention, the legal rule would not have been extended and no enforcement by the court would be possible. Judicial enforcement of conventions is quite possible, even if it is formally indirect.

The use of conventions as guides for interpreting statute and common law also opens up the question of whether the courts are employing conventions as 'legal rules' of interpretation. The answer is of more than just theoretical interest: if conventions are viewed as legal rules in this sense, then judges are under some obligation to consider them and to respect their terms in the course of resolving issues of interpretation. I would argue that judicial decisions of the past decade illustrate that most judges have in fact referred to conventions where they are relevant to the matters at issue. The need to account for the conventional setting of constitutional law seems particularly acute where fundamental and meso-conventions are involved. Without resort to these conventions, the courts would enforce a rather unreal set of rules.

Canadian judges will eventually have to deal more explicitly with the nature of the judicial enforcement already accorded to conventions. The issue may become quite critical in matters regulated by meso-conventions, or especially fundamental conventions. For instance, in 1981 the Supreme Court of Canada answered the reference dealing with the conventions governing an amendment to the Constitution because the questions raised 'a fundamental issue of constitutionality and legitimacy'.[28] I suggest that such crucial issues are posed whenever meso-conventions and fundamental conventions are involved. Courts should not shirk either from granting these conventions broad enforcement by authoritatively declaring their terms, or from indirect formal enforcement by utilizing these conventions to extend the application of an existing rule of positive law. Furthermore, a court might seriously consider whether formal enforcement should be given to a positive legal rule that conflicts with a fundamental convention. Rather than resting on legal formalism and declaring simply that the legal rule must prevail, the court might better fulfil its role of defending the constitution by declaring that conventions have so changed a particular legal rule that adherence to it cannot be actively given the court's sanction.

CONCLUSIONS

Although the particular scheme for classifying conventions suggested here certainly contains ambiguities, it is offered as a means of drawing attention to the distinctions that can be found among particular groups of informal rules operating in the constitution. Discussions about the obligation attached to a particular informal rule of the constitution, the general desirability of codifying conventional rules, or the broad role conventions should play in judicial decisions would be greatly enhanced by recognizing that differences exist among constitutional conventions. While there may be characteristics in common, one can identify significant differences between usage, infra-convention, semi-convention, meso-convention, and fundamental convention. If distinctions are not perceived among the informal rules of the constitution, an understanding of the nature of constitutional conventions is incomplete, and a study of the close relationship between law and convention will be made from an unsatisfactory foundation.

It is important that theories about the nature of constitutional conventions continue to evolve from those first propounded by Dicey a century ago. Even at the time when Dicey wrote that law and convention should be rigidly separated, constitutional conditions in Canada differed from those in Britain. With Canada's constitutionally entrenched provisions and some powers of judicial review, which are foreign to British jurisprudence, there can be more serious consequences in Canada than in Great Britain if outdated legal rules are enforced by the courts without regard for the relevant conventions.

We must recognize the full extent to which the constitution's legal framework has been indirectly, but fundamentally, transformed by conventions. By insisting on a rigid division between law and convention, Canadian jurists may imperil our constitutional system. The political arena gives birth to conventions so that constitutional laws can function acceptably. The most important conventions thus depend on a healthy marriage between law and politics. Any estrangement or divorce between the two would only produce grave consequences.

Notes

ABBREVIATIONS USED

AC—*Appeal Cases*

AG—Attorney General

ALR—*Alberta Law Reports*

All ER—*All England Law Reports*

BCCA—British Columbia Court of Appeal

BCLR—*British Columbia Law Reports*

CA—Court of Appeal

CSM—*Consolidated Statutes of Manitoba*

DLR—*Dominion Law Reports*

ER—*English Reports*

FC—Federal Court

FCA—Federal Court of Appeal

FCTD—Federal Court, Trial Division

FTR—*Federal Trial Reports*

HCJ—High Court of Justice

HL—House of Lords

JCPC—Judicial Committee of the Privy Council

NBR—*New Brunswick Reports*

Nfld and PEIR—*Newfoundland and Prince Edward Island Reports*

Nfld TD—Newfoundland Trial Division

NR—*National Reporter*

NSCA—Nova Scotia Court of Appeal

NSR—*Nova Scotia Reports*

NSTD—Nova Scotia Supreme Court, Trial Division

NZLR—*New Zealand Law Reports*

OR—*Ontario Reports*

PEIR—*Prince Edward Island Reports*

PEISC—Prince Edward Island Supreme Court

QAC—*Quebec Appeal Cases*

QB—Queen's Bench

QLR—*Quebec Law Reports*

Que.SC—Quebec Superior Court

RSBC—*Revised Statutes of British Columbia*

RSC—*Revised Statutes of Canada*

SC—*Statutes of Canada*

SCC—Supreme Court of Canada

SCR—*Supreme Court Reports*

SN—*Statutes of Newfoundland*

SNS—*Statutes of Nova Scotia*

SO—*Statutes of Ontario*

SQ—*Statutes of Quebec*

UCQBR—*Upper Canada Queen's Bench Reports*

WWR—*Western Weekly Reports*

YR—*Yukon Reports*

YTCA—Yukon Territorial Court of Appeal

1. THE ROLE AND NATURE OF CONVENTIONS

[1]*Reference re Amendment of the Constitution of Canada* (1981), 125 DLR (3d) 1 at p. 87.
[2]Peter H. Russell, 'The Supreme Court and Federal Provincial Relations: The Political Use of Legal Resources', *Canadian Public Policy*, vol. 11, no. 2, June 1985, pp. 161ff.
[3]*Stopforth v. Goyer* (1978), 20 OR (2d) 262 (Ont.HCJ)—rev. (1979), 23 OR (2d) 696 (Ont.CA); *Arseneau v. The Queen*, [1979] 2 SCR 136; *A.G. Quebec v. Blaikie et al.* (no. 2), [1981] 1 SCR 312; *Reference re Amendment of the Constitution of Canada* (1981), 125 DLR (3d) 1 (SCC); *Re A.G. Quebec and A.G. Canada* (Quebec Veto), [1982] 2 SCR 793; *Auditor General v. Minister of Energy Mines and Resources et al.* (1986), 23 DLR (4th) 210 (FCTD); *Re Ontario Public Employees' Union et al. and A.G. for Ontario* (1987), 41 DLR (4th) 1 (SCC); *Penikett et al. v. The Queen et al.* [1987], 2 YR 262 (YTSC)—[1988], 2 WWR 481 (YTCA); *Osborne v. Canada (Treasury Board)* [1986] 3 FC 206 (FCTD)—rev. [1988], 87 NR 376 (FCA).
[4]Geoffrey Marshall and Graeme Moodie, *Some Problems of the Constitution*, London: Hutchinson, 1959. This definition is a refinement of one first proposed by O. Hood Phillips in *Constitutional and Administrative Law* (5th ed.), London: Sweet & Maxwell, 1973.
[5]Eugene A. Forsey, 'The Courts and the Conventions of the Constitution', *UNB Law Journal* 33 (1984), p. 11.
[6]Peter W. Hogg, *Constitutional Law of Canada* (2nd ed.), Toronto: Carswell, 1985, p. 12.

[7]A.V. Dicey, *An Introduction to the Study of the Law of the Constitution* (8th ed.), London: Macmillan, 1924, p. 30.

[8]Hogg, op. cit.

[9]Henri Brun and Guy Tremblay, *Droit Constitutionnel*, Cowansville: Editions Yvon Blais, 1982. Other discussions may be found in A. Barbeau, *Le Droit Constitutionnel Canadien*, Montreal: Wilson and Lafleur, 1974; Gérald-A. Beaudoin, *Le Partage des Pouvoirs* (3e ed.), Ottawa: Université d'Ottawa, 1983; and F. Chevrette and H. Marx, *Droit Constitutionnel*, Montreal: Université de Montréal, 1982.

[10]Paul Gérin-Lajoie, *Constitutional Amendment in Canada*, Toronto: University of Toronto Press, 1950.

[11]Frank MacKinnon, *The Crown in Canada*, Calgary: McClelland and Stewart West, 1976.

[12]John T. Saywell, *The Office of Lieutenant Governor* (rev. ed.), Toronto: Copp Clark Pitman, 1986.

[13]Eugene Forsey, *Freedom and Order*, Carleton Library 73, Toronto: McClelland and Stewart, 1974.

[14]Peter H. Russell et al., *The Courts and the Constitution*, Kingston: Institute of Intergovernmental Relations, 1982; Forsey, op. cit.

[15]Marc Gold, 'The Mask of Objectivity: Politics and The Supreme Court of Canada', *Supreme Court Law Review* 7 (1985), 455.

[16]Dicey, op. cit.

[17]Sir Ivor Jennings, *The Law and the Constitution* (5th ed.), London: University of London Press, 1959.

[18]O. Hood Phillips, *Constitutional and Administrative Law* (5th ed.), London: Sweet and Maxwell, 1973; Marshall and Moodie, op. cit.; E.C.S. Wade, 'Introduction' to Dicey, op. cit.; H. Street and R. Brazier, eds, *de Smith's Constitutional and Administrative Law* (2nd ed.), London: Penguin, 1973; C.R. Munro, 'Laws and Conventions Distinguished', *Law Quarterly Review* 91 (1975), p. 218; see also Munro's reformulation of this article in his more recent book: *Studies in Constitutional Law*, London: Butterworths, 1987; T.R.S. Allan, 'Law, Convention, Prerogative: Reflections Prompted by the Canadian Constitutional Case', *Cambridge Law Journal* 45 (1986), p. 305; E.C.S. Wade and A.W. Bradley, *Constitutional and Administrative Law* (10th ed.), London: Longman, 1985.

[19]Geoffrey Marshall, *Constitutional Conventions: The Rules and Forms of Political Accountability*, Oxford: Oxford University Press, 1984.

[20]L.J.M. Cooray, *Conventions, the Australian Constitution and the Future*, Sydney: Legal Books, 1979. Cooray drew attention in this work to the importance of distinguishing between 'constitutional' conventions, which affect the basic operation of constitutional structures and processes, and what he called 'governmental' conventions, which regulate the internal workings of government departments.

[21]O. Hood Phillips, 'Constitutional Conventions: Dicey's Predecessors', *Modern Law Review* 29 (1966), p. 137.

[22]Dicey, op. cit., p. 417.

[23]Jennings, op. cit., p. 81.

[24]Dicey, op. cit., p. 23.

[25]Phillips, *Constitutional Law*; Munro, op. cit.; Marshall and Moodie, op. cit.

[26]Forsey, 'The Courts and the Conventions', p. 13.

[27]Jennings, op. cit., ch. 3.

[28]Illustrations of this can be found in Canada in the Ontario Cabinet Management Board Act, which presupposes the conventional creation of the Cabinet; also, the British Columbia Attorney General Act, RSBC 1979, c. 23, s. 2(e), grants the Attorney General such powers as belong to the Attorney General or Solicitor General of England 'by law or usage'.

[29]Wade, op. cit., pp. cxxxvi to cxlvi.

[30]J.R. Mallory, *The Structure of Canadian Government* (rev. ed.), Toronto: Gage, 1984, p. 442.

[31]*Madzimbamuto v. Lardner-Burke*, [1969] 1 AC 645; and, *Adegbenro v. Akintola*, [1963] AC 614.

[32]Munro, 'Laws and Conventions Distinguished', p. 228.

[33]Rodney Brazier and St J. Robilliard, 'Constitutional Conventions: The Canadian Supreme Court's Views Reviewed', *Public Law* 28 (1982) at p. 33.

[34]Forsey, 'The Courts and the Conventions', p. 42.

[35]This situation may well change in Canada, with redress being made, outside of reference legislation, for a declaratory judgement by a court concerning the terms or obligation of a party to respect a particular conventional rule. See, for instance, the unsuccessful application made by the Yukon Territory's administration to have a declaration made that the Meech Lake Accord contravened a convention the Territorial administration believed existed concerning the admission of new provinces to Confederation. *Penikett et al. v. The Queen et al.* [1987], 2 YR 262 (YSC); [1988], 2 WWR 481 (YTCA).

[36]Jennings, op. cit., pp. 122-7.

[37]Peter H. Russell, 'The Supreme Court Decision: Bold Statescraft Based on Questionable Jurisprudence', Russell et al., op. cit., pp. 20-4.

[38]Allan, op. cit, pp. 312-19.

[39]Marshall, op. cit., pp. 13-15.

[40]*Reference re Amendment of the Constitution of Canada* (1981), 125 DLR (3d) 1 at pp. 84-5.

[41]Ibid., at pp. 88-9.

[42]Marshall, op. cit., pp. 16-17.

[43]*Reference re Amendment of the Constitution of Canada* (1981), 125 DLR (3d) 1 at p. 16.

[44]Ibid., at p. 88.

[45]Gerald Rubin, 'The Nature, Use and Effect of Reference Cases in Canadian Constitutional Law', in W.R. Lederman, ed., *The Courts and the Canadian Constitution*, Toronto: McClelland and Stewart, 1964. See also Hogg, op. cit., pp. 180-1; Barry L. Strayer, *The Canadian Constitution and the Courts* (2nd ed.), Toronto: Butterworths, 1983, p. 292.

[46]*British Coal Corp. v. The King*, [1935] AC 500 at pp. 510-11.

[47](1979) 2 SCR 136 at p. 149.

[48]*A.G. Quebec v. Blaikie et al.* (No. 2), [1981] 1 SCR 312 at pp. 319-20.

[49]Hogg, op. cit., p. 10.

[50]Munro, *Studies in Constitutional Law*, pp. 59-60.

[51]Marshall, op. cit., p. 8.

[52]'A constitutional convention is worked out under the form of an understanding. A usage, practice, or a way of doing things becomes the object of an agreement. A convention is necessarily bilateral or multilateral; it implies several parties. It is a kind of contract. It is a way of doing things that happens to be sanctioned by agreement rather than by time, as in customary law; the determinative element of a convention is the agreement by virtue of which those in power consider themselves bound.' Brun and Tremblay, op. cit., p. 47.

[53]'This agreement . . . can be written, oral or tacit.' Ibid., 47.

[54]Gold, op. cit.

[55]Phillips, *Constitutional Law*, p. 77.

[56]Marshall, op. cit., pp. 10-12.

[57]Geoffrey Marshall, 'What Are Constitutional Conventions?', *Parliamentary Affairs* 38 (1985), p. 39.

[58]Hogg, op. cit., p. 16.

[59]Jennings, op. cit., p. 136.

[60]Ibid., p. 136.

[61]Forsey, 'The Courts and the Conventions', p. 34.

[62]Marshall, op. cit., p. 9.

2. CONVENTIONS OF THE GOVERNORS' POWERS

[1]Article I of the 1947 Letters Patent states: 'We do hereby constitute, order, and declare that there shall be a Governor General. . . .'

[2]Despite this broad wording, it must be noted that additional Letters Patent were issued by

the Queen in 1988 to permit the Governor General to grant armorial bearings in Canada: *The Canada Gazette*, Part 1, vol. 122, no. 24, 11 June 1988, pp. 2226-7.

[3]J.R. Mallory, *The Structure of Canadian Government* (rev. ed.), Toronto: Gage, 1984, p. 45.

[4]See, for example, the general comments of former Governor General Roland Michener about the desirability of appointing only Canadians to the position. *Proceedings of the Special Senate Committee on the Constitution*, Issue 2, 21 November 1978, p. 11.

[5]John T. Saywell claims that at the provincial level only residents of a province have been appointed as Lieutenant Governors since 1900. In addition, only francophones have served in this capacity in Quebec. These two practices seem to be invariably followed and appear to be viewed as binding rules in the appointment of Lieutenant Governors. *The Office of Lieutenant Governor*, Toronto: Copp Clark Pitman, 1986.

[6]A Gallup Poll conducted in early 1989 revealed that only 39 per cent of those asked thought that this alternation should continue; 48 per cent thought it should not; while 13 per cent had no opinion. However, 54 per cent of the respondents in Quebec thought the alternation should continue and only 30 per cent were opposed. The strength of the support in Quebec is an important reason to continue this symbolic alternation. *Gallup*, Toronto: Gallup Canada Inc., 20 February 1989, p. 3.

[7]Saywell, op. cit., p. 24.

[8]*Liquidators of the Maritime Bank v. The Receiver General of New Brunswick*, [1982] AC 437 at p. 443. See also *Bonanza Creek Gold Mining Co. Ltd. v. The King*, [1916] AC 566; and *The King v. Carroll et al.*, [1948] SCR 126, which held that a Lieutenant Governor holds office with respect to the government of the province and not of the government of Canada.

[9]See *A.G. Canada v. A.G. Ontario* (Executive Power), [1894] 23 SCR 458.

[10]Walter Bagehot, *The English Constitution*, Ithaca: Cornell University Press, 1966, p. 111.

[11]MacKinnon concluded that several other Lieutenant Governors have been ignored by their premiers. Frank MacKinnon, *The Crown in Canada*, Calgary: McClelland and Stewart West, 1976, pp. 103-5.

[12]*R. v. McLeod*, 8 SCR 1 at p. 26.

[13]Even Gough Whitlam, in his proposal for the abolition of the office of Governor General, conceded that someone was needed to act to appoint a new prime minister; he proposed that a committee of High Court Judges should undertake this task. *The Truth of the Matter*, London: Allen Lane, 1979, p. 184. Similarly, Tony Benn has suggested that the power of appointment should be placed in the hands of the Speaker of the House of Commons. 'Power, Parliament and the People', *New Socialist*, September-October 1982, p. 14.

[14]*Re Amendment of the Constitution of Canada* (1981), 125 DLR (3d) 1 at p. 86.

[15]Saywell has pointed out that the provincial premiers have often insisted on advising on their replacements; op. cit., pp. 92-3. Frank Miller is the latest example of this curious practice; when he offered his resignation after being defeated on the Throne Speech, he advised Lieutenant Governor Aird to appoint Peterson. *Toronto Star*, 20 June 1985, p. A4. Most authorities, however, conclude that governors are not obliged to follow such advice. For example: Eugene Forsey and Graham Eglington, *The Question of Confidence in Responsible Government: A Study Prepared for the Special Committee on Reform of the House of Commons*, Ottawa, 1985, p. 138; Geoffrey Marshall and Graeme Moodie, *Some Problems of the Constitution*, London: Hutchinson, 1959, p. 59; Harold Wilson, *The Governance of Britain*, London: Weidenfeld & Nicolson, 1976, p. 22.

[16]For a general discussion of the provisions of various Commonwealth constitutions, see S.A. de Smith, *The New Commonwealth and its Constitutions*, London: Stevens, 1964, pp. 90-100.

[17]Valentine Herman and Françoise Mendel, *Parliaments of the World*, New York: De Gruyter (for the Inter-Parliamentary Union), 1976, p. 806.

[18]H.F. Angus, 'The British Columbia Elections, June 1952', *The Canadian Journal of Economics and Political Science* 18 (1952), pp. 518-25.

[19]Eugene A. Forsey, 'Professor Angus on the British Columbia Election: A Comment', *Canadian Journal of Economics and Political Science* 19 (1953), p. 227.

[20]Fifteen Lieutenant Governors appointed since 1955 moved directly from a seat in a legislature to their new office. Between 1911 and 1955, 62 per cent of those appointed had held political office prior to their appointment; since 1955 this proportion has dropped slightly to just over half. Saywell, op. cit., pp. 266-7. (I include in my figures the eight new appointments made since Saywell's book was published.) Furthermore, all but two of the Canadian-born Governors General have held political offices at some earlier point in their careers.

[21]Sir Ivor Jennings, *Cabinet Government* (3rd ed.), London: Cambridge University Press, 1959, pp. 20-46.

[22]Forsey, op. cit., p. 227.

[23]Geoffrey Marshall, *Constitutional Conventions: The Rules and Forms of Political Accountability*, Oxford: Oxford University Press, 1984, pp. 32-5.

[24]Forsey, op. cit., p. 227.

[25]In Belgium, Norway, and The Netherlands the monarch appoints a respected politician to act as an 'informateur', who then conducts negotiations among the party leaders in order to compose a coalition that would have the support of parliament. See David Butler, *Governing Without a Majority*, London: Collins, 1983, pp. 88-9.

[26]J.R. Mallory, *The Structure of Canadian Government* (rev.ed.), Toronto: Gage, 1984, p. 49.

[27]MacKinnon, op. cit., p. 124.

[28]Henri Brun and Guy Tremblay, *Droit Constitutionnel*, Cowansville: Editions Yvon Blais, 1982, p. 259.

[29]It would be difficult to convey in any short description the wild and entertaining disarray that followed the elections of October 1971. Readers are directed to a clear and detailed account by Peter Neary, 'Changing Government: the 1971-2 Newfoundland Example', *Dalhousie Law Journal* 5 (1979), pp. 631-58.

[30]In 1979 the federal Liberal Party won 22 fewer seats in the House of Commons than the Conservatives, even though the Liberals had won almost 5 per cent more of the vote. In the 1985 Ontario election the Conservatives won 4 seats more than the Liberals, although they had won 1 per cent fewer votes. One should note also that in the 1986 Saskatchewan elections the Conservatives were able to form a majority government, with 38 seats to the NDP's 25, even though they received fewer votes than the NDP.

[31]Hugh McD. Clokie, *Canadian Government and Politics*, Toronto: Longmans, Green & Co., 1944, p. 52.

[32]*Toronto Star*, 29 May 1985, p. A1.

[33]Michael Atkinson, 'Parliamentary Government in Canada' in Michael S. Whittington and Glen Williams, *Canadian Politics in the 1980s* (2nd ed.), Toronto: Methuen, 1984, p. 336.

[34]P. Hogg, op. cit., pp. 206-8; Michael S. Whittington and Richard J. Van Loon, *The Canadian Political System* (3rd ed.), Toronto: McGraw-Hill Ryerson, 1981, p. 175; R. MacGregor Dawson, *The Government of Canada* (5th ed.), Toronto: University of Toronto Press, 1970, pp. 153-4.

[35]Ibid., pp. 124-6; Eugene A. Forsey, 'The Courts and the Conventions of the Constitution', *University of New Brunswick Law Journal* 33 (1984), pp. 19-21.

[36]Hogg, op. cit., p. 208.

[37]Ibid., p. 207-8. Mallory, op. cit., pp. 89-90.

[38]Forsey, 'The Courts and the Conventions'.

[39]Governments were dismissed in New South Wales in 1932, in Pakistan in 1953, in the Western Region of Nigeria in 1962, and, most recently, at the national level in Australia in 1975.

[40]Saywell, op. cit., p. 144.

[41]For a proper account of this incident, see Saywell, op. cit., pp. 131-3.

[42]S.A. de Smith points out, however, that some Commonwealth countries have overcome much of this problem with legal provisions requiring any incumbent government to resign after an election, with a successful government subsequently being reappointed. De Smith, *The New Commonwealth and its Constitutions*, London: Stevens and Sons, 1964, p. 95.

[43]Edward McWhinney, 'Prerogative Powers of the Head of State (Queen or Governor General', *Canadian Bar Review* 35 (1957), p. 370.

[44]Hogg, op. cit., p. 157.

[45]H.V. Evatt, *The King and His Dominion Governors*, London: Oxford University Press, 1936, chs 19, 20.

[46]Hogg, op. cit., p. 157.

[47]Dawson, op. cit., p. 162.

[48]Marshall, op. cit., p. 27.

[49]See MacKinnon, op. cit., p. 127.

[50]André Bernard, *La Politique au Canada et au Québec*, Montréal: Université de Québec, 1977.

[51]For a full discussion of this incident, see Saywell, op. cit., pp. 130-7.

[52]When Henri Joly, Lieutenant Governor of British Columbia, dismissed the Prior government in 1903 for corruption, he wrote: 'I am to my sincere regret unable to continue feeling that confidence in your judgement which could justify me acting any longer on your advice.' Ibid., p. 142.

[53]For a broader view of the episode, one should consult the book written by the Governor General: Sir John Kerr, *Matters for Judgment*, London: Macmillan, 1979; and the prime minister's own account: Whitlam, op. cit.

[54]Whitlam argued vehemently for the abolition of the office of Governor General: Whitlam, op. cit., ch. 12. Quite another view, but equally radical in its own vein, was taken by David Solomon in his book, *Elect the Governor General*, Melbourne: Nelson, 1976.

[55]Quoted in Kerr, op. cit., p. 343.

[56]B. J. Galligan, 'The Kerr-Whitlam Debate and the Principles of the Australian Constitution', *Journal of Commonwealth and Comparative Politics* 17 (1980), p. 247.

[57]See the criticisms of J. Archer and G. Maddox, 'The 1975 Constitutional Crisis in Australia', *Journal of Commonwealth and Comparative Politics* 14 (1976), p. 141; B.J. Galligan, op. cit., p. 258; Colin Howard, 'The Constitutional Crisis of 1975', *Australian Quarterly* 48 (1976), p. 5; George Winterton, *Parliament, the Executive and the Governor-General*, Melbourne: Melbourne University Press, 1983; Hogg, op. cit., p. 209; and those of Mallory, op. cit., p. 58. Kerr's actions have been defended by Lord Hailsham and Eugene Forsey in their respective Introduction and Epilogue to Kerr's book, op. cit., and by Francis West, 'Constitutional Crisis 1975—an Historian's View' *Australian Quarterly* 48 (1976), p. 48.

[58]Provincial writs contain a similar phrase relating to the first minister of the government as well.

[59]Eugene A. Forsey, *The Royal Power of Dissolution of Parliament in the British Commonwealth*, Toronto: Oxford University Press, 1943, p. 71.

[60]Forsey, 'The Courts and The Conventions', p. 22.

[61]Jennings, op. cit., pp. 400 and 428.

[62]Ibid., p. 410.

[63]Marshall, op. cit., pp. 26-7; Jennings, op. cit., pp. 411-12; Forsey, *The Royal Power of Dissolution*, p. 270.

[64]*Globe and Mail*, 22 January 1982, p. A8.

[65]Ibid., p. A8.

[66]Newfoundland was unique in that the electorate voted directly on whether to join Confederation.

[67]Forsey, 'Professor Angus . . .', p. 228.

[68]Forsey and Eglington, op. cit., pp. 170-85.

[69]Until 1878 the Instructions issued to the Governor General included a provision expressly stating that the Governor General could refuse the advice of his ministers, but such action and the reasons for it had to be immediately reported the British Secretary of State. K.C. Wheare, *The Statute of Westminster and Dominion Status* (5th ed.), Oxford: Oxford University Press, 1953, p. 56.

[70]Forsey, *The Royal Power of Dissolution*.

71Ibid., p. 262.
72Saywell, op. cit., p. 154; Mallory, *The Structure of Government*, pp. 51-7; Marshall, op. cit., pp. 36-42; Hogg, op. cit., pp. 209-11.
73Ronald Cheffins and Ronald Tucker, *The Constitutional Process in Canada* (2nd ed.), Toronto: McGraw-Hill Ryerson, 1976, p. 84.
74Most of the discussions of this incident are collected in R. Graham, ed., *The King-Byng Affair: A Question of Responsible Government*, Toronto: Copp Clark, 1967.
75Angus, op. cit; Jennings, op. cit., pp. 427-8.
76Bagehot, op. cit., p. 98.
77Jennings, op. cit., p. 400; R.M. Punnett, *British Government and Politics* (4th ed.), London: Heinemann, 1980, p. 273; K.C. Wheare, *Modern Constitutions*, London: Oxford University Press, 1951, p. 182.
78Saywell, op. cit., p. 221. Frank Mackinnon discusses three examples from PEI, where the Lieutenant Governor refused assent without the cabinet's concurrence, in *The Government of Prince Edward Island*, Toronto: University of Toronto Press, 1951, pp. 154-5.
79Constitution Act, RSBC, ch. 62, s.53. See Saywell, op. cit., p. 221.
80Ronald Cheffins and Patricia Johnson, *The Revised Canadian Constitution: Politics as Law*, Toronto: McGraw-Hill Ryerson, 1986, p. 82.
81Sir John Bourinot, *Parliamentary Procedure and Practice*, Montreal: Dawson Bros., 1892, pp. 645-56.
82Saywell, op. cit., pp. 207-8 and 267.
83*Reference re Reservation and Disallowance*, [1938] SCR 71.
84For an analysis of this example of reservation, see J.R. Mallory, 'The Lieutenant Governor's Discretionary Powers: the Reservation of Bill 56', *Canadian Bar Review* 27 (1961), pp. 518-22.
85The selective proclamation of parts of this act was upheld by the Supreme Court of Canada's examination of this instance in *Reference re Proclamation of Section 16 of the Criminal Law Amendment Act 1968-9* (1970), 10 DLR (3d) 699.
86Cheffins and Tucker, op. cit., p. 82.
87Marshall, op. cit., pp. 22 and 26-7.
88Van Loon and Whittington, op. cit., pp. 174-5; see also Hogg, op. cit., p. 202.
89*Re Amendment of the Constitution of Canada* (1981), 125 DLR (3d) 1 at p. 85 (SCC).
90*Gallant v. The King* (1949), 2 DLR 425.
91For instance, Forsey says that a defeated prime minister has no right to advise about his successor. 'The Courts and the Conventions of the Constitution', p. 20.
92MacKinnon, *The Crown*, p. 132; Hogg, op. cit., p. 211; Mallory, *The Structure of Canadian Government*, p. 16.
93MacKinnon, op. cit., pp. 47-8. When the Lieutenant Governor of Ontario agreed to make some appointments recommended by a defeated government in 1905, there were apparently many protests and criticisms. See A.B. Keith, *Responsible Government in the Dominions*, Oxford: Oxford University Press, 1928, p. 175.
94MacKinnon, op. cit., pp. 112-13.
95*Jollimore v. A.G. Nova Scotia* (1987), 75 NSR (2d) 191 at p. 193 (NSTD).
96Ibid., at p. 193.
97T. Franck, 'The Governor General and the Head of State Functions', *Canadian Bar Review* 32 (1952), pp. 10-97. See also A.B. Keith, *The Dominions as Sovereign States*, London: Macmillan, 1938, p. 214; Brun and Tremblay, op. cit., p. 258; *Currie v. MacDonald* (1949), 29 Nfld and PEIR 294 at p. 299 (Nfld CA) (Emerson C.J.).
98*Bonanza Creek Gold Mining Co. Ltd. v The King*, [1916] AC 566 at p. 587.
99Saywell, op. cit., p. 248.
100Forsey and Eglington, op. cit., p. 184.
101Special Senate Committee, op. cit., p. 2:28.
102Harold Nicolson, *King George the Fifth*, London: Constable, 1952, p. 481.
103A.B. Keith, *Letters on Imperial Relations*, London: Oxford University Press, 1935, p. 129.

[104]Marshall, op. cit., p. 174.

[105]Keith, *Letters*, pp. 126-32.

[106]The Judicial Committee of the Privy Council eventually ruled on the original dismissal of the prime minster by the Oni of Ife, and found it was quite constitutional. *Adegbenro v. Akintola*, [1963] AC 614. For a fuller account of the political crisis itself, see S.A. de Smith, *The New Commonwealth and its Constitutions*, London: Stevens & Sons, 1964, pp. 87-90.

[107]Reprinted in the Toronto *Globe and Mail*, 29 July 1986, p. A6.

[108]Keith, *Letters*, p. 130; Marshall, op. cit., p. 174.

[109]Franck, op. cit., p. 1096.

[110]*Proposals on the Constitution: 1971-1978*, Ottawa: Canadian Intergovernmental Conference Secretariat, 1978, p. 140.

[111]David Butler, 'Politics and the Constitution: Twenty Questions Left by Remembrance Day', in H.R. Penniman, ed., *Australia at the Polls: The National Election of 1975*, Washington: American Enterprise Institute for Public Policy Research, 1977, p. 328; Marshall, op. cit., p. 174; D.P. O'Connell, 'Canada, Australia, Constitutional Reform and the Crown', *Parliamentarian* 60 (1979), (1), pp. 9-10.

[112]See the accounts of this episode in *The Times*, London, 14, 15, and 25 September 1974.

[113]For a detailed account of both incidents, see Saywell, op. cit., ch. IX.

[114][1919] AC 935.

[115]Cheffins and Johnson, op. cit., p. 74.

[116]*Reference re Legislative Authority of Parliament to Alter or Replace the Senate*, [1980] 1 SCR 54 at p. 71.

[117]Peter H. Russell, review of Cheffins and Johnson, op. cit., in *Canadian Journal of Political Science* 19 (1986), p. 832.

3. CABINET, MINISTERS AND THE CIVIL SERVICE

[1]*Hansard*, 7 March 1966, p. 2281.

[2]However, the Minister of Justice or Attorney General may offer advice to the governor on particular judicial matters.

[3]Eugene Forsey and Graham Eglington, *The Question of Confidence in Responsible Government: A Study Prepared for the Special Committee on Reform of the House of Commons*, Ottawa, 1985, pp. 320-4. I add to their data the appointment of John Turner as Prime Minister in 1984.

[4]R. MacGregor Dawson, *The Government of Canada* (5th ed.), revised by Norman Ward, Toronto: University of Toronto Press, 1970, p. 179.

[5]Ibid., p. 179; J. R. Mallory, *The Structure of Canadian Government*, pp. 87-93; Joseph Munro, *The Constitution of Canada*, Cambridge: Cambridge University Press, 1889, p. 183; R.M. Punnett, *The Prime Minister in Canadian Government and Politics*, Toronto: Macmillan, 1976, p. 65; D.V. Smiley and R. Watts, op. cit., ch. 5; David E. Smith, 'The Federal Cabinet in Canadian Politics' in Michael S. Whittington and Glen Williams, *Canadian Politics in the 1980s* (2nd ed.), Toronto: Methuen, 1984, pp. 363-5; Richard J. Van Loon and Michael S. Whittington, *The Canadian Political System* (3rd ed.), Toronto: McGraw-Hill Ryerson, 1981, pp. 440-3.

[6]Punnett, op. cit., p. 66.

[7]Van Loon and Whittington, op. cit., p. 447; see also Dawson, op. cit., pp. 182-3.

[8]Dawson, op. cit., p. 178.

[9]*Arseneau v. The Queen*, [1979] 2 SCR 136.

[10]*A.G. Quebec v. Blaikie* (No. 2), [1981] 1 SCR 312.

[11]Ibid., at p. 320.

[12]Geoffrey Marshall and Graeme Moodie, *Some Problems of the Constitution* (3rd ed.), London: Hutchinson, 1964, p. 84.

[13]*Hansard*, 3 March 1976, p. 11575.

[14]Alistair Fraser, W.F. Dawson, and John Holtby, eds, *Beauchesne's Rules and Forms of the House of Commons of Canada* (6th ed.), Toronto: Carswell, 1989, p. 123.

[15]*Hansard*, 6 February 1978, p. 2567.

[16]A full list of improper matters that cannot be contained in a question is found in Fraser et al., op. cit., pp. 120-2. Examples of questions that will be disallowed by a Speaker include hypothetical questions seeking an opinion from a minister, queries about cases before the courts or royal commissions, and questions that seek legal opinions.

[17]*Hansard*, 14 March 1975, p. 4102; 14 April 1975, p. 4763; 3 March 1976, p. 11461.

[18]See specially the protests made by Opposition members to the Chair at *Hansard*, 20 June 1977, pp. 6846-50; and 6 February 1978, pp. 2551-65.

[19]For instance, *Hansard*, 18 May 1982, pp. 17536-7.

[20]Fraser et al., op. cit., p. 122.

[21]T.M. Denton, 'Ministerial Responsibility: A Contemporary Perspective' in Richard Schultz et al., eds, *The Canadian Political Process* (3rd ed.), Toronto: Holt, Rinehart and Winston, 1979, p. 347. Some individual officials in a department may also be vested with powers for which they are legally liable, rather than the minister; e.g. the Director of Investigation and Research of Combines and Investigation in *Hunter et al. v. Southam Inc.* (1985), 11 DLR (4th) 641 (SCC).

[22]*Bhatnager v. Minister of Employment and Immigration et al.* (1988), 82 NR 360 (FCA)

[23]For instance, Edmund Morris was declared guilty, when serving as Nova Scotia's Minister of Social Services, of a breach of the Nova Scotia Information Act, which forbids any department official from releasing confidential information about an individual. *R. v. Morris* (1988), 85 NSR (2d) 200.

[24]S.E. Finer, 'The Individual Responsibility of Ministers', *Public Administration* 34 (1956), p. 394.

[25]For example, Marshall and Moodie, op. cit., pp. 79-80; A.H. Birch, *Representative and Responsible Government*, Toronto: University Of Toronto Press, 1964, pp. 141-8.

[26]Philip Norton, *The Constitution in Flux*, Oxford: Robertson, 1982, p. 57. A similar position is also taken by Peter Bromhead, *Britain's Developing Constitution*, London: Allen & Unwin, 1974, p. 69.

[27]Marshall and Moodie, op. cit., p. 87.

[28]He does, however, allow that the resignation of Guy Favreau might be viewed in such a light. Denton, op. cit., p. 357. David Butler has also made this same claim about a lack of resignations in Australia: *The Canberra Model*, New York: St Martins, 1974.

[29]Kenneth Kernaghan, 'Power, Parliament, and Public Servants in Canada: Ministerial Responsibility Reexamined', in Harold D. Clarke et al., *Parliament, Policy and Representation*, Toronto: Methuen, 1980, p. 130. See also Michael Atkinson, 'Parliamentary Government in Canada' in, Michael S. Whittington and Glen Williams, eds, *Canadian Politics in the 1980s* (2nd ed.), Toronto: Metheun, 1984, p. 334; F.F. Schindeler, *Responsible Government in Ontario* Toronto: University Of Toronto Press, 1969, p. 267; Thomas d'Aquino et al., *Parliamentary Democracy in Canada: Issues for Reform*, Toronto: Methuen, 1983, p. 25; Denton, op. cit., pp. 344-62.

[30]Geoffrey Marshall, *Constitutional Conventions*, Oxford: Oxford University Press, 1984, p. 65.

[31]The Prime Minister's reluctance to accept the resignation was made clear in the correspondence between Thatcher and Carrington that was published in *The Times*, London, 6 April 1982.

[32]Indeed, an editorial in the Toronto *Globe and Mail* argued that Coates's actions were not such that they should require his resignation. 20 February 1985, p. A6.

[33]Finer, op. cit., p. 393.

[34]Kernaghan, op. cit., p. 130.

[35]For a comprehensive discussion of conflict of interest, see The Task Force on Conflict of Interest, *Ethical Conduct in the Public Sector*, Ottawa: Supply and Services, 1984.; I. Greene, 'Conflict of Interest, the Rule of Law and Equality: A Commentary on Conflict of Interest Rules', Paper Presented to the Annual Meetings of the Canadian Political Science Association, 1987.

[36]John P. Mackintosh, *The British Cabinet* (3rd ed.), London: Stevens and Sons, 1977, pp. 529-30.

[37]Toronto *Globe and Mail*, 1 September 1972, p. 3.

[38]See, for example, the *Financial Post*, 27 April 1989, p. 1; the Toronto *Globe and Mail*, 28 April 1989, p. A6; and the *Toronto Star*, 27 April 1989, p. A27, and 28 April 1989, p. A24.

[39]Toronto *Globe and Mail*, 28 April 1989, p. A7.

[40]Both Fox and Blair are quoted in the *Toronto Star*, 28 April 1989, p. A26.

[41]Ibid.

[42]Marshall, op. cit., p. 66.

[43]A broad-ranging discussion of this general topic is found in Kenneth Kernaghan, 'Political Rights and Political Neutrality: Finding the Balance Point', *Canadian Public Administration*, vol. 29, no. 4 (Winter 1986), pp. 639-53.

[44]*Re Fraser and the Public Service Staff Relations Board* (1986), 23 DLR (4th) 122 at pp. 135-6.

[45]*Re Ontario Public Service Employees' Union et al. and A.G. for Ontario* (1987), 41 DLR (4th) 1.

[46]*Re Fraser and A.G. Nova Scotia* (1986), 30 DLR (4th) 340.

[47]*Osborne v. Canada (Treasury Board)*, [1988] 87 NR 376 (FCA).

[48]Norton, op. cit., p. 57.

[49]Kenneth Kernaghan, 'Responsible Pubic Bureaucracy: A Rationale and a Framework for Analysis', *Canadian Public Administration*, vol. 16, no. 4 (Winter 1973). Robert Carman, 'Accountability of Senior Public Servants to Parliament and its Committees', *Canadian Public Administration* , vol. 27, no. 4 (Winter 1984), p. 544. Gordon F. Osbaldeston, *Keeping Deputy Ministers Accountable*, Toronto: McGraw-Hill Ryerson, 1989.

[50]*Royal Commission on Financial Management and Accountability: Final Report*, Ottawa: Supply and Services, 1979, pp. 573-8.

[51]See Carman, op. cit., p. 543.

[52]Kernaghan, 'Power, Parliament and Public Servants', p. 130.

[53]For the statement Goyer made to the Commons, see *Hansard*, 1 June 1976, pp. 14030-1.

[54]*Stopforth v. Goyer* (1978), 20 OR (2d) 262 at pp. 271-3. (Ont.HCJ).

[55]*Stopforth v. Goyer* (1979), 23 OR (2d) 696 at pp. 699-700. (Ont.CA).

[56]Kernaghan, 'Power, Parliament and Public Servants', p. 131.

[57]The Opposition cried loudly at the time that MacDonald was being sacrificed instead of the minister, Pierre Bussières. See *Hansard*, 29 March 1984, pp. 2547-9; 30 March 1984, p. 2561.

[58]Marshall and Moodie, op. cit., p. 47.

[59]Eugene A. Forsey and Graham C. Eglington, *The Question of Confidence in Responsible Government: A Study Prepared for the Special Committee on Reform of the House of Commons*, 1985, pp. 84-5.

[60]William A. Matheson, *The Prime Minister and the Cabinet*, Toronto: Methuen, 1976, p. 17; Dawson, op. cit., p. 175; Forsey and Eglington, op. cit., p. 86.

[61]Ibid., p. 86. One might add to this list the resignation of Suzanne Blais-Grenier in 1985, but this was widely thought at the time to be a pretext for resigning before Mulroney dismissed her for poor performance.

[62]R.K. Alderman and J.A. Cross, *The Tactics of Resignation*, London: Routledge and Kegan Paul, 1967, pp. 80-3.

[63]For Wilson's memoranda to his ministers at the time, see Harold Wilson, *The Governance of Britain*, London: Weidenfeld & Nicolson, 1976, pp. 191-3.

[64]In 1966 the vote on capital punishment centred on a private members' bill and the Cabinet took no official position on the issue; on this occasion six ministers dissented from their colleagues and voted against abolition. For a discussion of these votes, see Diane Pothier, 'Parties and Free Votes in the Canadian House of Commons: The Case of Capital Punishment', *Journal of Canadian Studies*, vol. 14, no. 2, Summer 1979.

[65]Matheson, op. cit., pp. 17-18.

[66]See Ian D. Clark, 'Recent Changes in the Cabinet Decision-Making System in Ottawa',

Canadian Public Administration 28 (1985), pp. 185-201; Richard J. Van Loon and Michael S. Whittington, *The Canadian Political System* (4th ed.), Toronto: McGraw-Hill Ryerson, 1987, ch. 15.

[67]'Background Paper on the New Cabinet Decision-Making System', Office of the Prime Minister, *Release*, 30 January 1989, p. 1.

[68]An exception to this general observation is found in the controversy that followed the resignation in 1944 of J.L. Ralston, who complained to the House of Commons about the matters revealed by the Prime Minister concerning his resignation: 'The doors to the Privy Council have been pretty well opened, and there is not very much that has taken place there, which one recollects, that has not been revealed to the House and to the public.' *Hansard*, 29 November 1944, p. 6659.

[69]*Hansard*, 10 October 1979, p. 25.

[70]*A.G. v. Jonathan Cape Ltd. et al.*, [1975] 3 All ER 484 (QBD)

[71]Ibid., at p. 494.

[72]*Stopforth v. Goyer* (1979), 23 OR (2d) 696 at pp. 699-700 (Ont.CA).

[73]*A.G. v. Jonathan Cape Ltd. et al.*, [1975] 3 All ER 484 at p. 495.

[74]Ibid., at p. 496.

[75]Ibid., at p. 496.

[76]The actual court case dealt only with the first volume of Crossman's diaries; but two further volumes were subsequently published that dealt with matters that happened as recently as seven years before: Richard Crossman, *The Diaries of a Cabinet Minister*, London: Jonathan Cape Ltd., vol. 1, 1975; vol. 2, 1976; vol. 3, 1977.

[77]Norton, op. cit., p. 61.

[78]Smith, op. cit., pp. 351-2.

[79]*Burmah Oil Co. v. Bank of England*, [1979] 3 All ER 700 (HL). See also the earlier case of *Conway v. Rimmer*, [1968] AC 910.

[80]*Fletcher Timber v. A.G.*, (1984) 1 NZLR 290 (CA).

[81]*Sankey v. Whitlam*, (1978) 21 ALR 505 (HCJ).

[82][1986] 2 SCR 637.

[83][1982] 2 SCR 686.

[84]*Carey v. The Queen*, [1986] 2 SCR 637 at 670.

[85]Ibid., at 673.

[86]*Auditor General of Canada v. Minister of Energy, Mines and Resources et al.* (1986), 23 DLR (4th) 210 (FCTD).

[87]*Canada (Auditor General) v. Canada (Minister of Energy, Mines and Resources)*, [1989] 2 SCR 49; *Auditor General of Canada v. Minister of Energy, Mines and Resources et al.* [1987], 73 NR 241 (FCA).

[88]*Nova Scotia (A.G.) v. Royal Commission (Donald Marshall Inquiry)* (1988), 87 NSR (2d) 183 (NSCA). The testimony had already been heard by the time the Supreme Court of Canada dealt with the appeal: *Nova Scotia (A.G.) v. Nova Scotia (Royal Commission into Marshall Prosecution)*, [1989] 2 SCR 788.

[89]See also *Sparling et al. v. Smallwood*, [1982] 2 SCR 686; *Gloucester Properties et al. v. The Queen et al.* (1981), 129 DLR (3d) 275. (BCCA).

[90]P. Gordon Walker, *The Cabinet*, London: Jonathan Cape, 1970, p. 34.

[91]Arthur Siegel, *Politics and the Media in Canada*, Toronto: McGraw-Hill Ryerson, 1983, p. 42.

[92]Birch, op. cit., pp. 135-7.

[93]Ibid., p. 138.

[94]*Report of the Special Committee on Reform of the House of Commons*, Ottawa: House of Commons, 1985, p. 6.

[95]*Report of the Special Committee on Reform*, p. 8.

[96]Australian Constitutional Convention, Standing Committee D, *Fourth Report*, vol. 1, 27 August 1982, p. 36.

[97]For example, Eugene Forsey, *Freedom and Order*, Carleton Library 73, Toronto: McClelland and Stewart, 1974, p. 114; Norton, op. cit., p. 69; Marshall, op. cit., p. 56.

[98]Personal interview with David Lewis, 24 March 1980.

[99]*Report of the Special Committee on Reform*, p. 8. Australian Constitutional Convention, op. cit., p. 36.

[100]For a review of these episodes, see *Hansard*, 21 January 1966, pp. 129-31.

[101]Personal interview with Eugene Forsey, 5 February 1980.

[102]*Report of the Special Committee on Reform*, p. 8.

[103]Marshall, op. cit., p. 56; see also Forsey and Eglington, op. cit., pp. 144-7.

[104]These two incidents are mentioned in ibid., pp. 298 and 300.

[105]See *Hansard*, 12 February 1923, p. 220.

[106]Special Joint Committee of the Senate and House of Commons on the Constitution of Canada, *Final Report*, Ottawa: Queen's Printer, 1972, p. 37.

[107]Toronto *Globe and Mail*, 29 May 1985., p. A4.

[108]Toronto *Globe and Mail*, 25 May 1985, p. A1.

[109]Ibid., p. A1; Toronto *Globe and Mail*, 25 May 1985, p. A4.

[110]*Toronto Star*, 28 May 1985, p. A1.

[111]*Toronto Star*, 30 May 1985, p. A1.

[112]*Toronto Star*, 28 May 1987, p. A8.

[113]*Toronto Star*, 20 June 1985, p. A4.

[114]S.M. Waddams, *The Law of Contracts*, Toronto: Canada Law Book, 1984, p. 114. See also G.H.L. Fridman, *The Law of Contract in Canada* (2nd ed.), Toronto: Carswell, 1986, pp. 25-30; P.S. Atiyah, *An Introduction to the Law of Contract* (2nd ed.), Oxford: Clarendon Press, 1971, p. 92.

[115]*Toronto Star*, 28 May 1985, p. A19.

[116]*Finney v. Township of McKellar* (1982), 133 DLR (3d) 351 (Ont.CA); *Vancouver v. Registrar of Land Registration District* (1955), 15 WWR 351 (BCCA); *Amalgamated Society of Railway Servants v. Osborne*, [1910] AC 87 (HL); *Egerton v. Brownlow*, (1853) 10 ER 359 (HL).

[117]*The King v. Dominion Postage Stamp Vending Co. Ltd.*, [1930] SCR 500 at p. 506.

4. THE LEGISLATURES

[1](1949) 2 DLR 425 (PEISC). The Privy Council had earlier underlined the importance of the Lieutenant Governor as part of provincial legislatures by holding that no new legislative power could be created that excluded the Lieutenant Governor: *Re Initiative and Referendum Act*, [1919] AC 935.

[2]For a detailed discussion of this topic, see Joseph P. Maingot, *Parliamentary Privilege in Canada*, Toronto: Butterworths, 1982.

[3]The privileges of the national parliament are said to be those of the British House of Commons at the time of Confederation. It is a curious hangover from Canada's colonial days that the statutory powers and privileges that the Canadian parliament may confer upon itself still cannot exceed those of the British House at the time of the Act. See Constitution Act, 1867, s. 18; Parliament of Canada Act, RSC 1985, P-1, ss.4,5.

[4]These rulings have been consolidated in a number of works on parliamentary procedure: Alistair Fraser, W.F. Dawson, and John A. Holtby, eds, *Beauchesne's Rules and Forms of the House of Commons of Canada* (6th ed.), Toronto: Carswell, 1989; *Selected Decisions of Speaker James Jerome, 1974-1979*, Ottawa: House of Commons, 1983; *Selected Decisions of Speaker Lucien Lamoureux, 1966-1974*, Ottawa: House of Commons, 1985. The leading compilation of the rules of the British Parliament is Sir Charles Gordon, ed., *Erskine May's Treatise on the Law, Privilege, Proceeding and Usage of Parliament* (20th ed.), London: Butterworths, 1983.

[5]*Hansard*, 11 July 1988, p. 17384.

[6]*Halifax Chronicle Herald*, 27 December 1988, p. 1.

[7]For a description of this episode, see C.E.S. Franks, *The Parliament of Canada*, Toronto: University of Toronto Press, 1988, pp. 133-4.

[8]Fraser et al., op. cit., p. 49.

⁹This information is calculated from House of Commons, *Journals*, vols. CXXVI-VII, 1980-86; *Status of Bills Report*, Ottawa: Canadian Law Information Council, 1986-8. For a listing of the success of private members' public bills in the Quebec National Assembly between 1867 and 1960, see Louis Massicotte, 'Le Parlement du Québec en Transition', *Administration Publique du Canada* 28 (1985), p. 560.

¹⁰W.F. Dawson, *Procedure in the Canadian House of Commons*, Toronto: University of Toronto Press, 1962, pp. 188-90.

¹¹David E. Smith, 'Party Government, Representation and National Integration in Canada', in Peter Aucoin, ed., *Party Government and Regional Representation in Canada*, Ottawa: Minister of Supply and Services, 1985, pp. 2-10.

¹²Martin Westmacott, 'Whips and Party Cohesion', *Canadian Parliamentary Review*, vol. 6, no. 3 (Autumn 1988), p. 16. Westmacott also cites Kornberg as having come to the same conclusion: Alan Kornberg, *Canadian Legislative Behaviour: A Study of the 25th Parliament*, New York: Holt, Rinehart and Winston, 1968, p. 131.

¹³John B. Stewart, *The Canadian House of Commons: Procedure and Reform*, Montreal: McGill-Queen's University Press, 1977, pp. 29-30.

¹⁴Massicotte, op. cit., p. 557.

¹⁵Roman R. March, *The Myth of Parliament*, Toronto: Prentice-Hall, 1974, p. 59. This figure excludes the free votes held on the flag debates.

¹⁶David Kilgour and John Kirsner, 'Party Discipline and Canadian Democracy', *Canadian Parliamentary Review* 11 (Autumn 1988), p. 10.

¹⁷Philip Norton, *The Commons in Perspective*, Oxford: Martin Robertson, 1981, p. 227.

¹⁸Richard Rose, 'British MPs, More Bark than Bite?'. in Ezra Suleiman, ed., *Parliaments and Parliamentarians in Democratic Politics*, New York: Holmes and Meier, 1985, p. 25.

¹⁹Kilgour and Kirsner, op. cit., p. 10.

²⁰*Débats*, 13 novembre 1975, p. 9032.

²¹*Report of the Special Committee on Reform of the House of Commons*, Ottawa: House of Commons, 1985.

²²Lucinda Flavelle and Philip Kaye, 'Party Discipline and Legislative Voting', *Canadian Parliamentary Review*, vol. 9, no. 2 (Summer 1988), p. 8.

²³Personal interview, 22 February 1980.

²⁴*Parliament of Canada Act*, RSC 1985, P-1, s.62.

²⁵For a fuller explanation of the duties of house leaders, see Paul G. Thomas, 'The Role of House Leaders in the Canadian House of Commons', *Canadian Journal of Political Science* 15 (1982), p. 125.

²⁶Martin Westmacott, op. cit., p. 15. A vivid description of the tribulations faced by MPs who have borne the range of the whip's disciplinary measures can be found in March, op. cit., pp. 85-6.

²⁷Franks, op. cit., pp. 105-6.

²⁸Quoted in Nancy Pawlek, 'Cracking the Whip?', *Parliamentary Government*, vol. 6, no. 4 (1987), p. 5.

²⁹Alan Kornberg, 'Caucus Cohesion in Canadian Parliamentary Parties', *American Political Science Review*, vol. 60 (1966), pp. 83-92.

³⁰Paul G. Thomas, 'The Role of National Party Caucuses' in Peter Aucoin, ed., op. cit., pp. 69-136.

³¹*Halifax Mail Star*, 1 July 1989, p. 1-WJ.

³²For various anecdotes and a general analysis of the role a government caucus can play, see McCormick, op. cit.; Howard Gold, 'Revitalizing Caucus: Enhancing the Role of Private Members', *Parliamentary Government*, vol. 4. no. 1 (1983), pp. 7-11; Lynda Rivington, 'Sanctum/Sanctorum: The Role of Caucus', *Parliamentary Government*, vol. 4, no. 1 (1983), pp. 2-7, 15.

³³Quoted in Rivington, op. cit., p. 15.

³⁴Norton, op. cit., p. 42.

[35]See the discussions in Keith Jackson, 'Caucus—the Anti-Parliament System?', *Parliamentarian*, vol. 59, no. 3 (July 1978), p. 160.

[36]*Toronto Star*, 16 May 1987, p. A4.

[37]For a general review, see John C. Courtney, 'Recognition of Canadian Political Parties in Parliament and in Law', *Canadian Journal of Political Science* 11 (1978), pp. 33-60.

[38]*Young and Rubicam Ltd. v. Progressive Conservative Party of Canada* (Unreported, 22 March 1971) (Que.SC); *McKinney v. Liberal Party of Canada et al.* (1987), 61 OR (2d) 680 (Ont.HCJ); *McKinney v. Mazankowski et al.* (Unreported, 23 November 1988) (Ont.HCJ).

[39]*McKinney v. Liberal Party of Canada et al.* (1987), 61 OR (2d) 680 at 684-5 (Ont.HCJ).

[40]Ibid., at pp. 682, 684.

[41]Ibid., at p. 686.

[42]*Re Resolution to Amend the Constitution of Canada*, [1981] 1 SCR 753 at 785.

[43]*Reference re an Act to Amend the Education Act (Ontario)*, [1987] 1 SCR 1148.

[44]*Retail, Wholesale & Department Store Union, Local 580 et al. v. Dolphin Delivery Ltd.*, [1986] 2 SCR 573 at 599.

[45]For a general discussion of these topics, see E.C.S. Wade and A.W. Bradley, *Constitutional and Administrative Law* (10th ed.), London: Longman, 1985, ch. 11; S.A. de Smith, *Constitutional and Administrative Law* (5th ed.), Harry Street and Rodney Brazier, eds, *Constitutional and Administrative Law*, London: Penguin, 1985, ch. 16.

[46]William R. Lederman reaches the same conclusion about 'the rules for orderly proceedings and discipline in the House'. But he argues that any use of the legislature's powers to bring someone 'before the bar' and order incarceration for contempt of parliament would be subject to the Charter. W.R. Lederman, 'Democratic Parliaments, Independent Courts and the Canadian Charter of Rights and Freedoms', in John C. Courtney, ed., *The Canadian House of Commons: Essays in Honour of Norman Ward*, Calgary: University of Calgary Press, 1985, pp. 100-1.

[47]*R. v. Therens*, [1985] 1 SCR 613 at 645; *R. v. Thomsen*, [1988] 1 SCR 640 at 651.

[48]For detailed descriptions of the two UK Parliament Acts, and their exceptions, see O. Hood Phillips and Paul Jackson, *O. Hood Phillips' Constitutional and Administrative Law* (7th ed.), London: Sweet & Maxwell, 1987, pp. 139-49.

[49]Donald Shell, *The House of Lords*, Oxford: Philip Allan, 1988, p. 119; *Senate Debates*, 1974-86; *Status of Bills Report*, 1986-8.

[50]*Hansard*, 7 June 1985, p. 5539.

[51]Franks, op. cit., pp. 190-1.

[52]Gregory Wick, 'Of Warhorses, Pastures and Power: An Interview with Allan J. MacEachen', *Parliamentary Government*, vol. 7, no. 4 (1988), p. 12.

[53]Robert A. MacKay, *The Unreformed Senate* (rev. ed.), Toronto: McClelland and Stewart, 1963, p. 199.

[54]*Senate Debates*, 1957-1988.

[55]MacKay, op. cit., p. 88.

[56]F.A. Kunz, *The Modern Senate of Canada 1925-63: A Re-appraisal*, Toronto: University of Toronto Press, 1965, p. 359.

[57]The Senate's refusal to pass the bill implementing the Free Trade Agreement is not included in these figures, since it was not technically an amendment to the legislation. However, this obstruction should be borne fully in mind in the following discussions.

[58]G. Ross, *The Senate of Canada*, Toronto: Copp, Clark Co., 1914, pp. 77-9; Kunz, op. cit., pp. 112-45; MacKay, op. cit., pp. 87-8.

[59]The number of Commons bills amended by the Senate was used as the dependent variable. The independent variables were: the percentage share of seats held by the PC Party; the percentage share of seats held by the Liberal Party; the size of the government caucus above or below the number needed for a majority as a percentage of the House; and the total number of Commons bills introduced into the Senate. When the last variable was controlled for, the following coefficients were calculated:

Government Majority:	.6696
Liberal Seats:	-.5957
PC Seats:	-.6481
$R^2 = .9395$ ANOVA $p = 0.0045$	

[60]Robert J. Jackson and Michael M. Atkinson, *The Canadian Legislative System* (2nd ed.), Toronto: Gage, 1980, p. 179.

[61]Kunz, op. cit., p. 365; MacKay, op. cit., pp. 110-11; Jackson and Atkinson, op. cit., p. 110; Thomas d'Aquino, Bruce Doern, and C. Blair, *Parliamentary Government in Canada: Critical Assessment and Suggestions for Change*, Ottawa: Business Council on National Issues, 1979, p. 98; J.R. Mallory, *The Structure of Canadian Government* (rev. ed.), Toronto: Gage, 1984, p. 263.

[62]Franks, op. cit., p. 190; Richard J. Van Loon and Michael S. Whittington, *The Canadian Political System* (4th ed.), Toronto: McGraw-Hill Ryerson, 1987, pp. 626-7. Some have gone so far as to argue that the Senate should be abolished altogether: Colin Campbell, *The Senate: A Lobby from Within*, Toronto: Macmillan, 1978, pp. 155-63.

[63]*Gallup*, Toronto: Gallup Canada, 5 October 1987, p. 2; 22 August 1988, p. 5.

[64]See specially a speech recorded in *Hansard*, 7 June 1985, pp. 5540-50.

[65]See, for example, Harvie André's endorsement of Senate amendments to the National Energy Board Act: *Hansard*, 11 December 1981, p. 13,987.

[66]MacKay, op. cit., pp. 112-23; Campbell, op. cit., pp. 6-9.

[67]Kunz, op. cit., ch. 11.

[68]The Standing Senate Committee on Legal and Constitutional Affairs, *Report on Certain Aspects of the Canadian Constitution*, Ottawa: Senate, 1980.

[69]MacKay, op. cit., pp. 123-8. However, he did feel that the Senate was more active in defending minority rights than those of individuals.

[70]Kunz, op. cit., p. 294.

[71]Norman Ward, *Dawson's The Government of Canada* (6th ed.), Toronto: University of Toronto Press, 1988, p. 153.

[72]*Hansard*, 11 July 1988, pp. 17382-4.

[73]Campbell, op. cit., pp. 10-19; ch. 5.

[74]MacKay, op. cit., p. 93; Kunz, op. cit., p. 185.

[75]In this respect there has been a consolidation of opinion since MacKay wrote in 1963, when he argued that no such prohibition appeared to exist: op. cit., pp. 93-4. The House of Commons has always included a provision among its Standing Orders (now SO 80(1)) stating its exclusive right to deal with money matters, 'which are not alterable by the Senate'. The Senate used to claim an ancient right to amend money bills, at least to revise downward a tax provision; see report of the Ross Committee that detailed the Senate's claimed rights: *Journals of the Senate of Canada*, 15 May 1918, p. 194ff.

[76]St John's: *Evening Telegram*, 23 July 1988, p. 6;
Halifax: *Mail Star*, 23 July 1988, p. 6;
Saint John: *Telegraph Journal*, 22 July 1988.
Montreal: *Gazette*, 22 July 1988, p. B3; *Le Devoir*, 22 juillet 1988, p. 8; *La Presse*, 22 juillet 1988, p. B2.
Ottawa: *Citizen*, 21 July 1988.
Toronto: *Globe and Mail*, 21 July 1988, p. A6 and 26 July 1988, p. A6; *Toronto Star*, 21 July 1988, p. A22 and 23 July 1988, p. A20.
Winnipeg, *Free Press*, 22 July 1988, p. 6.
Regina: *Leader Post*, 22 July 1988, p. A6.
Calgary: *Herald*, 21 July 1988, p. A4.
Vancouver: *Sun*, 21 July 1988, p. B2.

[77]Toronto *Globe and Mail*, 28 July 1988, p. A7.

[78]*Toronto Star*, 2 August 1988, p. A17.

[79]Toronto *Globe and Mail*, 21 July 1988, p. A4.

[80]Toronto *Globe and Mail*, 22 July 1988, p. A7.

[81]Gordon Robertson, 'The Global Challenge and Canadian Federalism', *Canadian Public Administration* 32 (1989), p. 128.

[82]Toronto *Globe and Mail*, 21 July 1988, p. A4.

[83]*Gallup*, Toronto: Gallup Canada, 22 August 1988, p. 3.

[84]Poll conducted for the CBC by *Canadian Facts*, *The National*, 8 November 1988.

[85]Fraser et al., eds, op. cit., p. 243.

[86]Gordon, ed., op. cit., p. 606.

[87]Ibid., pp. 606-7.

[88]*Pickin v. British Railways Board*, [1974] AC 765 at p. 787 (HL). The other Lords in this case made similar comments about the courts' inability to question the validity of an Act or the procedure followed within Parliament; see pp. 790, 796, 798-9.

[89]In this respect the courts would, initially at least, be conducting an accepted examination of the legal 'manner and form' requirements; see Peter W. Hogg, *Constitutional Law of Canada* (2nd ed.), Toronto: Carswell, 1985, pp. 262-4.

5. FEDERALISM

[1]K.C. Wheare, *Federal Government* (4th ed.), London: Oxford University Press, 1963, pp. 17-20.

[2]Peter W. Hogg, *Constitutional Law of Canada* (2nd ed.), Toronto: Carswell, 1985, p. 491.

[3]*Reference re Amendment of the Constitution of Canada* (1981), 125 DLR (3d) 1 at pp. 103, 106.

[4]Gerard V. La Forest, *Disallowance and Reservation of Provincial Legislation*, Ottawa: Department of Justice, 1955, pp. 83-115.

[5]The original articles have been reproduced in more recent compilations of these authors' works: Eugene Forsey, *Freedom and Order*, Carleton Library 73, Toronto: McClelland and Stewart, 1974, pp. 157-77; Frank R. Scott, *Essays on the Constitution*, Toronto: University of Toronto Press, 1977, pp. 175-89 and 209-43.

[6]Ibid., p. 179.

[7]Ibid., p. 238.

[8]J.R. Mallory, *The Structure of Canadian Government* (rev. ed.), Toronto: Gage, 1984, p. 373.

[9]For a description of this episode, see J.R. Mallory, 'The Lieutenant Governor's Discretionary Powers: The Reservation of Bill 56', *Canadian Bar Review* 27 (1961), p. 518.

[10]*Hansard*, 12 April 1961, p. 3577.

[11]*Hansard*, 28 March 1972, p. 1206.

[12]Pierre Elliott Trudeau, *Federalism and the French Canadians*, Toronto: Macmillan, 1968, p. 149.

[13]*Hansard*, 28 March 1972, p. 1206.

[14]' . . . an exception to the general principle that the federal and provincial parliaments are autonomous in their respective fields of legislative competence and take full responsibility for the measures they ratify.' Quoted in Henri Brun and Guy Tremblay, *Droit Constitutionnel*, Cowansville: Editions Yvon Blais, 1982, p. 309.

[15]The Special Joint Committee of the Senate and House of Commons on the Constitution of Canada, *Final Report*, 1972, p. 109; Task Force on Canadian Unity, *A Future Together: Observations and Recommendations*, Ottawa: Department of Supply and Services, 1979, p. 127.

[16]Standing Senate Committee on Legal and Constitutional Affairs, *Report on Certain Aspects of the Constitution*, November 1980, p. 7.

[17]Gérald-A. Beaudoin, *Le Partage des Pouvoirs*, Cowansville: Editions Yvon-Blais, 1982, p. 497; Brun and Tremblay, op. cit., pp. 309-10; Ronald I. Cheffins and Patricia A. Johnson, *The Revised Canadian Constitution: Politics as Law*, Toronto: McGraw-Hill Ryerson, 1986, p. 120; Hogg, op. cit., pp. 90-1; Garth Stevenson, *Unfulfilled Union* (3rd ed.), Toronto: Gage, 1989, p. 215; Richard J. Van Loon and Michael S. Whittington, *The Canadian Political System* (4th ed.), Toronto: McGraw-Hill Ryerson, 1987, p. 248.

[18]François Chevrette and Herbert Marx, *Droit Constitutionnel*, Montréal: Les Presses de l'Université de Montréal, 1982, p. 25; Mallory, *The Structure of Canadian Government*, pp. 370-

1; Norman Ward, *Dawson's The Government of Canada* (6th ed.), Toronto: University of Toronto Press, 1987, p. 226.

¹⁹P.C. Weiler, 'Rights and Judges in Democracy: A New Canadian Version', *University of Michigan Journal of Law Reform* 18 (1948), 51 at p. 86; Eugene A. Forsey, 'The Courts and the Conventions of the Constitution', *University of New Brunswick Law Journal* 33 (1984), 11 at pp. 24-5.

²⁰*Reference re Disallowance and Reservation of Provincial Legislation*, [1938] SCR 71. Previous court decisions suggesting that reservation and disallowance would be most properly used only when the provincial legislation is *ultra vires* or harmed the national interest include *R. v. Taylor* (1875), 36 UCQBR 183; *Severn v. The Queen*, SCR 70; *Quay v. Blanchet* (1879), 5 QLR 43; *The Corporation of Three Rivers v. Suite* (1882), 5 *Legal News* 330; *Mercer v. A.G. for Ontario*, 5 SCR 538; *In re Companies Reference*, [1913] 48 SCR 331.

²¹For the reason why the Supreme Court chose to answer the questions about the conventions concerning constitutional amendment, see *Reference re Amendment of the Constitution of Canada* (1981), 125 DLR (3d) 1 at p. 88.

²²*Reference re Disallowance and Reservation of Provincial Legislation*, [1938] SCR 71 at 78.

²³*Reference re Amendment of the Constitution of Canada* (1981), 125 DLR (3d) 1 at p. 43.

²⁴James McL. Hendry, *Memorandum on the Office of Lieutenant-Governor of a Province: Its Constitutional Character and Functions*, Ottawa: Department of Justice, 1955, pp. 20-2.

²⁵*Liquidators of the Maritime Bank v. The Receiver General of New Brunswick*, [1892] AC 437 at p. 443.

²⁶*The King v. Carroll et al.*, [1948] SCR 126.

²⁷See *Reference re Initiative and Referendum Act*, [1919] AC 935.

²⁸Scott, op. cit., p. 179.

²⁹*Reference re Amendment of the Constitution of Canada* (1981), 125 DLR (3d) 1 at pp. 43-4.

³⁰For a wide-ranging discussion of this topic, see Donald V. Smiley and Ronald L. Watts, *Intrastate Federalism in Canada*, Toronto: University of Toronto Press, 1985.

³¹He did point out, however, that PEI has more often than not been excluded from the Cabinet. R. MacGregor Dawson, *The Government of Canada* (5th ed.), rev. by Norman Ward, Toronto: University of Toronto Press, 1970, p. 179.

³²J. R. Mallory, *The Structure of Canadian Government*, pp. 87-93; Joseph Munro, *The Constitution of Canada*, Cambridge: Cambridge University Press, 1889, p. 183; Robert M. Punnett, *The Prime Minister in Canadian Government and Politics*, Toronto: Macmillan, 1976, p. 65; D.V. Smiley and R. Watts, op. cit., ch. 5; David E. Smith, 'The Federal Cabinet in Canadian Politics' in Michael S. Whittington and Glen Williams, *Canadian Politics in the 1980s* (2nd ed.), Toronto: Methuen, 1984, pp. 363-5; Van Loon and Whittington, op. cit., pp. 440-3.

³³Clark appointed these senators although his party had won two seats in Quebec; but even with both of these men in the Cabinet, he did not feel that Quebec was adequately represented. The addition of extra ministers from Quebec supports the general argument raised by Dawson that there are also guidelines about how many Cabinet positions the larger provinces should have: Dawson, op. cit., pp. 180-1.

³⁴*Hansard*, 10 October 1979, p. 31.

³⁵Smith, op. cit., p. 365.

³⁶Smiley and Watts, op. cit., pp. 81-5.

³⁷Dawson, op. cit., p. 181.

³⁸Robert A. Mackay, *The Unreformed Senate of Canada* (rev. ed.), Toronto: McClelland and Stewart, 1963, pp. 59-60.

³⁹For in-depth studies of the role and influence of regional ministers, see Herman Bakvis, 'Regional Ministers, and National Policies and the Administrative State in Canada: The Regional Dimension in Cabinet Decision-Making, 1980-1984', *Canadian Journal of Political Science* 21 (1988), p. 539; Herman Bakvis, 'Regional Politics and Policy in the Mulroney Cabinet, 1984-88: Towards a Theory of the Regional Minister in Canada', *Canadian Public Policy* 15 (1989), p. 121.

[40]Peter H. Russell, *The Judiciary in Canada: The Third Branch of Government,* Toronto: McGraw-Hill Ryerson, 1987, p. 169.

[41]Ibid., pp. 168-9.

[42]William R. Lederman, 'Thoughts on the Reform of the Supreme Court of Canada', *Background Papers and Reports,* vol. 2, Toronto: Ontario Advisory Committee on Confederation, 1970, p. 307.

[43]Russell, op. cit., p. 167.

[44]*Toronto Star,* 21 September 1988, p. A26.

[45]During the 1980s an increasing number of federal-provincial meetings also included representatives from the two Territorial governments.

[46]This information is calculated from the following publications of the Canadian Intergovernmental Conference Secretariat: *Federal Provincial First Ministers' Conferences 1906-1985,* Ottawa, 1986; *Federal Provincial Conferences Served by CICS, 1973-1986,* vol. 1, Ottawa, 1986; *Federal Provincial Conferences Served by CICS, 1986-1987,* vol. 2, Ottawa, 1987; *Federal Provincial Conferences Served by CICS, 1987-1988,* vol. 2, Ottawa, 1988. It should be pointed out that only those meetings held on a formal enough basis to be supported by the Canadian Intergovernmental Conference Secretariat are included in this data; a large number of more informal meetings are held each year.

[47]Canadian Intergovernmental Conference Secretariat, *Federal-Provincial First Ministers' Conferences, 1906-1985,* Ottawa, 1986, p. 80. Delegates to other conferences appear to fluctuate between two and three hundred.

[48]Richard Simeon, *Federal-Provincial Diplomacy: The Making of Recent Policy in Canada,* Toronto: University of Toronto Press, 1972, p. 127.

[49]J. Stefan Dupré, 'The Workability of Executive Federalism in Canada', in Herman Bakvis and William M. Chandler, eds, *Federalism and the Role of the State,* Toronto: University of Toronto Press, 1987, p. 244.

[50]Quoted in Canadian Intergovernmental Conference Secretariat, *Federal-Provincial First Ministers' Conferences,* p. 14.

[51]Gordon Robertson, 'The Role of Interministerial Conferences in the Decision-Making Process', R.D. Olling and M.W. Westmacott, eds, *Perspectives on Canadian Federalism,* Scarborough: Prentice-Hall, 1988, p. 225.

[52]All these departments also handle interprovincial relations, while Ontario and Alberta's departments also manage international affairs; Quebec has a separate international relations department. Stevenson, op. cit., pp. 226-7.

[53]By special arrangement, the federal government pays all of Manitoba's and a portion of British Columbia's shares.

[54]For a brief outline of the history, operations, and funding of the CICS, see *1989-90 Estimates, Part III, No. 58, Canadian Intergovernmental Conference Secretariat,* Ottawa: Department of Finance, 1989.

[55]Royal Commission on the Economic Union and Development Prospects for Canada, *Report, Volume Three,* Ottawa: Minister of Supply and Services, 1985, p. 261.

[56]On the various images of Canadian federalism, see J.R. Mallory, 'The Five Faces of Federalism', in J. Peter Meekison, ed., *Canadian Federalism: Myth or Reality* (2nd ed.), Toronto: Methuen, 1971; and Donald V. Smiley, *The Federal Condition in Canada,* Toronto: McGraw-Hill Ryerson, 1987, ch. 4.

[57]Canada-Newfoundland Atlantic Accord Implementation Act, SC 1987, c.3; Canada-Newfoundland Atlantic Accord Implementation (Newfoundland) Act, SN 1986, c.37; Canada-Nova Scotia Offshore Petroleum Resources Accord Implementation Act, SC 1988, c.28; Canada-Nova Scotia Offshore Petroleum Resources Accord Implementation (Nova Scotia) Act, SNS 1987, c.3.

[58]*Reference re Constitutional Questions Act* (1990), 46 BCLR (2d) 273.

6. JUDICIAL INDEPENDENCE

[1]For several critical views of the rule of law, see Allan C. Hutchinson and Patrick Monahan, eds, *The Rule of Law: Ideal or Ideology*, Toronto: Carswell, 1987.

[2]*The Queen v. Beauregard*, [1986] 2 SCR 56 at 72.

[3]J.R. Mallory, *The Structure of Canadian Government* (rev. ed.), Toronto: Gage, 1984, pp. 314-19.

[4]*Valente v. The Queen*, [1985] 2 SCR 673 at 702.

[5]Charter of Human Rights and Freedoms, SQ 1975, c.6.

[6]*Valente v. The Queen*, [1985] 2 SCR 673 at 694.

[7]Ibid., at 698.

[8]Ibid., at 704.

[9]Ibid., at 709. For further discussions on administrative independence, see Jules Deschênes, *Masters in their Own House*, Ottawa: Canadian Judicial Council, 1981, pp. 140-60.

[10]For modern discussions on the rule of law, see E.C.S. Wade and A.W. Bradley, *Constitutional and Administrative Law* (10th ed.), London: Longmans, 1985, ch. 6; Henri Brun and Guy Tremblay, *Droit Constitutionnel*, Cowansville: Editions Yvon Blais, 1982, pp. 476-82; F.L. Morton, ed., *Law, Politics and the Judicial Process in Canada*, Calgary: University of Calgary Press, 1984, ch. 1.

[11]*R. v. Wigglesworth*, [1987] 2 SCR 541.

[12]Gilles Pépin, 'L'Article 11(d) de la Charte canadienne: Une source d'inquiétude particulièrement pour les membres des cours inférieures et une source d'interrogation pour les membres des tribunaux administratifs', *Revue du Barreau Canadien* 64 (1986), p. 558.

[13]Ibid., p. 558.

[14]Charter of Human Rights and Freedoms, SQ 1975, c.6, s.56(1).

[15]*The Queen v. Beauregard*, [1986] 2 SCR 56 at 70.

[16]Ibid., at 72.

[17]Ibid., at 77.

[18]Such a two-pronged interpretation is favoured with respect to similar wording in British statutes by Harry Street and Rodney Brazier, eds, *De Smith's Constitutional and Administrative Law* (5th ed.), London: Penguin, 1987, p. 388.

[19]Peter W. Hogg, *Constitutional Law of Canada* (2nd ed.), Toronto: Carswell, 1985, p. 139; J.R. Mallory, *The Structure of Canadian Government* (rev. ed.), Toronto: Gage, 1984, p. 318; Ronald I. Cheffins and Ronald N. Tucker, *The Constitutional Process in Canada* (2nd ed.), Toronto: McGraw-Hill Ryerson, 1976, p. 98.

[20]William R. Lederman, 'The Independence of the Judiciary', *Canadian Bar Review* 34 (1956), 769 at pp. 786-7.

[21]*Valente v. The Queen*, [1985] 2 SCR 673 at 698.

[22]*Carey v. Ontario*, [1986] 2 SCR 637 at 673.

[23]See Deschênes, op. cit., pp. 173-7; Peter H. Russell. *The Judiciary in Canada: The Third Branch of Government*, Toronto: McGraw-Hill Ryerson, 1987, pp. 178-81.

[24]Gerald L. Gall, *The Canadian Legal System* (2nd ed.), Toronto: Carswell, 1983, p. 187.

[25]Ibid., pp. 187-8. The most recent instances occurred in 1933, and none have been removed since.

[26]Gall lists only three examples of removal, in Ontario, and four instances in three provinces where provincial judges have resigned before they could be removed. Ibid., pp. 188-9.

[27]Toronto *Globe and Mail*, 19 May 1989, p. A10.

[28]Toronto *Globe and Mail*, 20 August 1988, p. A4.

[29]Toronto *Globe and Mail*, 16 January 1987, p. A1.

[30]See Russell, op. cit., pp. 182-5.

[31]Toronto *Globe and Mail*, 22 March 1989, p. A5.

[32]Toronto *Globe and Mail*, 25 June 1988, p. A12.

[33]Montreal *Gazette*, 16 January 1987, p. A3.

[34]Deschênes, op. cit., pp. 121-3.

[35]Russell, op. cit., p. 181.

[36]Ibid., p. 178; Deschênes, op. cit., pp. 116-17.

[37]*Fleming v. Newfoundland and Provincial Judges' Association of Newfoundland* (1985), 56 Nfld and PEIR 196 at 210 (Nfld TD).

[38]R. MacGregor Dawson, *The Government of Canada* (5th ed.), Norman Ward, ed., Toronto: University of Toronto Press, 1970, p. 200.

[39]Gall, op. cit., pp. 185-96; Russell, op. cit., pp. 176-81.

[40]Now found in the Judges Act, RSC 1985, c.J-1, s.65(2).

[41]Russell, op. cit., p. 177.

[42]Toronto *Globe and Mail*, 27 September 1986, p. A2.

[43]Nova Scotia Judicial Council, 'Report of the Judicial Council convened to investigate the circumstances that gave rise to the suspension of His Honour Judge Ronald A. MacDonald', submitted to the Attorney General, 5 September 1989, p. 10.

[44]Gall, op. cit., pp. 204-5; Brun and Tremblay, op. cit., p. 514.

[45]*Sirrois v. Moore*, [1975] 1 QB 118; *McC v. Mullan*, [1984] 3 All ER 908.

[46]*Moirier and Boily v. Rivard*, [1985] 2 SCR 716 at 744. See also the decision of Judge Melvin L. Rothman of the Quebec Court of Appeal in *Royer v. Mignault* (1988), 13 QAC 39 at 46.

[47]Manitoba also dispels immunity for acts done 'without reasonable and probable cause': Provincial Court Act, CSM, c. C-275, s.49.

[48]*Charters v. Harper* (1986), 74 NBR (2d) 264 at 268. The suit, however, was later lost on merits: (1987), 79 NBR (2d) 28.

[49]*MacKeigan, J.A. et al. v. Royal Commission (Marshall Inquiry)* (1988); 85 NSR (2d) 219 (NSTD); (1988), 87 NSR (2d) 443 (NSCA).

[50]*Mackeigan v. Hickman*, [1989] 2 SCR 796.

[51]At the time of writing, the outcome of this hearing was unknown.

[52]Russell, op. cit., p. 185.

[53]Wade and Bradley, op. cit., p. 337.

[54]For a full account of these incidents, see Russell, op. cit., pp. 78-80.

[55]Drury's apology is recorded in *Hansard*, 12 March 1976, p. 11742.

[56]*Hansard*, 12 March 1976, p. 1171.

[57]Quoted in Russell, op. cit., pp. 80-1.

[58]Toronto *Globe and Mail*, 28 September 1988, p. A5.

[59]Toronto *Globe and Mail*, 25 January 1990, p. A1.

[60]An alternative proposal for dealing with sentencing disparities is offered in The Canadian Sentencing Commission, *Sentencing Reform: A Canadian Approach*, Ottawa: Minister of Supply and Services, 1987.

[61]Alistair Fraser, W.F. Dawson, and John A. Holtby, eds, *Beauchesne's Rules and Forms of the House of Commons of Canada* (6th ed.), Toronto: Carswell, 1989, p. 153.

[62]Ibid., p. 153.

[63]*Débats de l'Assemblée nationale*, 5 mai 1982, pp. 3294-6.

[64]*R v. Vermette*, [1988] 1 SCR 985.

[65]Public Issues Committee, Aukland District Law Society, 'Speaking Out: Members of Parliament and the Judicial Process', *New Zealand Law Journal* (1988), 300 at 302.

[66]*The Lawyers Weekly*, vol. 8, no. 32, 23 December 1988, p. 24.

[67]Gall, op. cit., p. 201.

[68]J.O. Wilson, *A Book for Judges*, Ottawa: Canadian Judicial Council, 1980, p. 92.

[69]On this general topic, see Gall, op. cit., pp. 200-4.

[70]Department of Justice, *A New Judicial Appointment Process*, Ottawa: Department of Supply and Services, 1988, p. 17.

[71]Gall, op. cit., pp. 201-2; Russell, op. cit., pp. 87-8.

[72]For a concise account of this episode, see ibid., pp. 85-9.

[73]Quoted in ibid., p. 86.
[74]J. Weber, 'The Limits to Judges' Free Speech: A Comment on the Report of the Committee of Investigation into the Conduct of the Hon. Mr Justice Berger', *McGill Law Journal* 29 (1984), p. 369.
[75]Gall, op. cit., p. 202; Russell endorses the involvement of judges in legislation relating to the justice system in Russell, op. cit., p. 97.
[76]Colin R. Munro, *Studies in Constitutional Law*, London: Butterworths, 1987, pp. 197-8, 201.
[77]Toronto *Globe and Mail*, 15 May 1989, pp. A1-2.
[78]Quoted in *Hansard*, 9 October 1986, p. 265.
[79]*Hansard*, 2 June 1986, p. 13854. See also the speech made by John Nunziata: *Hansard*, 16 June 1986, p. 14428.
[80]For an editorial comment strongly critical of Dickson's behaviour, see Toronto *Globe and Mail*, 3 June 1986, p. A6.
[81]*Muldoon and Teitelbaum v. Canada*, [1988] 21 FTR 154.
[82]Provincial Court Act, R.S.M. 1987, c.275, s.50.
[83]This story is recounted in a commentary by the Vice President of REAL Women of Canada, Gwendolyn Landolt, in *Lawyer's Weekly*, vol. 8, no. 32, 23 December 1988, p. 4.
[84]Quoted in ibid., p. 4.
[85]Quoted in ibid.
[86]Canadian Bar Association Committee on the Independence of the Judiciary in Canada, *The Independence of the Judiciary in Canada*, Ottawa: The Canadian Bar Foundation, 1985, pp. 43-4; see also Dawson, op. cit., pp. 405-8.
[87]Ibid., p. 43.
[88]Toronto *Globe and Mail*, 7 November 1985, p. A26.
[89]Toronto *Globe and Mail*, 22 November 1985, p. A4.
[90]For a comprehensive discussion on the appointment of judges, see Russell, op. cit., ch. 5.
[91]Dawson, op. cit., pp. 403-4; Russell, op. cit., ch. 5; Mallory op. cit., p. 332; Canadian Bar Association Committee on the Appointment of Judges in Canada, *The Appointment of Judges in Canada*, Ottawa: The Canadian Bar Foundation, 1985, ch. 6.
[92]Ibid., p. 57.
[93]Peter H. Russell and Jacob S. Ziegel, 'Federal Judicial Appointments: An Appraisal of the First Mulroney Government's Appointments', paper presented to the Annual Meeting of the Canadian Political Science Association, Laval, Quebec, June 1989, p. 50 (on microfilm).
[94]Russell, op. cit., pp. 135-7; Canadian Bar Association Committee, 'The Independence of the Judiciary', p. 44.
[95]Department of Justice, op. cit., p. 13.
[96]Russell and Ziegel, op. cit., p. 52.
[97]See Russell, op. cit., pp. 127-9.
[98]For a description of the federal system of appointment, see Department of Justice, op. cit., pp. 7-13.
[99]Toronto *Globe and Mail*, 12 July 1989, p. A4.
[100]*Retail, Wholesale & Department Store Union, Local 580 et al. v. Dolphin Delivery*, [1986] 2 SCR 573. For a concise criticism of this judgement, see Peter W. Hogg, 'The Dolphin Delivery Case: The Application of the Charter of Rights', *Saskatchewan Law Review* 51 (1987), p. 273.
[101]John McEvoy, 'Separation of the Powers and the Reference Power: Is there a Right to Refuse?', *Supreme Court Law Review* 10 (1988), p. 428.
[102]Nicolas Browne-Wilkinson, 'The Independence of the Judiciary in the 1980s', *Public Law* (1988), p. 54.
[103]*Gallup*, Toronto: Gallup Canada Inc., 9 February 1989, p. 2.
[104]Peter H. Russell, 'Canada's Charter of Rights and Freedoms: A Political Report', *Public Law* (1988), p. 398.
[105]Michael Mandel, *The Charter of Rights and the Legalization of Politics in Canada*, Toronto: Wall & Thompson, 1989.

7. THE VARIETY AND CHARACTER OF CONVENTIONS

[1]Much of the material in this chapter originally appeared in my article, 'Recognizing the Variety Among Constitutional Conventions', *Canadian Journal of Political Science* 31 (1989), p. 63.

[2]A.V. Dicey, *An Introduction to the Study of the Law of the Constitution* (8th ed.), London: Macmillan, 1924, p. 417

[3]Sir Ivor Jennings, *The Law and the Constitution* (5th ed.), London: University of London Press, 1959, pp. 134-6.

[4]John P. Mackintosh, *The British Cabinet* (3rd ed.), London: Stevens and Sons, 1977, pp. 20-1.

[5]Of course the central condition to be met for such a refusal is that either the current government, or an alternative one formed from the Opposition, could function with a legislative majority without the election.

[6]Geoffrey Marshall, *Constitutional Conventions*, Oxford: Oxford University Press, 1984, p. 211.

[7]For one example, see the use made of constitutional authorities in Pearson's defence of his refusal to treat the 1968 defeat of a tax bill as a loss of confidence. *Hansard*, 23 February 1968, p. 6923.

[8]For example, the Supreme Court of Canada referred extensively to academic authorities on the nature of the conventions relating to constitutional amendment in *Reference re Amendment of the Constitution of Canada* (1981), 125 DLR (3d) 1.

[9]For a discussion of the importance of viewing conventions as rules of critical morality, see Marshall, op. cit., pp. 10-12.

[10]John T. Saywell, *The Office of Lieutenant Governor*, Toronto: University of Toronto, 1957, ch. 2.

[11]Cheryl Saunders and Ewart Smith, 'Identifying Conventions Associated with the Commonwealth Constitution', Australian Constitutional Convention, Standing Committee 'D', Volume 2, 1982, 1. Unfortunately these authors did not attempt this classification, or suggest how it might be approached.

[12]The two lists of conventional rules remain as informal codifications of Australian constitutional rules. For analyses and lists of the conventional rules recognized by the Australian Constitutional Convention, see Charles Sampford and David Wood, 'Codification of Constitutional Conventions in Australia', *Public Law* (1987), p. 231; Charles Sampford, '"Recognize and Declare": An Australian Experiment in Codifying Constitutional Conventions', *Oxford Journal of Legal Studies* 7 (1987), p. 369.

[13]Some codified conventions in Caribbean constitutions, however, have been expressly prohibited from being subject to judicial review. Margaret de Merieux, 'The Codification of Constitutional Conventions in the Commonwealth Caribbean Constitutions', *International and Comparative Law Quarterly* 31 (1982), pp. 270-7.

[14]J.R. Mallory, *The Structure of Canadian Government* (rev. ed.), Toronto: Gage, 1984, p. 60.

[15]Dicey, op. cit., p. 24.

[16]O. Hood Phillips, 'Constitutional Conventions: A Conventional Reply', *Journal of the Society of Public Teachers of Law* 8 (1964-5), pp. 68-9; Colin Munro, 'Laws and Conventions Distinguished', in *Law Quarterly Review* 9 (1975), pp. 222-3.

[17]*Reference re Disallowance and Reservation of Provincial Legislation*, [1938] SCR 71.

[18]*Auditor General v, Minister of Energy Mines and Resources et al.* (1986), 23 DLR (4th) 210 (FCTD).

[19]*Madzimbamuto v. Lardner-Burke*, [1969] 1 AC 645 at p. 723.

[20]*Copyright Owners Reproduction Society Ltd. v. E.M.I. (Australia) Pty Ltd.* [1958], 100 C.L.R. 597 at p. 613.

[21]*A.G. v. Jonathan Cape Ltd. et al.*, [1975] 2 All ER 484 (QB).

[22]*Stopforth v. Goyer* (1978), 20 OR (2d) 262 (Ont.HCJ); this decision was overturned on appeal: (1979), 23 OR (2d) 696 (Ont.CA).

[23]*Re Fraser and the Public Service Staff Relations Board* (1986), 23 DLR (4th) 122; *Re Ontario Public Employees' Union et al. v. A.G. for Ontario* (1987), 41 DLR (4th) 1.

[24]*Arseneau v. The Queen*, [1979] 2 SCR 136; *A.G. Quebec v. Blaikie et al.* (no. 2), [1981] 1 SCR 312.
[25]*British Coal Corp. v. The King*, [1935] AC 500 (JCPC); *Reference re the Disallowance and of Reservation of Provincial Legislation*, [1938] SCR 71; *Currie v. MacDonald* (1949), 29 Nfld and PEIR 294 (Nfld CA); *Reference re Amendment of the Constitution of Canada* (1981), 125 DLR (3d) 1 (SCC).
[26]Ibid.; *A.G. Quebec v. A.G. Canada* (1982), 140 DLR (3d) 385.
[27]William R. Lederman, 'The Supreme Court of Canada and Basic Constitutional Amendment', in Russell et al., *The Court and the Constitution*, Kingston: Institute of Intergovernmental Relations, 1982, p. 52.
[28]*Reference re Amendment of the Constitution of Canada* (1981), 125 DLR (3d) 1 at p. 88.

Index